BBC Music in the
Glock Era and After

Leo Black (Felicity Vincent)

BBC Music in the Glock Era and After

A Memoir

Leo Black

edited by
Christopher Wintle

with
Kate Hopkins

drawings by
Milein Cosman

The Cosman Keller Art and Music Trust
in association with
Plumbago Books
2010

Plumbago Books and Arts
PO Box 55462
London sw4 oew

plumbago@btinternet.com
www. plumbago.co.uk

Distribution and Sales:
Boydell & Brewer Ltd.
PO Box 9
Woodbridge
Suffolk IP12 3DF

trading@boydell.co.uk
tel. 01394 610 600
www.boydellandbrewer.com

Boydell and Brewer Inc.
668 Mount Hope Avenue
Rochester
NY 14620, USA

Leo Black, *BBC Music in the Glock Era and After. A Memoir*
First published 2010

Logo by Mary Fedden, RA, OBE © Plumbago Books and Arts 2001

ISBN: 978-0-9556087-4-2 (hardback), 978-0-9556087-5-9 (softback)

Typeset in Adobe Minion Pro

Printed in Great Britain by the MPG Books Group, Bodmin and King's Lynn

Contents

Leo Black in the early 1950s (Studio Edmark, Oxford)

Introduction

This memoir recalls a vital and formative stage in British broadcasting. The BBC of the 1960s is by now swathed in hearsay; I offer a factual account of how the Music Programmes Department was organized, with character studies of its leading members from William Glock down. Nowadays those men are not so much forgotten as imprecisely remembered, so there is a need for a first-hand, more nuanced, less black-and-white account of them and their time.

One major omission is necessarily the concert series that has been probably the BBC's best-known and best-loved musical offering ever since Glock dragged it out of its committee-bound inertia: the Henry Wood Promenade Concerts. Despite their new lease of life, those concerts remained very much an empire unto themselves, hardly in contact with the departmental producers, something that changed a little under Robert Ponsonby, and more drastically with the advent in the mid-1980s of John Drummond as both Proms planner and Controller, Radio 3. During my twenty-eight BBC years I 'looked after' precisely one Prom, to mark the Assumption of the Blessed Virgin Mary, and even then it was a concert in whose planning I had had no hand.

At the end of the 1950s the BBC still enjoyed its monopoly, but a very limited range of stations had to cater for a wide variety of 'brows'. Culturally, ever since the end of the war it had led the way with its Third Programme, the first European radio network devoted exclusively to music, drama and 'the spoken word'. BBC Management, perhaps aware that its musical activities were in something of a rut, went in search of a dynamic, forward-looking new Controller for that output. As for me, I had spent two fraught years trying to prove myself in the strange and worldly business of music publishing, after a too-long five years in Oxford's ivory tower. At the London branch of Universal Edition, Vienna (Alfred A. Kalmus Ltd.), I was feeling as near a nadir as I had with the parent firm in Vienna three years earlier, aware that I was proving ineffective apart from keeping the copyright registrations up to date, and that my social and spiritual lives were going nowhere fast. With the BBC about to announce its new Controller, I had a pub talk with my closest friend, the composer Hugh Wood, which touched on the two most likely candidates. They were the publisher and notorious practical joker Howard Hartog (who, not that I knew it, had a background in broadcasting from his time with the British occupying forces in Germany) and the pianist, ex-music-critic and organizer of the Bryanston, later Dartington, Summer School, William Glock. Howard, then at the rival firm of Schott's, had his eye on me and was noticeably friendly. As for Glock, I proclaimed that he was quite unlikely, for some reason or other, to be a viable candidate.

He was duly appointed; Hartog went on to run a top artists' agency with Joan Ingpen, later a high-up at the Royal Opera House, and her dachshund Williams, whose subsequent life is not a matter of public record though the name survives. I became a small spoke in a large and involuted wheel that rolled waywardly on for a decade and more, until sociology caught up with it and classical music's place in people's lives began to change beyond recognition.

For a youngster, it was simply the time to add to his academic knowledge by learning from remarkable colleagues about music and life (an unending process still under way in his later seventies). Certain composers of particular importance to me meant little or nothing to Glock, particularly Franz Schmidt, who most strongly contradicts all the period's short-lived current assumptions linking 'progressiveness' with musical substance. His gradual illumination of my life, from a low-point in a Viennese hospital onward, will emerge in due course. His exact contemporary and opposite-number, Arnold Schoenberg, dominated my existence for a good ten years, a chance conversation after a recording by his literary executor, the pianist Leonard Stein, leading to the first hundred thousand Schoenberg words out of roughly a million that I eventually translated. Post-First-World-War pupils of whom he thought highly were Roberto Gerhard, still a force during my early BBC years, and Hanns Eisler and Nikos Skalkottas, neither of whom I met (Skalkottas, indeed, had been dead for ten years when I joined). A significant figure in my early BBC life was Luigi Dallapiccola, and he is recalled at some length with great affection. Hugh Wood was certainly noticed by Glock, who commissioned more than one of his major early works, but his role for me has always been that of close friend and conscience.

Such was the wealth of experience my BBC years offered that I have been unable to resist the temptation to run on into the post-Glock time (the 'Glock Era' ran from 1959 to 1972). On his successors direct and indirect – Robert Ponsonby, John Drummond, Nicholas Kenyon, Roger Wright – it is not for me to sit in judgement, since this collection amounts basically to a study in the palaeontology of English musical culture, offering the views and tastes of a traditionalist musician conditioned by his upbringing and immensely fortunate to find an important context into which he could fit for many years. However, a post-Glock Controller of Radio 3, Stephen Hearst, is recalled at length, such was the impression he made on me. Musico-political correctness

Hans Keller with Shirley Bignell outside the Stag pub in central London

in either direction is, I hope, absent from these pages: the views and blatant prejudices found here are all mine.

Nobody develops as I did without being profoundly influenced by certain distinguished musicians, and by personality as well as musical qualities, so a substantial tailpiece tells how I grew up and where my ideas and ideals came from. This clearly has much to do with my never having become an academic but rather a communicator and (I say it without shame) popularizer.

The book is 'dedicated to my former colleagues pictured within'. I hope that it adds up to a variegated account of a period in English music now gone beyond any other type of direct recall.

Leo Black
London, 2010

Editor's Preface

Every opera-goer knows how, early in *The Rake's Progress*, that charming young loafer Tom Rakewell cries "I wish I had money!" and Shadow – Old Nick – 'appears immediately at the garden gate'. Some months ago I was having a working lunch with Donald Mitchell and cried likewise, "I wish I had something on Paul Hamburger!" and – hey presto! – a book proposal arrived the next day from Leo Black with a chapter on the man himself. But there was a difference. I had wanted a Hamburger book to enrich my understanding of the émigré contribution to British musical life since the war – a project already under way with work many of us had done on Hans Keller and his circle. Yet rather than offer just 'Hamburger', Leo had included chapters on a host of other figures – and not just émigrés – who had helped mould the times. Some names, I must confess, were new to me – the 'contents page' alone was an education – and it was obvious I need look no further. Indeed, the limitation of my original wish had been put firmly in its place. It was as if, in his wisdom, Shadow had offered Tom not only money, but also a pocketful of ISAs, a Government-backed savings scheme and a final-salary pension scheme to boot.

Not that anything comes from nowhere. On 5 April 1995, Leo had followed up our first meeting – at the book-launch of Hans Keller's *Essays on Music* – with a letter about Schubert: he sensed a musical 'unity' to the great songs that 'the non-German music-lover responds to', especially in *Abendröte*. Would I have time, he wondered, to peruse his 'sizeable' essay on the subject? Peruse it I did, but in the great bustle of things, no more came of the matter. He was, in any case, proposing a monumental project that needed the support of a serious publisher, which in those days I wasn't:

> … for 28 years my enthusiasms [for Schubert] had an outlet … in making BBC programmes. So I must look to something a bit more serious, lest I vanish from the world and people say with Hardy's Lizbie Browne "And who was he?"

The 'something a bit more serious' duly turned into his study of *Franz Schubert: Music and Belief* (2003), to be followed by *Edmund Rubbra, Symphonist*

(2008) – Rubbra being another long-standing enthusiasm. But those twenty-eight years 'in the galleys' (to use Verdi's phrase) were by no means wasted. The BBC, William Glock, the personalities around him, the composers and performers involved (or not), and the consequent trajectory of British music in the 1960s and '70s – all these are now hot topics, as 'serious' as any for those who care about our recent history. And who, in any case, better to handle them than Leo Black, an eloquent and musical eye-witness who understood the system, knew the main players, and worked closely with top artists whose stature, if anything, has increased with time? *A Memoir* his book may call itself – and as autobiography it is certainly witty, judicious, personable, unsentimental and poignant – but it is still a key document for anyone who wants to grab the subject by the horns.

The division of labour in producing the book has been straightforward. Leo Black and I made the initial selection of chapters; Julian Hogg, Kate Hopkins, Leo Black and I shared the proof-reading; Stephen Hearst, Julian Hogg and Hugh Wood added information and comments, and Alison Garnham, Hans Keller Archivist in the Cambridge University Library and author of *Hans Keller and the BBC* (Ashgate, 2003) acted as a formal referee. Julian Littlewood once again happily took on the typesetting. Milein Cosman was as generous as ever in granting permission to use her drawings; Alexander Goehr kindly gave permission to reproduce a photograph of his mother's; and Felicity Vincent supplied the frontispiece. We have tried to contact the owners of other photographs but without success: so they are more than welcome to come forward. Not for the first time with a Plumbago project, Andrea Rauter of the the Austrian Cultural Forum (London) has offered unflagging encouragement; and the whole enterprise has been made possible by a generous grant towards the printing costs from the Cosman Keller Art and Music Trust.

A book that blends history with memoir needs an informal style, and it is informality that has guided editorial policy. For example, work titles appear either in English or in their original language, depending on what comes naturally, and usually without dates. Fifty years on, even first-hand information needs careful checking, and we have followed up references to people and places, works and performers, as best we can: if slips remain we apologize. The footnotes are predominantly the author's and are kept to the minimum; suggestions for further reading appear in the bibliography; and two appendices include materials that stand apart from the main text but are still obliquely relevant.

Christopher Wintle
King's College London, 2010

A Note on the Artist

MILEIN COSMAN was born in 1921 in Gotha, and educated in Düsseldorf and Geneva, and, from 1939, at the Slade School of Art in London. During the war she worked for the American Broadcasting Station in Europe, and after it settled in London, where she worked as a freelance artist. In 1947 she met and subsequently married the Viennese-born writer, broadcaster and musician, Hans Keller. Her first solo exhibition was held in London in 1949, and was followed by other exhibitions in Europe and America. Her work has been taken into several leading British collections: the National Portrait Gallery in London, the Ashmolean in Oxford, the Fitzwilliam in Cambridge and the Hunterian in Glasgow. Permanent collections of her drawings of musicians may be seen at the Wigmore Hall in London and the Palais des Beaux-arts in Brussels. As a specialist in portraiture, she has formed a voluminous and astonishing record of the figures that have shaped music, letters and the arts for the last 60 years.

Part One

William Glock (Milein Cosman)

Before the Music Programme

1 Yalding House

When in 1960 William Glock, the BBC's newly appointed Controller, Music, was in search of younger people to help him enliven things his eye fell on me; after a wholly friendly, un-competitive interview I was recruited. This book's chapter on 'The Making of a Music Producer' may offer some clue as to why he took it into his head to do any such thing; the worldly reader will wonder straight away how it was that a departmental head in a notoriously Civil Service-style organization could simply haul a young man in off the street with no such formality as an 'appointment board' and the presence of an all-supervising Personnel Department. In fact Glock was allowed to offer a few such people strictly-short-term contracts, keeping an eagle eye on how they performed and giving no assurance of continuing employment. 'Established' we weren't (nor was there for many years any suggestion that we should do anything about it); had there been a sudden financial crisis, as there had been in the not-so-distant past, it would have had to be 'last in, first out'. A good friend working for a rival publisher to my own declined an offer from Glock on precisely those grounds, going on to become a university professor. The insecurity weighed not at all with me; I happily began work, aged not yet twenty-eight, in May 1960.

My very first impressions, after inductions by Harry Croft-Jackson and Hans Keller, two strong personalities to be met pretty soon, were of an office in the outer and upper reaches of Yalding House, 156 Great Portland Street, previously occupied by Bernard Keeffe, who had left to pursue his conducting career. Yalding was and is halfway down Great Portland Street, between the tube station of that name and Oxford Circus. In terms of internal BBC organization, I was a member of the Music Programmes Department (Radio) of a larger entity, Music Division. When I arrived I found I was one of the Chamber Music group of producers, which briefly disappointed me since so much of my promotion work for my previous employer had been on behalf of the Universal Edition orchestral catalogue. But a few minutes with my first boss, Hans Keller, saw to that. The BBC worked on the principle of 'Planning and Supply'. Air-time was at the disposal of the Planners (Heads of Home Service, Light Programme and Third Programme), based in Broadcasting House, who were 'supplied' with programmes by the Output Departments, most of them based wherever there was office space in the near hinterland. The system had, of course, been devised in the dim and distant past by planners, not suppliers, so there was potential for friction, but with Music Division and the Networks it never became an issue during my early years. The London-based BBC Symphony Orchestra, largest of the many the Corporation ran up and down the country, was and continued to be de facto outside the Music Programmes Department, reflecting the everlasting dilemma with 'a radio orchestra' – it's there to give concerts, not to 'make programmes'. A Light Music unit was also technically part of Music Division, but Glock took no interest in it. Before his arrival the Department had Organizers who 'offered' programmes to the Home Service and Third Programme respectively; but, so far as the general run of programmes was concerned, Glock saw things in a new way. He split the production of the majority of the London output between an orchestral group of producers headed by the former Home Service Music Organizer, Leonard Isaacs, and a chamber music and recitals group, where he bypassed the Third Programme Music Organizer, Robert Simpson, and instead promoted, as the relevant 'Chief Assistant', Hans Keller, whom the previous year he had recruited, with due regard for procedure, as Music Talks Producer. Opera remained in the hands of Peter Crossley-Holland, whose main interest in life seemed to be the collection of folk music in places like Nepal. Music Talks remained a domain of its own, which was what had so entranced Hans Keller about the job during his short time doing it: ideas went straight to the Third Programme's 'offers meeting', though they could of course be shot at there like everything else. Hans having moved on and up, they were soon in the hands of another young man from Oxford (a contemporary of mine), Robert Layton.

Both Home and Third planned a quarter of a year at a time. The Home Service was headed by a formidable military historian, Ronald Lewin; at my very junior level I never had to meet him but the reports brought back from Broadcasting House by the seniors gave a vivid idea. Some years later, after his retirement, he produced a documentary showing that George III had not been mad but had suffered from a rare hereditary disease, porphyria; I was impressed and moved. Lewin's office issued a quarterly skeleton schedule not totally unlike later essays in 'strip planning', with few specific programmes apart from agreed series, and many spaces to be filled week by week. There was room for live orchestral concerts in the evening, and for live recitals, most but not all of them at an ungodly hour of the morning; the latter had by my time shaken off their exclusive live-ness, singers and wind-players being allowed to record if they so wished. At one point early on, Hans Keller called me in and we considered how to fill a Sunday evening space mysteriously denominated as 'GTS Recital'. This had clearly to be no run-of-the-mill recital, but something out of the ordinary – a Gran Turismo Special perhaps. Suitably prestigious names were thought of, and the results evidently satisfied Captain Lewin's exacting ear. Only later did it dawn on us that GTS meant Greenwich Time Signal.

The Third Programme functioned differently. Its Controller, Chief or Head – the BBC in the early Carleton-Greene era havered over the designation of its top officials, though the people and the jobs they did seemed to change not at all – was P. H. (Howard) Newby, an experienced talks producer and a far-from-negligible novelist. I duly read most of his books, often with some pleasure, and was quite surprised to find myself almost the only person at the time who had, apart from the omniscient Basil Lam; he was rated obscure and boring, which I find a good example of the British intelligentsia's favourite attitude, *"Know it? I don't even like it!"* Newby had a quite small amount of air time at his disposal, so the channel's mix of speech and music was thought about very hard indeed. At his weekly 'offers meetings' the Chief Assistants and other direct suppliers of programmes were of course principal contributors, but producers were welcome too, and discussion was both civilized and lively, especially once Hans Keller came to play a part in them. (Newby's engaging account of his relationship with Hans can be found in Alison Garnham's *Hans Keller and the BBC.*) What it boiled down to was discussion among intellectual equals, and cross-fertilization. The offers to Lewin's Home Service could be criticized only from above; those that the Chief Assistants and others made to the Third Programme were fair game for anyone sufficiently well-informed and interested. Out of the resulting mess of pottage an admirable lady named Pamela Orr constructed a quarterly schedule, which, once laid down, seemed to change very little with week-by-week developments.

Newby held that 'even the Controller' was entitled to Have a View as to what went out on his network; he wouldn't have dreamed of hazarding opinions on the musical merits of a proposal, but a nice example of his intervention came when he was offered a recital by an up-and-coming pianist, evidently of a standard to justify promotion to the 'elite' channel. Newby was sympathetic, but noted the fee proposed, which was low even for those pre-inflation days: the artist in question simply hadn't been broadcasting long enough to be offered more. Newby reasoned "if this man's of a standard for my channel, he shouldn't cost me so little." Fees were settled by a relatively autonomous unit, Music Bookings, which formed part of the Legal Adviser's empire, and were treated on a Civil Service-style incremental basis, with quality less of a factor than 'length of service'; it took a bit of negotiation with the relevant Manager to get The Man jumped up the queue to some such princely sum as £20.

Settled into Yalding, I met a variety of new, strong characters: William Glock, Hans Keller, Harry Croft-Jackson, Robert Simpson, Leo Wurmser, Basil Lam and Deryck Cooke were by no means the only remarkable people with whom I worked, played and at times squabbled. My first decade in the BBC, a period when the rest of the country was engaged in the newly-found pastime of Swinging, would have to be described rather as the Singing Sixties. Work in those early years meant making programmes with singers, pianists, chamber music groups and ensembles as large as the English Chamber Orchestra, which had developed out of the Goldsbrough Orchestra and was into a period when it seemed to be on the air every week. (In the 1970s the London Sinfonietta would enjoy a comparable vogue.) For the time being, I naturally chose artists of whom I had experience, such as the soprano April Cantelo; five years before, I'd written an article for *Isis* praising her and her then husband, Colin Davis, for their part in the Chelsea Opera Group's concert performances of Mozart operas in Oxford. By the early 1960s the days when 'artists rendered selections' were over; but it was still normal for a BBC music producer to offer a performer or performers an engagement ('date') and accept without demur whatever was suggested by way of programme, provided it was timed to match the available space. That soon changed, though, when I invited April to give a recital: her suggested programme of Shakespeare settings by Castelnuovo-Tedesco and others was all her own and couldn't have been improved on.

I also had strong enthusiasms from listening to broadcasts by pianists like Clifford Curzon and Geza Anda (with neither of whom I ever worked) and relays from abroad, notably those broadcast from Bayreuth. Few of the remarkable generation of singers who appeared there were for me, partly because of the general difference between the kind of singing required for Wagner's heroic roles and that needed for Lieder, and partly because they rarely came here.[1] I especially admired some magnificent baritones – the noble Hermann Uhde, the sinister Gustav Neidlinger – but had to leave it at that; someone who did come, just the once, was the third in the triumvirate, Benno Kusche, who must have been one of the best Beckmessers ever. His agent duly offered him for a recital, it duly took place, and I'm appalled to realize that I had for some reason to let someone else look after it in the studio, that I have no longer any idea what the programme was, that I have no memories of what it sounded like when broadcast, and that the tape, which I'm sure was magnificent, didn't go into the Archives, so that the programme is now the merest non-memory. How little we knew in those early years!

Some of my most vivid impressions as a very new producer, before I was let loose on my own account, were of major figures (from the past, one would have thought, but there they still were) observed at older producers' shows. The most powerful personality I've ever shared a room with, however briefly, was the very elderly Leopold Stokowski, who came to record with the London Symphony Orchestra. I remember him as a brooding presence, motionless and monosyllabic in a chair in the control cubicle. The veteran violinist Mischa

Elman paid his last visit; I heard a live broadcast of his with an extraordinarily weighty, 'this-is-how-it-goes' performance of Brahms's G major sonata, and was allowed to sit in when Hans 'produced' him in the studio. The overriding impression of gravity and total absence of doubt remains with me, even if the results, re-sampled thirty years later in the Archives, had lost their magic. My some-time idol among Lieder singers, Irmgard Seefried, got the Keller production treatment; a stickler for accuracy, he picked her up on some point or other, whether note-length or text I no longer recall. She expressed herself duly grateful; when it happened a second time, she didn't.

The first 'show' I was allowed to look after with nobody senior there to bale or bail me out was a live Home Service recital by a Hungarian-American violinist, Victor Aitay, and Ernest Lush. It was Peter Gould's programme but he couldn't be there. I no longer have the first idea what they played, nor did I come into any kind of sensible contact with them; the tradition that the studio manager managed the studio and the announcer spoke his lines was very much alive. Nearly twenty years later I flew to Chicago for the first of our live relays of the Symphony Orchestra; there was Aitay, still firmly installed as co-leader – he hadn't been that young when I almost met him in 1960, but the States showed a marked reluctance to invoke age as a reason for stopping work. I gathered even later still that he continued, to everyone's general satisfaction, until the new millennium, when a whole swathe of super-veterans was finally persuaded to take it easy. In my first BBC years there were our own veterans of broadcasting to make me feel duly small, since I'd grown up listening to them. The baritone Bruce Boyce was outstanding among home-grown Lieder singers in combining a fine line with a great ability to deliver a text. My contact with him was less than happy, for he had begun to feel overlooked and reacted badly when I politely enquired whether he could oblige me by changing a recording date to suit the soprano with whom he was sharing the programme. To the best of my recollection it ended up as two separate Schubert recitals.

Someone who proved unfailingly friendly and accommodating, not to mention inventive, was the elderly pianist Maurice Cole. He had broadcast since Savoy Hill days but wasn't in the least grand on the strength of it. The most thoughtful and un-pushy of men, he played for me several times, his most memorable contribution coming when I thought up a programme of 'last thoughts' with the Intermezzo from Franz Schmidt's late piano quintet, a solo for the left hand which demands a real sense of colour and awareness of time having passed, and an equally late but far more peculiar Mozart Adagio and Allegro originally written for an ensemble featuring the glass harmonica. The virtually unique thing about that rare instrument is that its sound grows, whereas that of the piano dies. It's a very uncanny effect, but, given the extreme rarity of performers interested in it, the piece tended to be played, if at all, on instruments that didn't share its qualities, and much too fast, in which case it could turn out rather boring. Maurice was well aware of the problem, and came up with a piano sound that in the strangest way satisfied the demand for something almost impossible and rather desperate (like Mozart's situation in his final months): it was all down to finger legato and, above all, resourceful use of the sustaining pedal. Mozart's companion composer in the programme would have been intrigued, since his own reluctance to compose for the piano stemmed largely from the way its sound immediately begins to die, imposing intolerable demands on a pianist's faculty of 'active hearing'.

NOTES

1   One evident exception was a veteran German baritone named Robert Titze, who brought to Schubert, Brahms and Hans Pfitzner a sensitivity and intensity I have rarely experienced again; he at one point showed us a picture of himself made up as Alberich in *The Ring*, which was stunningly scary. If his singing of the role came anywhere near that visual image, he must have been an intimidating figure.

2   *New Recruits*

Once recruited, I had relatively little to do with William Glock, who operated at a level far above me; that changed for only a short while when I was put in charge of the Invitation Concerts. My fellow-recruits were my boyhood friend Alexander Goehr, and David Drew, who had lately produced a marathon guide to the music of Roberto Gerhard for Glock's publication, *The Score*. It looked as if some year or other, after a forthcoming enquiry by a Committee with the glass-making magnate Sir Harry Pilkington at its head, there might well be a big increase in music broadcasting, perhaps even with a dedicated channel carrying it for quite a proportion of the day, and David was felt to have a specially comprehensive knowledge, indispensable as contingency plans were laid. So of us three he was the one who saw Glock at closest quarters; yet within a year he was gone – manoeuvred out, or so the rumour ran. If anything similar was tried on me I never became aware of it. Nobody thought to explain that if you wanted a permanent post on the 'Establishment' you waited till one fell vacant and then applied; so I remained, on a series of short-term, non-pensionable contracts, till in 1967 I became restless and took half a departure. David went on to a most distinguished career with the publishers Boosey and Hawkes, and continued the research that made him a world authority on Kurt Weill; Sandy left in the mid-60s for a university career and to devote as much of his time as possible to composing.

Subsequent recruits in the early 1960s were Stephen Plaistow, a Cambridge music graduate who came from reviewing for *The Times* and proved an outstanding, totally unflappable producer, and the Australian pianist John Douglas Todd, who had it in him to flap when occasion offered. He came in as producer for the BBC Symphony Orchestra, though his ambition was to become a staff accompanist and he certainly had a rock-solid piano technique; from sharing a flat with him for a few weeks I remember that his idea of practice was to play through Brahms's Paganini Variations, note-perfect, then play through them again. I could only stand and wonder, my own pianism having taken me as far as the same composer's quite complex Handel Variations while stopping short of the sheer athletic qualities needed for music like the Paganini ones. Todd eventually came into contact with Stockhausen, who told him he was a genius, and things were never quite the same again: an irascible and talented man, never 'made the most of', whose standard mode of address to me was "my boy?". Not long after his arrival we welcomed into the chamber music group the 'cellist Eleanor Warren, whose familiarity with most of the musical profession stood her in good stead in the studio.

3   Artists (I)

Since we were all there to make programmes not with circular pieces of plastic (a quite separate Gramophone Programmes Department dealt with those as well as the long-running *Music Magazine*) but with real people coming to perform in our studios, the greatest trouble had clearly to be taken in choosing them, and the assessment of unknown artists at concerts, as well as auditions, was part and parcel of a producer's work. There were copious 'reports' available on which to base suggestions for performers, and the BBC was particularly conscientious at the start of a broadcasting career. Newcomers from the United Kingdom or the Commonwealth, once through their audition (which was held under conditions of strict anonymity), normally had three chances ('Test Dates') to prove themselves before a decision needed to be made as to whether they were now 'On' or 'Off' The Books, i.e. eligible for further booking. The Ministry of Labour had strict rules about the employment of non-Commonwealth performers; the BBC had to put its hand on its heart and declare that they had something to offer which nobody here could provide, and their fee then had to be set at an appropriate level.[1] For them there was no question of 'test dates', but in either category the producer of a programme would often be required to file a report on how it had gone. As a further measure of quality control there was often outside or 'special' listening commissioned by the Music Bookings unit from prominent musicians, most of them retired and so no longer 'competing'. The assessors' comments, and those of the producer, were considered at a regular committee meeting, and though no artist was the worse for one critical report, a series of them could lead to the not-in-itself-unreasonable conclusion that they were going through a period of being at less than their best. (Nobody mooted the possibility that they might have had an incompetent or unsympathetic producer or, indeed, balancer.) That might affect the frequency with which they were engaged (if at all). Enormous files of those artist reports were circulated for the information of all producers; the folder was colloquially known as The Yalding Bugle because of the irate or frivolous comments added by producers as it wended its months-long weary way through production offices.

The outcome of all that was enshrined in the printed Artists' Census, listing those who were 'on the books', though not yet the ones yet to complete their three 'test dates'. (A girl friend at the time came down hard on me for my 'pomposity' when I said that artists 'needed to know how they stood with us'. They did, though.) While on the one hand the procedure could lead to anomalies like later-famous musicians failing their BBC audition, and while a minute such as 'Janet Baker: proceed to Test Date' would with hindsight look prim and uptight, it all to some extent helped maintain standards. The pressure of agents' hype and record companies' bottom lines was not yet the all-pervading thing it later became, but caution was still the watchword, and basically, we trusted BBC ears over anyone else's. The same applied to the assessment of new works. Prizes, in particular, were not thought an applicable criterion, a reasonable precaution given the notorious habits of juries, though it could lead to incidents and accusations that a composer was being 'blacklisted'. A further source of misunderstanding and bad feeling was that the standard letter to a composer whose work had not been recommended by the reading panel used language like 'we are not prepared to broadcast it on any of our national networks', rather than simply saying that for the moment Music Division could find no outlet for it; Glock's writ didn't run in the Gramophone Programmes Department, who could broadcast anything they pleased on a national network so long as it was off a gramophone record. Not many such obscure works could hope to be recorded, but the language was wrong and reflected, I fear, the self-importance of the writer, Harry Croft-Jackson.

Before the Wigmore Hall under William Lyne became the arbiter of taste, a far larger proportion of its concerts were given by unfamiliar artists who could afford the hall's then-less-exorbitant hiring fee. There's now a myth that everything pre-Lyne was of utter mediocrity, but in fact I heard some excellent new artists and was once or twice able to go straight to the office next morning and suggest they be offered an engagement, either now if still here and a studio were free, or at least on their next visit. There were no formalities about 'second opinions'; Keller, Isaacs and his successor Peter Gould alike trusted my enthusiasm. A very fine Swedish baritone, Erik Saedén, is one I remember trawling in that way, and his performance of a set of *Songs of Death* by Yrjö Kilpinen came close to converting me to someone I'd so far found rather insipid on the basis of HMV's special-issue Kilpinen Society records. Erik Saedén went on to become Intendant of the Stockholm Opera. With artists from outside the Commonwealth there was no question, under prevailing legislation, of making an 'experimental recording' (see 'Hans Keller') – we had to commit ourselves, which suited me very well.

Some most distinguished performers occasionally appeared as assessors at audition sessions, the grandest of all being a former idol of my father's, Dame Eva Turner, who would come out with phrases like "When Ai Sang The Ritornah Vincitor at La Scah-Lah' (I'd grown up with her record of that great aria). Her written reports on auditions and broadcasts were, on the other hand, succinct in the extreme, with cryptic wording like 'tops off' or 'lazy tops'.

NOTES

1   With Britain's entry into the European Common Market the situation reversed itself, the Commonwealth now being beyond the pale and subject to restrictions, with Euro-members bookable as if they were a 'home product'.

4   *Announcers and Presentation*

In the 1960s BBC Radio's squad of announcers covered all programmes that needed announcing: the later concept of the 'specialist' announcer developed only with the dedicated networks of the 1970s. Home, Light and Third were marked off from each other by height of brow, and the announcers had infinitely adjustable foreheads. Of the legendary war-time newsreaders, Stuart Hibberd, Bruce Belfrage and Joseph Macleod had moved on, but we still had Alvar Lidell and Frank Phillips, both well aware of their status and not above presuming on it. One of the musical fixtures on the Home Service was *Music at Night*, broadcast live after the 11 pm news. That in itself could make for the odd problem, as when one half of a piano-duet team who was an early riser and early-to-bed man found himself dropping off during the broadcast. On one occasion the programme's producer sent in a long report detailing the unique contribution of Frank Phillips, who had clearly regarded the programme as an occasion for putting the listener (but not the artists) at ease; "If Derek Collier came to your house to play, you'd expect him to tune his instrument a little" (encouraging gestures to soloist and faint tuning noises from violin), and far too much more in the same vein. The Head of Presentation, a legendary figure named H. Rooney Pelletier, politely admonished him, in terms befitting a war veteran, to keep it more basic next time. From Alvar, on the other hand, I learned more about the relationship of written to spoken English than from anyone else. He was always at pains, even when provided with a script rather than notes, to ensure that what he read out was what he could deliver: miracles of adaptation went on, but the factual content was never touched, except for things he found totally incomprehensible, which he would roundly declare to be out of the question both for him and for any reasonable listener. It was a matter of style, and he was the supreme master.

Another indelible impression is of the times when Wallace Greenslade of the Goon Show ("Mr. Secombe, it is the *sworn duty* of a BBC announcer to Talk Posh!") would show up at balance tests for live Home Service morning recitals, rubicund and mouthing curses about the earliness of the hour; he was the greatest possible tonic, but also an impeccable deliverer of the goods. The most interesting and engaging of those all-purpose figures was the young John Dunn, who once or twice came and did the job with inimitable charm, but made it clear that while we classical musicians had a wonderful product, we really had no idea at all how to sell it. *That* he could do, both in the not-very-adventurous context of the Morning Recital and later as a Radio 2 host whose grace of manner made him into a cult figure. A gentle giant whom it was a privilege to know, however slightly.

At other times the all-purpose announcers were stretched to capacity and beyond. Foreign languages were usually a problem, if not for Alvar with his native Swedish and faultless German and French. Listening to a Bach programme on the Third one night, the back-announcement after a church cantata, *O ewiges Feuer, o Ursprung der Liebe* (O Eternal Fire, O Fount of Love) engraved itself indelibly on my mind; the unfortunate fellow got a good pass-mark for "O" but otherwise sent no fewer than ten hurdles flying: "that was Bach's cantata number 34, O efigess Veuer, o Ersprung da Lieder ... in which the obbligati were played by Emanuel Hurvitz [his name, unexpectedly, was to be pronounced with a 'w'] Terence Wweil [his, expectedly, was to be pronounced with a 'v'], Richard Adderney and Peter Grame [those two distinguished wind principals were in fact Adeney and Graeme = Graham]."

With names like Baker, Watts or Young the singers came off better, but the dedicated music team was already well overdue. On top of all that, much of the announcing of the time, as and when I have occasion to re-hear it, seems to sit in a comfortable bath of self-satisfied RADA euphony, saying nothing beyond "Am I not lovely?". It can be creepy – though, by the same token, it avoids today's ever-increasing trend to cocky knowingness, memorably summed up long ago by Ian McIntyre in the phrase "handing out sticky buns". 'Editorializing' of any kind was strictly forbidden under the BBC's charter, so producers were not allowed to express opinions or comment on the music in their programmes, nor even to refer to performers as 'distinguished' (they were that by definition if they broadcast for us): they were there to deliver facts. It was a distinction naturally amenable to some bending of the rules (it didn't take me too long to realize that the basic principle for doing useful and satisfying work within the BBC was the bending of briefs), and the edict about editorializing could be circumvented by the 'attribution' of material that showed more originality than usual. At one point a good joke made the rounds of the Gramophone Programmes Department: "Leo Black has written, 'Mozart was born in 1756 ...' ". The advent of human voices and communicators like Peter Barker and Andrew Gemmill (the latter staying too little time before his departure for incomparably better-paid work as a head-hunter) was a great relief, augmented when experienced former announcers like Patricia Hughes and John Holmstrom returned to add their knowledge of what would engage a listener's attention. The other half of the problem lay in the scripts they had to read, but that's another story.

5 *Staff Accompanists*

In my own field of recital programmes the 'staff accompanists' played a valuable role. They were endlessly versatile and partnered anyone from the BBC Chorus (later the BBC Singers) in its most skittish, 'riding-down-to-Bangor' mood, to home and visiting instrumentalists and singers who might have just passed their audition but might equally be of the calibre of a Pierre Fournier, with whom Ernest Lush not merely broadcast but gave concerts for some years. When I joined, Ernest had already been there for three decades; he was rightly a legendary figure and soon became quite my favourite accompanist-chamber music player, with the obvious exception of Benjamin Britten, who appeared only with Peter Pears and then once in a blue moon. Ernest's playing was a constant delight, with a command of the piano equal to Gerald Moore's, an ego unequal (as I would discover) to that great man's, and the true chamber-music-player's ability both to match his partner and to present his own very viable ideas. Editing an Ernest Lush recording, on the other hand, could be a nightmare, for in any retake there would invariably be some minute but crucial difference that made it unusually difficult to bring off an undetectable edit. Either version was absolutely musical, splicing them together another matter; and usually the partner had occasioned the retake in the first place.

The other staff accompanists when I joined were the urbane Clifton Helliwell, who left to go to the Northern School of Music before it became the Royal Northern College, the cheerful but sensitive Frederick Stone, and Josephine Lee. 'Joey' was invaluable when working with really temperamental performers, for example a Polish baritone named Alfred Orda who 'came in handy' when Russian or Polish songs were wanted. I was never asked how I judged the correctness of someone's pronunciation in languages I didn't speak, and had I been I should have had no convincing answer. Alfred Orda's rather beautiful voice and talent rightly earned him a place on the air, but a recording could be a tempestuous affair if he was on less than top form. We were prepared to re-take passages which had gone less than well, though that was the thin end of a wedge that grew to monstrous proportions with the advent of the 'new music' movement, whose practitioners were scarcely used to doing anything else but play bits and pieces in a recording studio. During the 1960s we tried to keep retakes and editing within limits, and to the end some of us aimed to maintain the illusion of a 'performance'; but it depended, among other things, on how any given performer reacted when something went wrong. Joey could calm the Alfred Ordas of this world marvellously. For me, however, Alfred's most memorable moment came as we walked down Farringdon Street after a recording had been successfully concluded: he suddenly came out with "Mr. Black, the only way to stay healthy is TO LEAD A CLEAN LIFE". I don't know what he'd noticed but I wasn't going to disagree.

New accompanists were now recruited. Charles Spinks came in for harpsichord continuo, at which he was supreme; the infinitely sensitive and musical Viola Tunnard came, to leave all too soon when struck down by (as we thought) multiple sclerosis, though I eventually learned that, as with Hans Keller, it had been motor neurone disease; Wilfrid Parry was endlessly genial and sympathetic with his artists and producers, and capable of both creating and appreciating beauty. He told me of the day when as a young man he'd played the Elgar Piano Quintet with a group of his contemporaries; hearing the violist play the tender melody that opens the second movement, he told himself "I'm going to marry that girl". Her name was Eileen Grainger, and he did. A rare moment came when he was involved in Mátyás Seiber's *Two Jazzolettes*, for which we had booked some real and rather fierce jazz musicians. At rehearsal it emerged that they couldn't start in the usual classical way, but needed the (to them) customary "A-one-a, a two-a, a one-two-three-four," which Wilfrid provided from the piano stool. Finally, Paul Hamburger was a near-genius and one of Hans Keller's greatest admirers, the friendship going back to their internment on the Isle of Man during the early years of the war (a period described by Alison Garnham in her forthcoming *Hans Keller and Internment* (Plumbago, 2010)).

All those 'new' accompanists are now dead, Paul having worked on as a leading vocal coach into his early eighties and the new millennium. Whoever made four such marvellous appointments had his head screwed on right; the artistic decision presumably rested largely with Hans Keller, though the posts were 'managed' by Harry Croft-Jackson.

6 *Artists (II)*

As I picked up the rudiments of programme-making, a flood of new impressions broke over me. There were so many performers and such an infinite variety of music that could be made into programmes. The first real revelations were the violinist Wilfred Lehmann whom I'd heard while he was leader of the City of Birmingham Orchestra – his playing of the 'Fiedel' solo in Mahler's Fourth Symphony had greatly impressed me – and a new, definitely 'stellar' soprano, Elizabeth Harwood. Wilf was Australian, with a blonde flute-playing Australian wife, Frances, and they'd lived in this country for some years. He left very soon to become leader of a newly-founded Japanese orchestra, at which time his family life also rearranged itself; but before he went I was able to give him several mostly-quite-short Home Service broadcasts. The elegance and precision of his playing are still with me; they set a precedent for my reactions of sheer pleasure a decade and more later when I first heard the American Joseph Silverstein. Wilf's repertoire for me included lollipops such as the Intermezzo from Kodály's *Háry János*, but extended through Smetana's short but deeply felt *From Bohemian Fields and Groves*, to the culmination of his broadcasting work here – a major masterpiece for unaccompanied violin, Bach's D minor Partita, which ends with the famous and much-transcribed Chaconne. His recording of it was like a farewell gift to me, but in the fullness of time it suffered one of those special BBC nonsenses. Contact between music producers and the Sound Archives eventually grew into a major collaboration with the advent of music selectors like Jill White, later senior music producer for BBC Bristol and then Director of the National Youth Orchestra, and Gordon Clarke, but was more or less non-existent in the early '60s. Someone evidently found Wilf's D minor Partita worth preserving: so far so good. Unfortunately, what was preserved was the Prelude with its ensuing dance movements, while the crowning Chaconne somehow got left out and was therefore 'washed', since tapes, once taken in by Archives, were out of the normal recordings library and one's original 'hold' on them automatically cancelled. I only discovered this amazing lacuna many years later when I remembered the performance and wanted to repeat it, and was livid as seldom in my BBC career: the Chaconne on its own would have been useable without the opening movements, but in programme terms the opening movements without the Chaconne made very little sense. I had to be content with finding some excuse or other for repeating the Sarabande. Of Liz Harwood, more, much more, in due course.

7   *Travels*

In the first flush of my notoriety as a Young Lion I was sent to report on the Kranichsteiner Musiktage at Darmstadt. Boulez's *Pli selon pli* impressed me, even in its unfinished state with the opening *Tombeau* played as a piano solo by Maria Bergmann, and I wrote in *The Score* that it had stood out 'like a bear with a sore head in a zoo full of the smaller mammals'. On the other hand, its long stretches of relentless orchestral fortissimo had had me shifting about in my seat, and when Boulez gave a talk about his work, mooting the possibility of 'dynamic' and 'static' elements, I took the chance at question time of asking how long a static section could go on before stasis degenerated into boredom. This clearly meant nothing to him; he was talking compositional method, not listener-reaction, and simply smiled indulgently. However, one of his fellow avant-garde composers, André Boucourechliev, came up to me afterwards and said he'd very much appreciated my question.

As for the smaller mammals, once safely back in Yalding I showed myself sceptical in a way that could have had Glock pricking up his ears and wondering whether I'd so soon shot my bolt as a paragon of avant-garde agitprop. A nine-page report to him (and foolscap pages were longer than A4 ones) covered some thirty works but recommended scarcely anything save a piano piece by Richard Hoffmann, Schoenberg's Austro-American amanuensis in his final years, Krenek's 'Cello Concerto and an Oboe Sonata by the Jugoslav composer Milko Kelemen, who figured in the UE catalogue. I certainly failed to spot György Kurtág as someone to watch, but a four-minute early piano piece wasn't the best introduction. Harsh words were reserved for Karl Amadeus Hartmann's *Concerto funèbre*, using the odd if suitably monochrome combination of violin and strings, despite my having been mightily impressed a few years before by his apocalyptic Sixth Symphony, and for an electronic piece by Bruno Maderna, whose sheer musicianship should have made him a sacred cow. Glock must have wondered what was going on; but I'd still stand by one comment on a 1960s-vintage 'open form' piece – 'the form was *so* open that the music had slipped out'. And my reservations about much of the fare on offer (not all that different in content, come to think of it, from anything Hans Keller would have come up with in the same circumstances, though the tone would have been different) was summed up by something I wrote the following year, apropos of similar things at the ISCM festival: 'The impression is of someone using all the clichés of "expressive" music without even wanting to "express" anything (i.e. the diametrical opposite of Webern's cliché-less expressiveness).'

It was also suggested that I go on an exchange visit to the West German Radio in Cologne, where the latest developments in electronic music were under way in the trendy hands of Otto Tomek: during my time at UE Wien he had been in charge of the firm's publicity. The idea never came to anything, and I can only suppose that no-one from Köln was prepared to sweat it out in a *Scheiss-Stadt* like London, capital of *Das Land ohne Musik*.

Nothing daunted, The Boss next sent me to the 1961 festival of the International Society for Contemporary Music. Since it was in Vienna, I was very happy to go, but came back equally sceptical. The major point of interest was the newly-excavated torso of Schoenberg's *Die Jakobsleiter* (Jacob's Ladder), conducted by his ex-pupil Winfried Zillig. My notes reveal the presence in a small role of my supreme idol, the veteran tenor Julius Patzak. The extraordinary nature of this unfinished oratorio, with its many spoken or shouted parts, made for a very convoluted first reaction, duly communicated to Glock.[1] *Die Jakobsleiter* was to play an interesting role in my life when I was asked to translate its difficult text for a BBC Festival Hall concert. Checking my efforts, Hans Keller paid me one of the best compliments ever – "I must admit that just now and again I caught myself looking at the translation to find out what the original meant." Before that, Sandy Goehr had homed in on the work and put it on in the studio, causing an incident, a case in point illustrating how, despite the existence of a Music Division Book of Reference, young producers were told nothing. A passage near the end of what Schoenberg completed calls for a second orchestra. In Sandy's production that was recorded with the one-and-only orchestra playing 'over itself'. It emerged that the BBC's agreement with the Musicians' Union forbade any such thing; the music in question should have been played, and, more to the point, paid for, at a separate session. The one couldn't be remedied, the other could and had had to be, and it was all found serious enough to warrant a special departmental meeting, with a visitation from Michael Standing, famous years before as the voice that 'stopped the mighty roar of London's traffic' in the programme *In Town Tonight* but by now a very senior figure in radio management. Anyone who ever saw Richard Wattis playing a civil servant will have a good idea of the fully matured Michael Standing. He duly appeared and said it was inconceivable that anyone could have failed to spot a problem like that: we must All Do Better. For the first time, and by no means the last, I noted that no heads rolled; on a few future occasions I was to be thankful for that kindly BBC attitude.

NOTES

1   My views on Schoenberg's *Die Jakobsleiter* began with a diatribe against the ISCM International Jury's selection of works for that year, and continued:

> The ISCM, with its way of judging new works purely by the most superficial kind of 'newness' is in the great tradition of 'Schoenberg's Viennese public'; but, of course, all is now forgiven, things have changed. Anyone who thinks most of the Viennese have really seen the error of their ways should read Lothar Knessl's article in the June issue of *Melos*; all the same, the concert performance of the existing sections of *Die Jakobsleiter* was a sentimental occasion greeted with enormous enthusiasm and (curiously) televised. The first part of the work, which Schoenberg completed in short score and which has been orchestrated by Winfried Zillig, lasts 35 minutes; the extant half of the symphonic interlude separating it from the second part (which would have been much longer) lasts seven minutes. Thus the complete work would have been enormous. Schoenberg sketched most of what exists, in that dry, cerebral fashion we are always being told about, in roughly three months, before he was called up for military service. The music is vivid, powerful, immediately impressive, and sweeps along as a full-scale oratorio should: all critical references to Mahler's Eighth Symphony, the First Chamber Symphony and cognate works are justified, though it would be wrong to say that Schoenberg had in any way 'gone back' from 'the stage he had reached' in the Five Orchestral Pieces. He had simply altered his scale to suit his subject, and the work is a step forward in his development. Only repeated hearings would show whether there is quite such pure musical distinction in *Die Jakobsleiter* as in the best of the works before it, but as an orchestral score it is a most exciting new acquaintance.
>
> There is, however, also a text. Schoenberg's libretto is immensely interesting, if not always easy to appreciate; it pin-points not one spiritual predicament but practically all the available ones, mercilessly tracking down the failure of attitude in each of them. The second half, which remains unset, does much more. As a libretto it must be unique for its psychological penetration and present-day relevance. A document such as this presents correspondingly unique problems when it has to be set to music. At a first hearing I felt the moods of the music too generalized to go ideally with the text. (Incidentally the scoring is so thick as to make the voices mostly inaudible, until the entry of the soprano soloist, with her clearer timbre and the quieter writing that accompanies her.) It might indeed be thought that the speaking-voice used for most of the first half (at 'definite pitches' but nevertheless speaking) is a blunt instrument with which to work, especially on so subtle a text; alternatively, one can take it as a sign that Schoenberg realized his libretto was 'unsettable' in the traditional way. One may appreciate his intention to create a new blend between text and music, while remaining less than wholly convinced by any particular solution proposed. In this case, the text comes to resemble a difficult lecture-course shouted by sonorous male voices, and I had a feeling of being subjected to propaganda

insufficiently strained through the sieve of musical organization; this impression was compensated, though not dispelled, by the orchestral score, which besides being absolutely disciplined, imaginative and musically virile, manages to follow or counterpoint the rhythm of the text. This combination of musical invention and prosodic exactness is itself a product of genius, paralleled perhaps only by the similar interplay in the *Ode to Napoleon*. But the Ode's text is in rhymed verse, which immediately sets up another field of purely aesthetic organization missing from the prose text of *Die Jakobsleiter*; hence, perhaps, my unease. It is impossible to say whether the rest of the work, once composed, would have solved this problem, whether by the end one would have come to see the first half in a different light. Probably Schoenberg would have simply said it was his work, that a religious work of the twentieth century must be like that, and no apologies. In any case, *Die Jakobsleiter* is incomplete, it raises apparently unsolved problems, and we have to take it or leave it. It is music that must be heard.

8   All Change in the Middle – Invitation Concerts

After a year or two, Glock decided to transpose the two Chief Assistants. Keller went to try and liven up the orchestral output, with Isaacs moving to the 'quieter' pastures of chamber music. The change of boss was something I personally regretted, though Leonard was a most kindly and cultured man. His enthusiasms were above all Francophile, yet his version of *The Art of Fugue* for chamber ensemble had become staple fare on the Third Programme. He proved a tolerant boss, sometimes slightly at sea trying to make out what this young lion that'd been wished on him was up to, but indulgent to a fault. He was still in charge of chamber music when I was pitched into the main firing line. One 'quarter' after another of Invitation Concerts supervised by Peter Gould had come out well over budget and with endless changes long after they were supposed to be set in concrete. Howard Newby complained that he 'expected the schedule for these concerts to have the reliability and predictability of Admiralty tide tables,' Peter was at a loss, and with about a year's BBC experience under my belt I was asked to take over. One of the earlier concerts I produced included the British premiere of a late Stravinsky jewel, an anthem from 1962 entitled *The Dove Descending Breaks the Air*. Its text-author, no less a figure than T. S. Eliot, was prevailed upon to attend, solemnly escorted by Controller Newby to sit in lonely splendour in the normally untenanted balcony of Studio 1, Maida Vale. The *Four Quartets* had been among my staple reading ever since I'd written a pastiche of their form for the Cheltenham Grammar School magazine, and now I had sight of their author, a wizened old man who looked as if since time immemorial he'd had far too much on his mind.

Somehow I managed to get the financial side of the Invitation Concerts in hand, mainly by looking very hard at rehearsal schedules (each ensemble day cost an extra half-fee); some of the legendary caution over money displayed at UE by Dr. Kalmus had rubbed off on me. I also learned to cope with Glock's famous last-minute changes of mind. Postcards would arrive from places like Corfu, saying 'I think that on … we should do … rather than …', performers having long since been 'pencilled', i.e. half-contracted, for the work that was now not going to be given. From the autumn of 1961 until I went on sick leave with pulmonary TB in the summer of 1963 I looked after the concerts, and distinctly remember my very first. Luciano Berio and Cathy Berberian provided the up-to-the-minute element, and Berio put me on my mettle by asking in a letter for two large heavy springs 'such as can be obtained from any yard where old cars are broken up'. I didn't go in person to obtain these musical instruments, but Central Services did their usual admirable job and the great man seemed happy.

Another fashionable visitor was Luigi Nono, whose conducting ability I found could be summed up by the word he used when asking the ensemble to pause – 'wanting'; I had no much higher opinion of his composing ability, as distinct from his instinct for the politically-correct bandwagon, but that of course is something history must decide. Roberto Gerhard's new works of the time were genuinely exciting, and for me he became one of the elder statesmen. John Ogdon's performance of Messiaen's *Vingt regards sur l'Enfant-Jésus* was a major occasion, even for someone like me who distrusted the composer's methods of construction: that lack of sympathy was to persist and after I incautiously agreed to book a young Czech pianist for a recording of the half-hour *La Rousserolle effarvatte* from the *Catalogue d'oiseaux* it struck me that one version of Penance and Purgatory for me would be to have to sit through a complete performance of that formidable collection of pianistic birdsong. Where Messiaen could find it in him to be succinct and even charming, as in the songs of *Poèmes pour Mi*, I warmed to him, but it didn't happen often enough. For the *Vingt regards* a second Steinway and a tuner were on hand throughout the evening just in case of accidents, but music and instrument survived unscathed.

There were occasional surprises, as when at a concert, just before I took over, George Malcolm played one of Couperin's harpsichord *Ordres*, and his page-turner turned at what George had thought was the end, to reveal a further page he'd never played and had to sight-read. He was one of the most regular contributors, since William and Hans admired his musicality and dynamism not only at the harpsichord but also at the piano. He was the supreme example of a performer who would never admit to feeling the slightest degree of satisfaction at the way he'd just played.

One coup on William's part was a full-length recital by Elisabeth Schwarzkopf, whose presence brought home to me for the first time the force of the dictum 'keep well away from the Truly Great'. For some reason the venue was not Maida Vale, but Broadcasting House's Concert Hall, which was just as well, given what went on during the balance test. The performance was typical – colours and effects laid on with the most impeccably-judged trowel – and the personality alarming: such total self-involvement, and just a few modest requests, as that the piano be moved back several yards onto the next level up because she, one of the world's leading and most publicized singers, HATED being exposed to public gaze. Apprised of her request, our studio attendants reported back that last time they'd tried it someone had broken his arm and it was a job for a piano-removal firm. None being available at six in the evening, the Diva had to be told, and proved philosophical – probably she expected nothing better of the BBC. She thought a powerful spotlight shone in her eyes should keep the enemy adequately at bay; it emerged that Broadcasting House had a small television-interview studio down in the bowels of the earth, and we were able to have her suitably dazzled. Apart from something about raw eggs to soothe her throat, that was about it: but the atmosphere of surface charm, arrogance and general strung-upness has stayed with me. And to help put everyone at their ease we had her husband, the great Walter Legge of EMI, sitting in the control cubicle running his remarkable ear over the balance. Since the microphone placings were in the hands of the ultra-talented James Burnett, even a Walter Legge could find nothing to improve. Madam's comment to Geoffrey Parsons as they were about to go on for the second half summed it all up: "I suppose we'd better give these lovely people what they want." I never worked with Fischer-Dieskau.

There was a contretemps when William had commissioned a wind quintet from the London composer George Newson and we'd booked, as we thought, the very best to play it – the London Wind Quintet, whose members were top men like the bassoonist Gwydion Brooke. It backfired because George included in his score passages where the players were instructed to improvise. That was something Mátyás Seiber had already done in his Violin Sonata, but probably he was there to advise the first performers, and there were moreover only two of them. The five great men in this case would have given a spotless performance of even something as new to them as the Schoenberg Wind Quintet, but improvisation had never been on the agenda. Young and green as I was, I didn't cotton on to the fact that George was expecting of an older generation something only the newest generation would take in its stride, and that in any case it always helps if composer and performers get together, well in advance, to talk about a new piece. At the afternoon balance test George was greatly put out by the lack of improvisation, the players were put out by his dissatisfaction, and you didn't rub two explosive characters like Newson and Brooke together without a spark (a letter from George a year or two later refers to 'the belligerence I normally feel when facing another musician'). He walked out of the rehearsal and the performance went ahead without his taking a bow.

Nobody in my time with the Invitation Concerts followed the example of Stravinsky and Yvonne Loriod in insisting that they be paid before they performed, rather than after. The custom was to hand cheques to those who didn't have an agent here; I was only once expected to cash them on the spot, by the members of a French ensemble who had just performed a new Berio piece. I somehow escaped lynching and they got their money the next day. Certain piano music can make me intensely dislike the piano, and at one or two of the concerts I had my fill of it. Loriod I only overheard, during Peter Gould's time in charge of the concerts; when I took charge the avant-garde piano repertoire was in the hands first of an industrious Belgian lady named Marcelle Mercenier and later of Frederic Rzewski, to be encountered shortly.

A far more refreshing figure, Imogen Holst, was a gifted choral conductor who also followed modestly in her father's footsteps as composer and eased Britten's daily routine as amanuensis. Basil Lam claimed knowledge of a postcard sent by Holst to Vaughan Williams while on his honeymoon with the words "I say, Ralph, aren't women a funny shape!" Funny or not, in terms of passing on profound musicianship something had clearly worked. 'Imo' came a couple of times to conduct the Purcell Singers, an excellent small choir made up of potential or indeed actual soloists. She introduced me not only to some of her father's best choral music, but also to minor Baroque masters such as Franz Tunder. Her technique in charge of a group was summed up by her most frequent reaction after a first run-through – "Lovely, darlings … BUT!!" She was eminently balletic and could transmit some of her natural rhythm to those with whom she worked. A memorable lady.

The 'TIX', or Thursday (later Tuesday) Invitation Concerts, happened not only in Studio I, Maida Vale, and later in the Concert Hall, Broadcasting House, but, at the start of the season, in four out-of-London centres. Hans looked after the one in Belfast with Heather Harper's second performance of Schoenberg's *The Book of the Hanging Gardens*; Janice Williams, an intensely musical pianist whom I had recommended, played John Field and reported Hans's practising his ball control with a scrumpled-up sheet of paper in an attempt to make her give herself a rest. She'd been determined to go on practising her piano control, and wasn't appreciative: for a prominent 'analyst', Hans could be a hopeless psychologist. I travelled to Newcastle to produce the Lukas Foss Improvisation Group, my boss Leonard Isaacs gladly touring the city to fetch an extra percussion instrument for the group, and to Coventry for a concert as part of the celebrations on the opening of the new Cathedral.

Leonard Isaacs soon received an irresistible offer to become head of a new Conservatoire in the middle west of Canada, and with a young Canadian wife he wouldn't have hesitated: his best BBC time had been and gone and it was a wonderful opportunity. He took Canadian nationality in 1973 and died in Winnipeg in 1997. His successor in charge of 'chamber music and recitals' was Peter Gould, a producer since leaving the Navy just after the War and a fascinating pianist who had never had the confidence to go after a solo career: during his BBC years he was persuaded by Hans, who cared nothing for rules and regulations, to make very occasional appearances as a pianist, notably in two programmes where he accompanied Janet Baker. That was permitted, though no money could change hands. From the moment I arrived as one of 'Glock's lot', Peter had been invariably kind and helpful, with not a shade of animosity, and although the far more senior David Stone, soon to become Principal of the Royal Scottish Academy of Music, was made his deputy, I had any amount of scope for my ideas. He evidently admired the fluency with which I came up with them and the range of music I offered, and trusted my choice of artists.

The late spring of 1962 saw a concert in the old Jubilee Hall at Aldeburgh as part of the Festival. A new Tippett cantata, *Crown of the Year,* was the centre-piece, with its ineffably genial composer conducting, if that was the word for his giggly direction, and Maureen Lehane well cast as the soloist in delightfully spring-like music with a children's choir. The all-embracing composer immediately garnered in the young man from the BBC, who after the morning rehearsal found himself part of the daily group lunch at the Wentworth Hotel. He then walked briskly back to the station, which Aldeburgh still had in those happy pre-Beeching days, and waved along the way to a splendidly sporty car containing William Glock and Peter Gould off to the concert itself. Peter had been a totally unflappable producer and must have done the honours at least as well as I could have done. What I recall of the rest of the programme is that Peter Pears and Osian Ellis delivered Schubert's *Songs of the Harper* in an unauthentic but plausible version for voice and harp; I supposed that Osian could, on demand, have delivered them single-handed, judging by his prowess at the old Welsh musical technique *penillion,* where a melody is played on the harp after which the performer improvises a vocal line against a second hearing of it. (The only song I know of that does the same in classical music is Richard Strauss's eminently well-titled *Morgen.*) Someone, probably Basil Lam, raised the objection that transferring the piano part to the instrument it was supposed to be imitating meant stripping away a layer of artistic ambiguity from the music. But then he'd been suckled on Empson. I left it to him to put the point to Osian Ellis.

There were also concerts in two of the City of London's mediaeval guild halls. Stationers' discommended itself by having a thick carpet that deadened the sound, despite which the violinist Tibor Varga made Schoenberg's arcane Violin Fantasy extremely persuasive; hearing it was a pleasure denied its composer, who ten years earlier had written to Varga one of his last letters, saying of his performance of the Violin Concerto that he had never known a work of his performed so totally sympathetically except when he himself had coached it, and ending with the hope that he would soon hear Varga play the Fantasy. My main memory of the Goldsmiths' Hall concert is that the members of the Allegri Quartet wandered off limits into the basement and were challenged by a fairly rough young man worried about the security of several million pounds' worth of silver stored there. Their 'cellist, William Pleeth, always a combative character, was at the centre of a mild altercation, which ended with my being told I should keep my staff in better order. A thought to chill the marrow.

Input from William could make not only for bizarre novelties but also for interesting surprises, as when he returned from a visit to Switzerland to dump on my desk the programme of a concert that had included (or even consisted of, since it was the size of work publishers' catalogues refer to with the ominous word '*abendfüllend*' (evening's length)) an Elegy by Othmar Schoeck for singer and chamber orchestra, to poems by Lenau and Eichendorff. I knew more or less nothing by or about this ultra-conservative contemporary Swiss composer, the UE's not-much-less conservative Frank Martin being more or less the A and O of my acquaintanceship with Swiss music – apart from one rather lovely piece, *Auf die ruhige Nachtzeit* by the much younger Klaus Huber, which Hans had run across at an ISCM Festival. (I'd then had Mary Thomas perform it in the studio with the Melos Ensemble, whose members she proved perfectly capable of conducting through the trickier 'corners'.) William's handwritten gloss on the concert programme was 'I thought this a very beautiful piece, which we should do'. And so it turned out. An outstanding Swiss bass-baritone, Heinz Rehfuss, sang the solo part (which led to a number of equally outstanding BBC recordings of Lieder: he is an unjustly forgotten artist, one of the best), and the Virtuoso Ensemble of London was conducted by Jacques-Louis Monod, enjoying the chance to make less spiky music than usual. The evening proved hauntingly memorable. So much for Glock as the Enemy of Euphony.

Other surprises and new works were less welcome and enlightening, for the concerts threw up extraordinarily silly things that exasperated me, as when a pianist named Frederic Rzewski flew in all the way from Naples to soil a concert-grand Steinway with the talcum powder required to execute Stockhausen's glissandi in a new *Klavierstück*. The very influential Steinway office in London had an energetic new chief man named Bob Glazebrook, and on learning of the pollution he waxed eloquent, prompting Peter Gould to issue a long-overdue edict that for piano pieces involving 'preparation' of any kind the Steinways were on no account to be used. An over-enthusiastic or gullible or maybe influenceable official had some years before purchased about forty Challen pianos for Music Division; they were eminently suitable to have talcum powder strewn inside them, and (so far as we were concerned) useable for little else. I dropped William a line about it all, saying I could think of better things to do than provide material for Deryck Cooke to savage in *The Listener*, and he was soon obliged to take me at my word, for halfway through 1963 a routine mass X-ray showed up a shadow on one of my lungs. Not long before, I had spent much of a visit to a UNESCO programme-exchange conference in Paris fighting fever and exhaustion, and now enjoyed three weeks in Brompton Chest Hospital, where in a few days I put on five pounds without treatment even having begun. Many more weeks were spent convalescing.[1] Stephen Plaistow looked after the autumn 1963 concerts that I had planned, and liked the job so much better than I by now did that he stayed on as their regular producer, transforming the series into a pure showcase for recent music. William's main interests by then lay elsewhere. Stephen was succeeded for the concerts' final stage by Tim Souster, one of two composer-producer recruits from 1965. I returned with relief to my great loves, the Lied and chamber music.

NOTES

1   Convalescence included a brief holiday on one of the Canary Islands, during which I came across a mineral water whose label insisted that it produced an immediate sensation of well-being (*el sensacion de benestar*). One of my productions on my return was with a group supreme at arousing such instant euphoria, the Italian String Trio (Franco Gulli, Bruno Giuranna and Giacinto Caramia). I quoted the bottle and said that was how their playing affected me, which pleased them very much.

9 *The Lieder Recital*

I found a rich field for the deployment of such craftsmanship as I had in giving a more digestible form to the Lieder recital, or for that matter to recitals of songs in any language that needed translating: for example, when I eventually awoke to Fauré's fascination I found works such as *La Bonne chanson* a true challenge. Perhaps I should have been one of those obscure nineteenth-century literary men who in their spare time from doing a boring job set down their inmost, unrealizable longings in third-rate verse, for a part of the secret fascination many songs held for me was that I was sufficiently behind the times to take seriously, at least as genuine attempts at emotional expression, the often mediocre texts of many great Lieder. (Wolf had impeccable literary taste, Schumann's was usually very good, Schubert found grist to his mill in a variety of things high and low, while Reger, I came to feel, had been able to set only turgid and off-putting lyrics.)

Broadcast song translations when I joined were literal in a way such material simply wouldn't bear, and their delivery entrusted to the all-purpose announcers, who were understandably embarrassed by the bald, naively-phrased emotions they were required to read out. The educational standard in the earlier 1940s, even before the implementation of the Butler Act, had been such that I'd learned to précis and paraphrase, which I now did with those awful soppy song-texts. Their poets had been in earnest, something the composers recognized and allowed to guide their inspiration; now it was up to me to encapsulate it all in a few words well-enough chosen and down-to-earth enough for an intelligent fellow like a BBC announcer to empathize with and deliver. So in a Lied programme I aimed at a fusion of music and two sets of words, in text and script. I needed to remember also that no listener can hold more than two or three quite brief summaries in his mind: with major Lieder cycles one had either to let the listener sink or swim, or interrupt at the least intrusive points. That lesson, like so many others, seems to have been forgotten again.

In the fullness of time some sort of synthesis was achieved, though the tension between announcer and script could rarely be fully resolved. Producers were more or less banned from going on the air themselves, the doctrine being that in our safe jobs we were there to provide employment for those with the talent and knowledge to lay claim to air-time; if, quite exceptionally, there were some matter on which a producer was better informed than anyone else, then subject to vetting by the Personnel Department he could be invited to write about it in the *Radio Times* or *Listener*, against payment of a 'staff contribution'. (The payment was to, not by, the producer. There was a story of an old don, supreme expert in his field, given to railing against his younger colleagues' 'demeaning their discipline' by appearing on television, who, when entreated to give of his expertise with the rider 'the fee will be twenty-five guineas', replied by return 'Dear Sir, I will appear in your programme and enclose my cheque for twenty-five guineas'.) The staff contribution was, however, a relative rarity; what we were allowed, indeed expected to do, apart from occasionally writing an 'attributed' script of the kind already described, was appear and 'trail' our programmes for a minute or so. That counted as part of our work, and could be illuminating or embarrassing – it depended on how tolerably one spoke and whether one had a good idea that would attract the listener (I ended one trail with "Come on in, the water's lovely!"). It could also be mildly disastrous, as when a ham-fisted studio manager trying to record me holding forth about Brahms managed to press the record-button on the machine that should have been delivering the musical illustration. The resulting 'howl-round', an alarming noise not unlike the sort of thing an epileptic may hear in his head just before an attack, immediately told us what was wrong. But by the time he could stop the tape a bar or two of the piano introduction to Brahms's *Abenddämmerung*, the most numinously beautiful thing Viola Tunnard ever played for me, was gone beyond recall: it had seemed to conjure up the most solemn moments in the *St. Matthew Passion*'s evening music and also the magical '*Soave sia il vento*' trio from *Così fan tutte*. Viola was by then too ill to help (recordings often waited a long time before being transmitted), so we had a tricky recording and editing session with Paul Hamburger playing the missing bars on the same piano. He did his best but he wasn't Viola. The programme containing the song was broadcast and certainly the deception wasn't apparent to the uninitiated.

Of course I could never have delivered a complex script as well as an announcer, who might well have an actor's training, merely because I'd thought it up in the first place. There was something in the doctrine of separation of functions. The best Third Programme/Radio 3 announcers got on a script's wavelength quite remarkably, and if one had written anything presentable some of the old guard could respond with remarkable vigour: I remember Ronald Fletcher, he of Cyril Fletcher's comedy show, at the announcer's table, his mind clearly on the racing results, but delivering high-quality goods when his moment came. And Joy Worth with the wonderful throaty gin-voice was equal to anything on any level of brow. But on balance, and re-hearing some of the cringe-making presentation from the 'golden years of broadcasting', I have to agree with another of the late John Drummond's better dicta, "I don't like being read at". Whether the 'personality presenter' is any better is a different question; first-hand knowledge delivered at arm's length, versus quick study delivered with charm and smarm? Some choice.

One curiosity came my way around 1970 after a broadcast of Schumann's classic female song-cycle *Frauenliebe und -leben* (Woman's Love and Life). A very angry lady wrote in complaining that both the words and the music were hopelessly male chauvinist and how could I put such a work on the air!? I took the point about Chamisso's text (even though it in fact reflected the events leading up to his own marriage), but should have been genuinely fascinated to know how music can be male chauvinist. Unfortunately the writer had in her indignation omitted to include an address to write back to. I'm sure that during the intervening decades there have been many dissertations purporting to show precisely how music can be male chauvinist; those haven't come my way, but recent studies of Schubert's musical language are beginning to show that it does indeed make sense to try and identify 'male and female' traits, just so long as it doesn't carry automatic inferences about a composer's own sexuality (after all, does it matter?), and doesn't descend to words like 'chauvinist'.

Lieder recitals brought out the chronic over-preparer in me: to achieve a good programme countless songs needed looking at, with many ruled out only to be looked at anew since one was bound to have missed something first time. After I left, Siegfried Lorenz's recordings made in the DDR during the 1970s and '80s showed me how much there was in some of the simple, one-page strophic Schubert songs I had passed over time after time in those days of quiet research. And to write an interesting, informative script it might be necessary to go quite deeply into the background. The BBC's Central Reference Library went to endless trouble getting hold of authoritative works on any subject or person one cared to name, and the major German poets in particular had to be boned-up on. The greatest of all was not so much a chapter to himself as a veritable library, some of which inspired in me the epigram 'Goethe was a Turd'. I only found out much later how very shamefully the real-life Hatem had treated the real-life Suleika, Marianne von Willemer, but had long since come to understand why D. H. Lawrence wrote that Goethe 'began literally millions of intimacies, got as far as "How d'ye do?", then lapsed off into his own infinite ego'.[1] There was, however, no denying the magic of the writing. Then there was the super-sensitive Mörike and the other poets set by Hugo Wolf, not to mention Schubert's other favourite, Mayrhofer, who in turn led on to the rest of the circle, such as Schober, whom my Goethe characterization also fitted but without the caveat. Knowing less of French literature, I felt impelled to work still harder there; from wading through an 800-page life of Mallarmé my memory can now salvage merely that he was determined never to express similarity with the word 'comme', but with some alternative such as 'selon' – all part of the Symbolist ethic, different things and forms being basically the same anyway; that he spent endless evenings closeted with men of equal distinction considering the French language from every angle; and, surprisingly, that he had a long catalogue of likes in British food, such as 'Cockaleekie Soup'. And then there was poor Baudelaire with his wicked guardian, and after him poor Verlaine with his cheap cigars and expensive ideal of woman, achieving '*sagesse*' only at the end of a life filled with anything but. And so on and so forth. Gradually I acquired what Cormac Rigby used to call a 'well-stocked mind'. The strangest side-effect came when I needed to check a Biblical reference; I did so on a London bus, whose conductor, on reaching me, said to this atheist-by-upbringing and (at the time) agnostic-by-temperament "I hope you'll pray for me, sir, you doesn't see moch folks readin' de Bible dese days."

NOTES

1   Even Goethe's amendments to Marianne von Willemer's poems before their inclusion under his own name in the *Buch Suleika* of the *Westöstlicher Divan* do little more than smooth out a few roughnesses and bring about the music one expects of a Goethe lyric. Once or twice he falsifies her psychology, as at the end of the first stanza of '*Was bedeutet die Bewegung?*' where Marianne's hope of sitting quietly at her lover's feet becomes the more glorious prospect of being greeted by a thousand kisses from the ever masterful poet.

10   *Artists (III)*

An essential part of programme-making was to identify and exploit talent. A wide range of artists had got themselves 'on the books' on their merits, and broadcasting wasn't just for the 'biggest names', which it often couldn't afford anyway outside prestige series such as the Proms. To make a programme with Janet Baker was a supreme pleasure and privilege, collaborations with major overseas artists like Elisabeth Grümmer an education (she was the incarnation of womanly musicality); but other singers, some far less prominent, could come up with valuable performances. Among sopranos, for example, the procession – and what proportion of the names are now widely remembered? – ran something like this: Jennifer Vyvyan, April Cantelo, Jacqueline Delman, Heather Harper, Dorothy Dorow, Wendy Eathorne, Elizabeth Harwood, Jeannette Sinclair, Angela Beale, Margaret Price, Jenifer Eddy, and (if I not for the last time allow myself to run on beyond the time-frame of this particular piece) Sheila Armstrong, Margaret Neville, Victoria Sumner, Alison Hargan, Jill Gomez, Norma Burrowes, Sandra – "Mister BUNthorne!" (*Patience*) – Dugdale, Lucia Popp, Patricia McCarry, Bozena Betley, Margaret Marshall, Yvonne Kenny, Elizabeth Gale, Caroline Friend, Edith Wiens, Barbara Rendell and Harolyn Blackwell. The list could be matched in other areas of solo and chamber-music performance, though given my inborn love of the soprano voice there the lists would be shorter. Ironically, the BBC's demarcation between the Music Programmes Department of Music Division and the Gramophone Programmes Department of Recording Services, which indeed grated with us since it meant that records were off limits except by special dispensation, was an incentive to trawl for talent among those not so 'distinguished' as to be recording commercially (a rarer activity then than it later became). For that matter, some of the ones who made records often seized the opportunity to learn for me lesser-known music of no immediate interest to their record company. The degree of cooperation I received from artists like Janet Baker and John Shirley-Quirk when it came to taking on probably un-reuseable repertoire still amazes me and makes me think a devout vote of thanks.

With such talent around, I had a sneaking feeling that the producer's contribution could lie only in realistic and responsible 'casting', the right performer for the right music. To which, add the duty to do everything possible to help the artist give of his or her best, and refrain from anything counter-productive (the balancer Keith Wilson observed to me of one over-sensitive producer, "She can fuck it up in ten seconds flat"). Producers were there for their ears and knowledge, and it was our job to offer an opinion when asked by artists whether they had done themselves justice. A programme might well be heard more than once, but it was not a gramophone record; though standards of accuracy needed to be high, I must have advised against proposed 're-takes' almost as often as I asked for them. Inspiration and a sense of continuity were just as important.

Before Glock, even the producer's presence at a broadcast was not thought essential – 'the performers know their stuff, the studio manager's in charge of the studio and the announcer has his notes to work from'; an earlier Head of Music, Herbert Murrill, was quoted as saying the producer's place was at home by his wireless set judging the quality of the finished product. That changed, though I sometimes think with surprise of the number of my early programmes where for one reason or another I wasn't there. When it came, as it mostly did, to recordings, Glock's new 'highly musical/creative' producers tended to be of a cast of mind that wanted not merely to monitor proceedings, but also to contribute ideas – meaning coach: they were often frustrated performers, as indeed was I somewhere in the dimmer recesses of my mind. The Dartington Quartet, with whom I made countless programmes, didn't feel they had the measure of an unfamiliar work till they'd been through it, in both senses, with Hans Keller, and even then they could be in some doubt, particularly about minuets: one of them said to me once, only half jokingly, "we never know what to do with Haydn's minuets, we have to ask you". Glock, too, certainly believed in sharing his ideas with people, though he never acted as their producer in the studio, and in my prime I was surely as active and interventionist as anyone. The sheer effrontery of expecting experienced and thoughtful artists to change even a small detail of what they'd prepared over perhaps years, at no notice and into a microphone, never crossed our minds. And very many of them put up with it amazingly or even seemed grateful.

Maybe we producers were not so much frustrated performers as embryonic teachers? Belief in the BBC's educative role was still strong in our time, but given many listeners' tendency to turn to music for entertainment rather than education it could be a touchy subject. Newby was still of the Reithian, improving turn of mind, though when an American heard his account of what the Third Programme set out to do and said "But that's education!", the Controller's reply was, "No: pleasure and enlargement". (It was a dictum that, without anyone's realizing it, echoed down the decades into Ian McIntyre's time and his much-misunderstood title for the Radio 3 'Evening Sequence', *Mainly for Pleasure* – hence the frequent puzzlement over why a programme should be called that, and suggestions of alternatives such as *Partly for Pain*.) The BBC did, after all, have a Controller, Education, whose writ ran immeasurably wider and with more draconian authority than that of Controller, Music. When at one point the post was advertised it was possible to read a summary of his job description, which made it clear that everything, but everything, had to be done as he prescribed. Since education programmes were geared to national curricula that should have been no surprise, but at the time I thought, "if only C. Mus. had as authoritative a brief!" An idle thought, for even if he had, he wouldn't have presumed on most of it. Hans Keller would have, though.

11   *Programmes*

Peter Gould's openness to my programme ideas led to a variety of series broadcast on the Third Programme and in due course the daytime Music Programme. One project that gave me immense satisfaction immediately after my return from sick-leave was a weekly series with six broadcasts of lesser-known Schubert songs at the start of 1964. The singers were Heather Harper, Janet Baker, the Swiss tenor Ernst Haefliger, already a veteran and with a touching mellowness to his conception of the composer, Jeannette Sinclair, a deeply musical soprano who after Sir Georg Solti's arrival at Covent Garden had found herself with time on her hands, Robert Titze, a remarkable German baritone of an older, bel-canto school, and, above all, Peter Pears with the incomparable Benjamin Britten playing the piano parts. The recital by these last two was given live from the Concert Hall of Broadcasting House on 3 January 1964, and included rarities such as *Der blinde Knabe*, *Der Winterabend*, *Der Geistertanz*, *Vor meiner Wiege* and the great Pyrker setting, *Das Heimweh*, which about the same time prompted Paul Hamburger to leap from the piano stool as he and a singer were about to record it, exclaiming "You know, this *Heimweh* is ZE GREATEST SCHUBERT SONG OF ALL!!". The Pears-Britten recital was a momentous occasion for me, though not the easiest: Pears proved gracious to a fault, but Britten acted surly until he could establish the pecking order, enquiring 'from which NAAFI we'd inherited this piano' (a 9-foot Steinway, for my representations down the years that microphone balances in chamber music and recitals would greatly benefit from something smaller fell on deaf ears).[1] After which, he became almost genial and expounded to me his idea that the low repeated notes in the accompaniment to *Der blinde Knabe* represent the tapping of a blind person's stick as he makes his way through the world. I was convinced, repeated the idea here and there, and eventually began to see it put forward as other people's original thought.

From the pianist Andor Foldes I learned a good deal about Bartók, and he was also hospitable. I remember our walking out of a Chekhov play that starred an unbelievably wooden Ingrid Bergman. His posthumously published memoirs tactfully say he remembered nothing of the evening, for in principle he adored the ground Bergman stood on: it was just that 'stood' was too much the watchword that night. The most purely exciting pianist I ever worked with was the Hungarian-American György Sándor, a keyboard lion from a bygone age but still in his prime (which went on for very many years!). He had left his native land quite early to settle in the United States, less on political grounds than because he simply liked the place and its way of living. He had the most stupendous technique and a fantastic rhythmic sense.

With me at my most Schoenbergian stage we had mild arguments about modern music, which he felt had disintegrated once tonality, an absolute necessity to his ears, was dismantled, but in the studio he was extremely pleasant and matter-of-fact to work with. The first thing in his repertoire that amazed me was a Bartók transcription of Bach's G major organ trio sonata, seemingly written entirely in octaves for both hands; it came over as the most dynamic and bouncy music imaginable. That encouraged me to let him loose on the same composer's B minor 'French Overture', which thrilled me to the core but prompted the most vigorous protests from our Old Music guru, Basil Lam, not to mention his hyper-sensitive secretary, because of its total disregard of any period style, even to the extent of double-dotting dotted rhythms. I suppose he was really most in place in the early twentieth century. One revelatory weekend was spent when Martin Dalby, the other 1965 recruit, asked me to look after Sándor recording for him the entire Prokofiev piano oeuvre. I had my reservations about Prokofiev's piano music, going by what I'd so far heard from more modestly-endowed pianists, but I happened to be free and said yes to Martin, knowing it would be a make-or-break experience from which I'd emerge either vowing never again to hear another note of the stuff, or else a total convert. The latter duly happened. György had seen and heard Prokofiev playing his own work, and vividly described the poker-faced way in which he would sit at the keyboard, body motionless, building up the most colossal crescendi; he himself was capable of similar things, but what I remember most of all, among the welter of notes and virtuosity, was one of an early set of pieces, entitled Scherzo for Four Bassoons. I've always wanted to hear that splendid little piece transcribed for its rightful performers, but there are few bassoon quartets about. The best comment on Sándor came from Hugh Wood's pianist wife, Susan McGaw, after we'd been to his South Bank recital – she said she loved these old-style virtuosi with whom in quick passages the hands moved so fast as to become invisible or at most a blur! (Or, as the immortal Schnozzle Durante put it, "I coulda gone foider but I ran outa pie-anno!")

NOTES

1   The 'Navy, Army and Air Force Institute' was a welfare provision that accompanied our armed services wherever they went. NAAFI pianos were notorious for the high risk that they would be come upon by personnel whose idea of a bit of fun was "Go on, give it a drink!".

12   *Words and Music*

Words and music mingled happily in the song recital, but at one point in the middle 1960s, which is to say after the Music Programme began (there will be a certain amount of such dovetailing as the narrative develops), I devised, under some internal emotional pressure, six programmes that combined them in a cheekier way. Half a day of a major actor's time could be had remarkably cheap, since it didn't encroach on whatever he or she was doing in the evening, so I was able to call on readers of the calibre of Micheál McLiammóir in Yeats, Jack MacGowran in Beckett, Michael Hordern in Philip Larkin (between the songs of Mussorgsky's *Sunless*) and the vinegary-voiced Anthony Jacobs in William Empson and, later, Christopher Logue (the music in that programme being Hugh Wood's set of Logue songs). My manifest idea was to point up certain coincidental or at most synchronistic similarities of mood or procedure between the different arts, such as a tendency to set out boldly and immediately wilt, found both in Yeats poems read by Cecil Day-Lewis and in the Debussy songs I put with them. I originally thought up the programmes for the early days of the Music Programme, but communication broke down and they were finally ruled ineligible, after which it took a private talk with a puzzled Howard Newby before he could be persuaded to allow them, very reluctantly, onto the Third. His point, that people tended to listen either for speech or for music and would find an alternation of the arts within a single programme puzzling, accurately forecast the reaction of more or less everyone who heard the programmes.

Undaunted, I then compiled an enormous conflation of readings from the sedater pages of Henry Miller's *Tropic of Capricorn* with various composers' music (late Beethoven to Charles Ives!), under the authentic Miller title *Opus Izzit of My Sadly Corrugated Clavichord*. It too was withdrawn from the Music Programme schedule at a late stage, though I did use some of it as a separate account of a 'Bohemian Christmas' in Paris; that one I didn't even try to sell to Newby, who had a few years earlier been visited by the Vice Squad after the critic Peter Duval Smith quoted Miller's F-word over the air. For this curiosity I called not on an American actor but on the redoubtable announcer Douglas Smith, who had exactly the right mix of high spirits and newsreader-quality voice, which he used to corpsing effect in *Round the Horne*. The *Words and Music* broadcasts brought home to me the civility of great writers: I received letters or cards, naturally all short and unmemorable except to me, from Beckett ('I hope all went the way you wished'), Empson ('I am sorry I could not hear the programmes. It sounds as if I should have done'), Larkin ('I can see that lovers of music 24 hours in the day might be upset if they found poetry coming at them instead') and Logue ('never mind, it is best to expect a

Paul Hamburger, Milein Cosman and Leo Black
at the Arnold Schoenberg Institute, Vienna, 2000

ratio of 6/1 in terms of effort and positive result. Viva Ché!') when I'd let them know either that the programmes would be broadcast or that they wouldn't. Contact with Henry Miller was left to his publisher John Calder, who reported him as Not Amused.

Those 'mixed programmes', for all their problematic reception, were the least unreal embodiments of my constant urge to make links: a natural Symbolist, I. Whatever I liked, loved, I wanted to work into programmes, though it seldom got that far. A boyhood passion for jazz had persisted, and with Hans Keller constantly going on about Gershwin and trying to get 'acceptable' versions of him (if by Hans's lights there were any) onto the music network, I was inclined to follow suit. My first attempt came very early on, when I got as far as almost contracting an excellent jazz pianist, Dave Lee, heard and enjoyed on the Light Programme, for a live quarter-hour recital – I had (and have) no idea what he would have played or how we would have set about it. He was game, till it became clear to him that quarter to nine meant am not pm: as he reasonably pointed out, he normally went to bed around then, and the idea was dropped.

Oscar Peterson was a great idol, also Erroll Garner. When the latter visited London I was so emphatic about his stature to William Glock (I had him in mind, so help me, for an Invitation Concert), that the poor man actually took himself off to a South Bank concert of Garner's. His sole comment to me afterwards was "He has slicked-back, greasy black hair". My ideal of promoting some new Benny Goodman, equally apt in jazz and classics, remained a pipe-dream, for which the listening public can probably be profoundly grateful.

Another enormous enthusiasm, contracted in the UE Vienna days through films and alive to this day (she is a year older than me), was for a supreme dancer-singer named Caterina Valente, immensely beloved in Germany. She struck me as the most 'musical' popular singer I'd come across. Her equal talents at dance and song made her a kind of Michael Jackson of her day, without the extreme peculiarities. She sang in twelve different languages, with her best-known English song *The Breeze and I*. Given this country's relatively low degree of familiarity with her I could keep my love private, though I did breathe her name to Hans now and again.

Sport, too, crept in – had not Hans, after all, commissioned World Cup Variations for 1966? I got up to nothing so ambitious; on an FA Cup Final day when Leeds United played Arsenal I devised a brief morning programme with the Leeds pianist Kathleen Jones and the Highbury flautist Gareth Morris. That elicited a suitably sniffy commment in a periodical from my BBC predecessor, Bernard Keeffe. More viable (though only just in Glock's time and again way beyond the strict time-frame of this essay) was a series of three talks at the time of the 1972 Olympics. When the Baron de Coubertin resurrected that great festival, he made sure it included arts as well as sports; it's just that nowadays one never hears anything about them, which is probably just as well given what passes for 'the arts' in our day and age. My reading of Sir Roger Bannister's memoirs, *The First Four Minutes*, inspired the idea of having the passages about his youthful experience of blending with the universe in 'rapturous running' read out, with a suitable linking text; he came to the recording and seemed pleased. A strong recollection from the session is of the enormous capacity of his barrel-chest. The other two programmes were a talk about Music and the Olympic Ideal by my fellow-producer Michael Pope, a man of great dignity and decorum who had taken part in the 1948 London Olympics as a 400-metre hurdler (the 'man-killing event'), and one on the similarities between athletic and artistic performance from the soprano Anne Pashley, who had run as a sprinter in the 1956 Melbourne Olympics and later established herself in the musical profession.

13   Training? What Training?

'The Olympics' provide a timely cue for the theme of Training. Looking back, I find it hard to believe how untrained we young producers were when we set out, and how much was done for us. Our departmental managers held the producer responsible for everything about his or her programme, but the lifelike reproduction of the artists' contribution was in the mostly very safe hands of the 'studio managers', i.e. balance engineers, who had any amount of training, both technical and musical, and who would, nay did, look with some amusement on the idea that anyone else should answer for what they achieved. The best ones – James Burnett, Paul Reding, Ronald Cooke, John McCulloch, John Sadler (who to our great sorrow died all too young), Keith Wilson, John Rushby-Smith and, later, Margaret Steven, James Hamilton, Martin Page and Geoffrey Klinton Parker – were masters of their craft, as we (hopefully) of ours, but with a more realistic idea what it was. If we wanted anything to sound different and knew how to ask for it tactfully, they were duty bound to try, but were rightly in charge. For producers, microphones were strictly off limits except in the direst emergency. One morning early, with the Brahms Piano Quintet bearing down at a rate of knots, the studio manager had clearly overslept, and after waiting rather a long time I decided that something needed doing. We were in Maida Vale, so a call for a replacement from Broadcasting House would have meant a crucial further delay. Positioning one of the BBC's faithful monophonic PGS ribbon mikes (they needed no plugging into an electrical socket) near the piano and another over the centre of the quartet, I got a balance that, once arrived, the balancer checked approvingly and altered very little. But that was definitely a one-off, in extremis, and with the onset of stereo I should have been out of my depth. Strict demarcation was the watchword; when I first worked in America with the team from station WFMT who looked after the Chicago Symphony, I was flabbergasted to see the producer, Norman Pellegrini, casually stretch out an arm and alter the level of a fader controlling one of the mikes set up by his supremely expert balancer Mitchell Heller. With us that would have provoked a strike.

14 Oops!

Even 'quality monitoring' was for many years left to others. We had nothing in our offices on which to play recorded tapes – whether because we were thought dangerously incapable or to save expense I neither knew nor thought to ask – but relied on copious notes to ensure that when a programme had been edited after recording it didn't contain anything unwanted. Naturally there were 'errors and inclusions', and it was only a matter of time before I too experienced what should be every producer's worst nightmare, the moment when he hears a 'false start' or other 'unwanted mod' going out over the air to the listening dozens in a programme of his. I had it happen only two-and-a-half times in three decades, but for the first I chose an artist as famous as the veteran violinist Szymon Goldberg. He'd recorded two of Bach's solo works for me, and when I heard it broadcast I found to my horror that I'd left in a false start in a movement of the B minor Partita. Since three of his pupils made up the Oromonte String Trio, with whom I worked a good deal and who might have been expected to be listening to their old teacher's broadcast, I expected ructions and more when the mistake got back to him. In fact I never heard a thing about it.

A few years later I credited the equally distinguished Annie Fischer with a second shot at the end of Beethoven's 32 Variations in C minor for piano, but the only such trauma that actually led to even a phone conversation was when Susan McGaw, wife of my best friend Hugh Wood (I surely knew how to pick them!), was broadcast playing the piano part in Webern's early Piano Quintet. This was a very strange one: listening to the transmission, I clearly heard the work start, go on for a few seconds, stop, and start again after a few more seconds' pause – and so did she. I went straight to my 'phone, and before Susan could have time to react she heard hers ringing and my voice saying "SHIT!!". I duly crawled and was forgiven. I ordered the tape for my next editing session to remove the offending section, in case of a repeat broadcast. Great puzzlement: no false start was to be found, the performance was spotless but not more than complete. Nobody else would have taken in the tape meanwhile to remove anything, and I had to conclude that what had happened had been an error on transmission: the engineer starting the tape in the continuity suite must for some reason have thought he'd missed the beginning, run the tape back and started it again. But nothing was mentioned in the continuity log, so it remained one of those mysteries.

To offset those minor catastrophes, I should tell the story of the Stravinsky Elegy. An interlude near the end of my time with Kalmus had been a visit to the little festival of new music at the south German spa town of Donaueschingen, where I heard the premiere of a 90-second tribute by Stravinsky to the festival's late founder, Count Max Egon zu Fürstenberg. It eventually found its way into a BBC programme that I produced. Following the score at the balance test, I got the impression that something sounded wrong, and realized it was up to me to tell the top clarinettist Jack Brymer, whom Sir Thomas Beecham had summoned a decade earlier with an invitation to play his 'clarionet' in the newly-founded Royal Philharmonic Orchestra, that he was playing the piece on the B flat instrument instead of the A; or maybe it was the other way round. I surprised myself by the tact with which I was able to tell the great man – though given his supremely calm and magisterial nature a more forthright reminder would probably have given no offence either. Another feature of that Donaueschingen weekend had been that the leading modern-music conductor Hans Rosbaud fell ill, his enormously difficult and obscure programme being taken over at no notice by an unknown (to me!) from Paris: on my return I duly wrote to the BBC's new Controller, Music about that feat by Pierre Boulez. Not so many years later Boulez became the BBC Symphony Orchestra's Chief Conductor.

15   At Last, the Music Programme

Sweating on the second two-year renewal of my short-term contract, I knew it would all depend on what Pilkington said. If radio was to remain a quiet backwater, then nobody as new as me could assume he was entitled to outlast those already 'on establishment'; but were there indeed to be a day-long music programme, and the assured funding to run it, then many more people would be needed and I could hope, if I went on doing good work, not assaulting my secretary and not stealing the petty cash, to have an enduring future with Music Division.

Not everyone agreed that a day-long music programme, which in effect, meant that music could be allowed into the home as easily as turning on a tap, was desirable. Benjamin Britten had expatiated in his Aspen Lecture of 1964 about the 'alarming availability of music', and figures nearer home had their doubts too – for example, Alvar Lidell, who was very much against it. I saw the force of the arguments about cheapening music by making it too easily available, and the danger of people's using it as mere background, but my joy in my work of the past few years was such that I fervently hoped for a larger-scale broadcasting scheme that would let me go on doing it and more. For once in my life I displayed a healthy self-interest, and there was also something in my feeling that you can't tell people how to behave – it would be up to them what use they made of the programme were it once there.

In the fullness of time Pilkington He Spoke, and the Music Programme was ensured. It began in December 1964, going on the air at 8.00 am, and continuing until 2.00 pm on weekdays, noon on Saturdays and 5.00 pm on Sundays. Administratively it was run by the managers in charge of the Home Service, with John Manduell, an experienced ex-producer, doing the outline planning. It therefore had a Home Service-level musical brief, though with a couple of concessions to the natives' funny ways in the form of strands called *Music in Our Time* and *Further Hearing*. As I've said, much of the joy of programme-making lay in bending the brief, and at one stage, a year or two in, Gerard Mansell, the Controller of Home and Music and the future architect of *Broadcasting in the Seventies*, exploded at Manduell, saying he'd realized not merely that the thing was no longer what it was meant to be, but also that it never had been!

The years of innocence were over, the years of experience followed, and long they were indeed. The later chapters of this book afford just a glimpse of them.

Part Two

Paul Hamburger (I) (Milein Cosman)

Personalities

1 William Glock

From the outset, which is to say a year before I came into the picture, Glock began to update BBC music, remoulding it nearer to his heart's desire. One innovation was a series of 'Invitation Concerts' on Thursday (later moved to Tuesday) which mixed different eras and forces in a way not previously heard on the radio, nor indeed anywhere else. The very first placed Boulez and UE's *Le Marteau sans maître* between two Mozart string quintets. With the UE catalogue in the frame I made a point of turning up at some of the early concerts, notably when Wilfrid Parry and Yfrah Neaman were the soloists in the Berg Chamber Concerto.

During the interval of that or a similar concert in February 1960 I found myself addressed by Glock's French wife, Anne. I'd done a small piece of work for his publication *The Score*, and when she said "My husband wants to see you," I thought "more of the same". In due course his secretary Betty Evans rang to make an appointment for me to go to Yalding House. At that point I began to wonder if something was afoot, for he was known to be re-organizing the place – but then she rang again to say he'd double-booked himself and must postpone seeing me, which seemed to me to squash the whole idea, supposing there ever to have been one. (In fact it was standard practice with him.) I'd also heard meanwhile that the new producer was David Drew, he of the Roberto Gerhard study. I had no idea Glock was looking for several new people.

O ye of little faith! Came the second call and day, went the young man, to find himself facing not only Glock in his Controller's office, but the equally formidable Hans Keller, who was by then Chief Assistant, Chamber Music and Recitals.[1] Glock didn't beat about the bush but asked straight away whether I'd like to join the BBC and help organize radio's classical music output. As well as saying, in effect, 'would a duck swim?!' I did prudently ask to know a few details of what the work entailed. He said it might be more 'planning', or more 'producing', whichever I preferred. Being a shy type, I opted for planning, as likely to involve less contact with those whom at an abortive interview in 1955 a high BBC official had described as 'temperamental artists'. I soon learned that 'planning' was strictly speaking something done by a different area of BBC Radio, Music Division being what was known as a 'supply department', but supposed that Glock had in mind the likelihood of extended music-broadcasting hours once the Pilkington Committee had carried out its imminent investigation into the BBC. I did murmur about money, the great man asked me what I was earning, so I told him, Kalmus having just upped me from £12 a week to £13. He beamed and said he could certainly double that. When some weeks later I finally went to see 'Personnel Officer, Radio' – a classically rotund bespectacled figure named Hetley on whom one could almost see the indispensable bowler hat – he said rather grandly "I'll put you down for two thousand", i.e. three times my UE pittance. In 1960 that felt like money.

At the Glock interview I tried briefly to see things from the point of view of UE's Dr. Kalmus, who had, after all, given me my chance even if I felt I'd blown it, and I asked if I could allow him a bit more time to find a successor. Glock agreed that during the first two months (May-June) I should work half-time for him and half for Kalmus.

Purely in passing, for a long time I shrewdly or cynically put down my life-transforming piece of luck to opportunism on the part of the BBC's top management with the Pilkington Committee due. After the arrival and challenge of ITV, BBC Television had perked up amazingly whereas radio remained a bit of a backwater, and there seemed to be some risk that it would be superseded altogether. I came to suspect that The Board had been in agreement: 'For Pilkington a Show Must Be Put On' – a radio show. Since the Controller of Music was coming up to retirement age, they hit on that as the field for 'Putting on a Show' and looked around for a Showman. Hence the appointment of William Glock, pianist, Schnabel-pupil, music critic sacked from *The Observer* for writing once too often about Bartók, and notably head of the music summer school at Bryanston, later Dartington, to liven things up. It was a theory.

When I told colleagues and acquaintances of my impending departure from UE London, one reply came from a sombre lady at Boosey & Hawkes New York, Dr. Eva Wiederer, who said I'd seemed genuinely interested in copyrights and that to that extent she'd miss me. What more could I ask? On a more serious tack, my Oxford instructor Bernard Rose wrote that, though he felt Glock's appointment would do untold harm to British Music, a few people like me around might help keep it within bounds. My first-year Oxford harmony and counterpoint tutor, Bernard Naylor, simply asked "What can you do for me in your splendid new position of power?" (I did, in fact, place a group of his motets in a programme, but they deserved it.)

Although Glock's writ extended in theory to music on television, the Music and Arts people there, including iconic figures such as Huw Wheldon, were more than happy that he never showed any interest, and would doubtless have resisted strongly if he had. The BBC ran orchestras up and down the country within flourishing music departments in Glasgow, Manchester, Cardiff, Birmingham, Belfast and Bristol, each of which also had its own 'artists' census'; 'the regions' still contributed occasional programmes to the national services, as well as employing musicians at an earlier stage or more modest level for broadcasts within their own area. The staff orchestras were the main element in Music Division beyond the bounds of the Music Programmes Department. Glock saw that, for a while at least, he had to influence the content of programmes, something rarely attempted by his one predecessor, R. J. F. Howgill. The latter had come from an oil company, and his desk, or so the seniors reported, had seldom been encumbered by anything more than the day's London *Times*. The Controller embodied Management beyond the Rubicon, meaning in this case Great Portland Street, London W1; he was a Proconsul, responsible for seeing that the natives implemented high-level policy, which certainly never touched on music beyond the need to maintain a dignified Reithian worthiness and not frighten the horses.

Glock, however, was a horse of a different colour, and the management of the time surely failed to realize the full Trojan implications of his appointment. It wasn't a matter of the Proconsul's going native, for he was profoundly native already – to his new recruits, a charismatic figure who played the piano like an angel, could talk to Stravinsky, had put his job on the line for Bartók, understood music as we could only hope with great good luck to do some day, and was from the start referred to, addressed even, as William. Bliss was it in that dawn to be alive; the feet of clay were spotted only as the day unfolded. He was, pro tem, for hands-on rather than arm's-length management. He had long-term plans to improve the BBC Symphony Orchestra in London and did so, persuading the money-bags to finance his inveiglement of other London orchestras' top players, who deserted in droves and came to enjoy a principal's salary on a co-principal's workload. Another major aim was to modernise the Henry Wood Promenade Concerts, as David Wright has shown in detail in his recently co-edited book on *The Proms*. Nearer my own field, he instituted the Invitation Concerts with their mixture of periods and styles, and took an active role in planning them.

In much of that indispensable work, perhaps too diplomatically described in his 1991 memoirs, *Notes in Advance*, he found himself obstructed by the Head of Music Programmes, a minor composer named Maurice Johnstone, whose orchestral tone poem *Tarn Hows* was heard from time to time over the air, as were a variety of pieces by other still lesser composers on the staff (of course the producer-composer Robert Simpson by no means fell into that category, though with Glock there he suffered along with the others).[2] Given Howgill's role in life, 'Maurice' had been a very powerful figure, in fact The Boss. A parting of the ways became inevitable, and with Johnstone gone William wanted to avoid having anyone comparably influential under him, though he found it perfectly possible to work with Johnstone's Assistant Head, Eric Warr.[3] The most amiable of men, Eric stayed on till retirement age, did yeoman service helping run the BBC Symphony Orchestra's public concerts, and kept a watching brief on departmental employment of artists in general via a weekly assembly known as Artists' Committee. He could be a benevolent, calming influence when the lion cubs showed signs of sticking out a paw to biff their elders and betters on the muzzle.

During my twelve years working for Glock, his presence and our background combined to create a powerful ethos; but the idea of a 'Glock regime' is an illusion. The conditions for a monolithic regime simply didn't exist. For a start, William himself was two musicians, the Schnabel pupil deeply in love with the Viennese classics and capable of uttering fascinating truths about them ("In Mozart a scale is a melody; in Beethoven it's the way from one point to another"); and the missionary of modernity, who knew he must try to reflect not only the more-or-less undeniable greatness of the recent past but also the still-questionable prominences of the present, at the risk of falling for things whose spuriousness would only show up in the fullness of time. Some of his producers were longer in one suit, others in the other, while the very occasional one, such as Stephen Plaistow, seemed equally strong in both. If the programmes with which Glock was directly concerned showed what he memorably called a 'creative unbalance', that 'unbalance' could be corrected, at least in part, by what his underlings did off their own bat: one need only consider the amount of Brahms and Richard Strauss broadcast despite his (at best) indifference to both composers. With a voice-fetishist like me on the rampage, Strauss was bound to figure! I wouldn't like to say where that voice-fetishism came from – not, surely, my father's efforts, but perhaps records of people like Elisabeth Schumann with which I'd grown up, and extra-musical factors of which I'm no longer aware.

One thing about which Glock's recruits were, pro tem, in no possible doubt was that we were working for a man whose word in all matters musical could be taken as law. The feeling didn't recur during my BBC time, for all his successors' conviction that they fitted the bill, while I only gradually became aware of the gaps in his knowledge and the limits of his sympathies. One moment when the scales fell from my eyes was when the widow of Roberto Gerhard, whom William had made a focal point of his 'new music' output, observed to me "William doesn't really like Roberto's music – he plays it because he knows he ought to". But then she was at least as strange and eccentric an old lady as many a composer's widow.

He had a reputation for taking people up and then suddenly going off them, especially manifest in his other life running the Dartington Summer School; I kept away from there, I think uniquely among the generation he recruited, and I also think it wasn't just shyness and pressure of work that made me do so. Obviously it meant missing a great number of very interesting and stimulating people. I remember declining an invitation to lecture there about Schubert; he had already featured in many of my programmes, but I simply didn't feel ready to talk about him yet.

Part of the challenge of 'dragging the radio listener screaming into the twentieth century' was that there was often a yawning divide between the new and the worthwhile, and Glock took it as part of his remit to cover both. The composer Philip Cannon tells of a conversation between himself and Glock at a party shortly after his return from Australia in the late 1950s, when Glock allegedly said he had no particular belief in contemporary music – "nothing really special was written after Mozart so all one can do is encourage experiment." (Some party to make him forget Schubert!) Cannon, a fearless young man, told him roundly that it was a disgraceful attitude for someone in his position to take, and spent the next few decades telling himself that was what had got him 'blacklisted'. I think William was in fact blissfully unaware of many composers who imagined him as terribly down on them, though personal taste was bound to come into it to some extent; much of the tension between him and Hans Keller, as Alison Garnham points out in *Hans Keller and the BBC*, derived from the fact that Glock didn't really like Schoenberg either, his ideal twentieth-century composer being Stravinsky, with the no-longer-controversial Bartók a close second.

Much of the 'new music' had been written before the Second World War and a fair amount before the first, so it was more a musico-political matter. Certainly there was a lot of catching up to be done, hence that 'creative unbalance' theory. The problem with creative unbalance is that if it goes on long enough it can be tantamount to blacklisting; for that reason Bob Simpson argued passionately and in public that the planning of the Proms shouldn't stay with the same man for more than five years.[4]

The Bartók-Stravinsky generation hadn't done that badly before William's arrival; what he felt he must concentrate on was in the first place the post-Second World War avant-garde, and then the Second Viennese School, though that he soon began to leave in Hans Keller's safe and enterprising hands. Down to the time he left, it paid off, thanks to intelligent recruitment. Where the 'newest' music was concerned, a rift gradually revealed itself between William and Hans, in terms not only of taste but also of value-judgements. William was unprepared for a radical experiment wished on him by Hans and Susan Bradshaw. There had been warning signs: I remember a memorable broadcast report on the 1959 Kranichsteiner Musiktage, beginning with a collection of seemingly disconnected notes followed by a sinister foreign voice – "Ladies and Gentlemen, That was the Beginning of *A Piece of Music* [in fact Stockhausen's first opus, *Kontra-Punkte*]." Hans and Susan now slipped into a BBC studio with a recording engineer to thrash about and concoct an entirely spontaneous and meaningless collection of percussion noises, which Hans then had broadcast on 5 June 1961 within a recording of a genuine Invitation Concert as *Mobile for Tape and Percussion* by one Piotr Zak. The composer's name, he told me, originated with Harry Croft-Jackson, who as arbiter on the acceptance of unknown scores had of necessity to be in on what was otherwise a well-kept secret: he asked his Polish barber for the most typical Polish name, and that was what the man came up with.

When the secret was revealed, there was not a vast amount of critical reaction to quote as proving Hans's point that for the first time in music's history something could be regarded as music which was not even bad music but no music at all. All the same, a broadcast discussion with Donald Mitchell and Jeremy Noble generated a certain amount of heat. As for William, he was furious, saying to me "I don't like own goals," and the two of them never got on as well again.[5] However effectively Hans dealt with opposition, it saddened him to lose a friend. He said to me more than once "When I arrived here, William was my only friend; now he's my only enemy".[6]

There was never much press comment on music broadcasts. I always found it strange that a London concert attended by a couple of hundred people might be written up whereas a programme heard by many thousands or tens of thousands very rarely was, despite the best efforts of successive radio publicity officers. One effort that struck me as misguided came in *Private Eye*, a profile of Glock neither particularly funny nor at all fair. Its best feature was a well-drawn small cartoon of a pianist turning to the audience with a worried look, rather as would Rolf in The Muppet Show, saying "Here comes the hard bit"; but in particular its closing salvo, '*Private Eye* is always prepared to be sued; William Glock always has been,' seemed perverse, when here was a guy doing his damnedest to liven up a great Establishment institution long thought the epitome of stuffiness. But 'pseud' was and is, of course, one of the prime *Eye* words, as 'phoney' was one of Keller's. Hans, however, made it abundantly clear what were the things he found not phoney, whereas 'these swine' (to use a favourite expression of Basil Lam's) never let on what they regarded as the real thing rather than pseudo (i.e. 'false, apparent, supposed but not real,' as the *Oxford Concise English Dictionary* has it). Shun those who know not how to admire but piss indiscriminately on anything that shows a sign of life.[7]

To those who made music programmes for BBC Radio in the 1960s, that time now looks like some kind of golden age. Not that anything was necessarily better than it is now (chorus of oldsters from the floor: Oh Yes It Was!), merely different in keeping with the times – but there did seem unlimited money to use up on music: just as I joined, even the very simple costing form producers had so far filled in after a broadcast was abolished. The bills weren't scrutinized but the products of our inexperience were, and it took a year or two to get the hang of the job. We were there to think about spending money well – nor did anyone worry much about feedback from the public on whether it was noticed to have been well spent: we knew just enough about listeners to know we knew better. It was a crusading age, through the pioneering work of Glock and his producers in making carefully selected tranches of the twentieth century known when it was at most a mere sixty years old. The 1960s were the time (or yet another time, given Edward Clark's inter-war enterprises) of 'the new music', though, curiously, recent works by an Edmund Rubbra, an Anthony Milner, a Philip Cannon and a myriad others seemed to some of his new producers anything but 'new' – they were there simply to be overlooked. That Glock, for all his achievements, also reflected a more general atmosphere is suggested by the fact that a *Listener* article by Edmund Rubbra, 'Letter to a Young Composer', contains the sentence, 'to dismiss a work merely because it does not fit into the critics' category of what constitutes modernity is a fatal narrowing of vision'. That dates from 1956, as long as three years before Glock joined the BBC. Our vision was, indeed, for a while quite narrow: in due course the 'Glock regime', not to mention the ensuing regimes, squeezed out Rubbra and many others. Glock himself saw to it that when Rubbra had had a *Cantata di Camera: Crucifixus pro Nobis* commissioned and performed in New York, it duly appeared in an Invitation Concert, as had a very fine choral predecessor, *Lauda Sion*, written at Hans Keller's suggestion and premiered in 1961. For the 1966 Proms Glock commissioned the next Rubbra choral work, *Veni Creator Spiritus.* He did, unfortunately, remain impervious to the virtues of Rubbra's symphonies, which show the composer's stature at its clearest. The truth can be inconveniently complex.

That opens up a range of speculations and half-truths about 'the Glock regime' and its attitude to the more traditional British composers. At one end of the scale there are 'old believers', many of them composers or former composers, who insist that figures of the stature of Rubbra were 'blacklisted' under Glock, and that he had once said he'd rather resign than have to broadcast all Rubbra's symphonies. The latter remark can be dismissed as fantasy – in the first place, nobody over Glock would have dreamed of issuing such an order to the Controller of Music, and, secondly, any such series would in any case have been the business rather of the subordinate figure in charge of the orchestral output. That was, in turn, Leonard Isaacs, one of the old guard who'd grown up revering Rubbra, and after him Hans Keller, a great admirer, as witness his suggestion that led to *Lauda Sion.*

At the opposite end of the scale is the view of Glock as the sole redeemer of an outdated and fusty department, the rejuvenator of broadcast music in Great Britain, without a wart in sight. David Wright has argued that point in the *Musical Times* (Winter 2008) with much statistical back-up. Certainly Glock was able to point out that in 1961 there had been twenty-six broadcasts of Rubbra's music as against three works by Boulez and one by Stockhausen, but down the years that kind of old-style representation diminished, not through ill-will on the part of the Controller but because older producers who had grown up with the Rubbras of this world retired and were succeeded by younger men and women with different tastes. Here is the crux of the matter: the music output of Home and Third, as later of Radio 3, depended on the initiative and energy and knowledge of producers given every encouragement by line managers devoid of any sense of 'I have the power here' – which in turn ruled out a balanced output in the profoundest sense, that of representing everything worthwhile and not merely what each individual producer thought worthwhile. The managers intervened, if anything, too little, not too much. At my pre-recruitment interview Glock said, a-propos the abortive idea of my having to do with 'planning', "You'll meet with a certain amount of resentment – they've had twenty years of laissez-faire". When I retired they'd had, we'd had, twenty-eight more. Output planning was a chimera, hankered after by the more elevated spirits (Keller and Plaistow, to name but two), but not the business of those exclusively in the firing line. Two cheers for democracy, then; it certainly made for a more interesting output than that of commercial radio with its computerized play-lists.

'William' has gone down in history, and many of his innovations still mark off BBC music from its competitors. We may well see his like again, but will he or she then be allowed to achieve anything?

NOTES

1   In the BBC's hierarchy a crucial fault line normally separated posts with titles such as Chief Producer from those called Chief Assistant: the latter seemed part of a Management Club for which one had to have had one's name put down at birth. It's a measure of the confusion attending the 'Glock regime' that posts with that title could have existed in Yalding, but they were, after all, virtually sub-heads of department. It's also a measure of something or other about the BBC's treatment of its staff that despite the constant shrinking of Hans Keller's field of action over his storm-tossed final years he never had his title taken away, only adjusted.

2   That was another thing Glock determined to take in hand, so complicating the careers of various young creative figures from Alexander Goehr onward, whose creativity was a main reason for their being in the department.

3   In fact, an Assistant Controller was eventually appointed, to 'try and get to the bottom of William Glock's in-tray', words used to Hans Keller by the Radio Personnel Officer when they heard a pneumatic drill in the street outside. The lot fell initially on a distinguished scholar and former Head of BBC Gramophone Programmes, Gerald Abraham. His new post had nothing to do with programme-making.

4   In a booklet published in 1981, *The Proms and Natural Justice*, Simpson commented sharply on BBC policy, something which under the standard producer's contract he would have undertaken not to do, even after retirement. BBC staff, on appointment, used to sign as part of their contract a clause saying that neither during nor after the termination of their employment would they write or speak in public about 'any confidential matters that had come to their notice', and you had to be quite high up in the Management Club to ride rough-

shod over that one. But so far as I know, there were no repercussions such as followed, for example, the appearance of Barrie Hall's post-retirement book on the Proms after the 1980 orchestral strike, or indeed Bob's fatal 'statement to the press' about dissatisfaction over the orchestral 'cuts' and ensuing strike. Glock's successor Robert Ponsonby retained the planning of the Proms for all of his decade and a half, but ironically enough the next incumbent, the all-dominating John Drummond, did so for precisely the period Bob had suggested.

5   Like Hans, who harboured a latent passion for football going back to the great Viennese Jewish club of the 1930s, Hakoah, and in the 1960s developed an overt one for Tottenham Hotspur, William was a fan, namely of West Ham United. He also claimed to have seen the uniquely graceful Kent and England cricketer Frank Woolley, which to me was like saying he'd heard Schubert sing and play the piano. For that matter, the future Controller Radio 3, Stephen Hearst, had during the same youthful years in Vienna harboured a fierce passion for the far-distant players of Arsenal; I discovered that only long after my retirement, let alone his.

6   Hans had in fact greeted Glock's appointment with euphoria. In 'Welcome to William Glock', *Musical Opinion*, Vol. 82, April 1959, p. 463, he wrote that it 'will prove a milestone in the history of British broadcasting … I consider him *the* man for this key position.' Reprinted in: *Hans Keller, Film Music and Beyond*, London, Plumbago, 2006, pp. 222-24.

7   Radio 3 was, however, immortalized at least once, the week *Private Eye* ran a spoof Radio 3 column. It worked on the tried and trusted Goon Show principle that if jokes come thick and fast enough they needn't all be very good, and naturally made great play with a certain Hans Killer, at what time the model was promoting short radio talks in which the word 'problems' often featured. One of the cracks I liked best duly came when a running gag about the kazoo (=comb and paper) reached a climax with 'Cecil Aronowitz considers problems of playing the kazoo after a lifetime spent playing the viola'; in some new pieces stranger things did indeed happen to well-respected elder statesmen. The rubric 'News and Weather' was acknowledged, with one very short piece by each of the said composers within its five-minute slot. Some of it was well researched, and at times so near the mark as to make one suspect inside information, but whoever thought up 'Hans Killer discusses problems of after-lunch speech coherency under the influence of Mouton Cadet' knew not his man, for HK was strictly Best Bitter with a whisky chaser. Nor did that give rise to any 'problems of speech coherency'; I never saw or heard him even minimally altered by alcohol, and noted in him a natural state of openness and 'suppressed censors' that most of us achieve, if at all, only after a drink or two. In fact to my mind he was constitutionally drunk, and I had read just enough elementary physiology to identify that with lowered synaptic resistances. Given the eventual effect on his life of motor neurone disease, I'm profoundly relieved never to have put this theory to him in person, and to very few people altogether. I was allowed a couple of token appearances as Leo Bleck, but their heart wasn't in it; maybe my beautiful conducting of Kreisler's Beethoven Violin Concerto (see 'The Making of a Music Producer') got me off the hook.

2 Hans Keller

I became aware of Hans Keller a whole decade before I went to work with him at the BBC in 1960. During student years in Oxford, *Music Survey* and *The Music Review* would turn up in the Music Faculty library, both with trenchant contributions by him – anything from a regular survey of film music to a winning entry in a *New Statesman*-style competition for an imaginary newspaper review of an opera. I'd sent in a very feeble entry and was most impressed with Hans's impersonation of Hanslick reviewing *Wozzeck*. Those pieces established him in my mind as a formidable personality; long before *Private Eye* satirized him as 'Hans Killer' in the 1970s, my mind had arrived at a similar nickname. By the time he became BBC Radio's Music Talks Producer in 1959 he had worked out an early version of his wordless method of musical analysis, four examples of which had been broadcast, and I heard the very first one in 1957. It treated music I thought I knew very well, Mozart's D minor string quartet K. 421, studied as a 'set work' both at school and at Oxford, yet it made me realize things that had never crossed my mind before, things as elementary as the fact that it ends on the very same falling octave with which it began.

During my two years working in London for Universal Edition/Alfred A. Kalmus Ltd. (1958-60), he visited our office once; the reason I forget, his request for a discount I still remember. One of the odd jobs I did for *The Score* around then was to translate Schoenberg's 1931 radio talk on his Orchestral Variations, and when Hans became the BBC's Music Talks Producer in 1959 he homed in on that as obvious material.

And little more than a year later, there I was, working under this extraordinary man, this mixture of Socrates, Karl Kraus, Donald Tovey and Groucho Marx.[1] I was Hans's subordinate, or he might have said 'insubordinate', for I lost count of the number of times he felt obliged to call out to his secretary Pauline Beesley in the next office, "Pollini, Mr. Black is being obstreperous, will you kindly take him for a walk round the block." That was the atmosphere, fed by a shared sense of humour, yet it took many years for him to call me by my Christian name. He'd been promoted over the heads of far more experienced producers, and I suspect that once he learned to trust them he let them get on with things they understood, but over this very raw recruit he took endless trouble. In the preface to his book *1975*, later reissued as *Music, Closed Societies and Football*, he confessed to his 'one act of BBC-style management', when he declined to let a certain Mr. Black include in a programme the Carl Nielsen wind quintet. He wrote, 'Leo Black grumpily disagreed, but far from having a proper discussion on the matter, far from showing proper respect for his opinion, I simply ruled the work out of the programme.'[2] What Hans didn't write was that in true Keller fashion Leo

Black went off and pretty soon got the work in anyway. So much for BBC-style management.

But by and large he was a joy to work for – totally encouraging, willing to discuss any subject, and with his normal reaction to a programme idea "Yes, get on with it". He knew and had assessed a fantastic range of music within the Austro-German tradition – he knew everything, it seemed to me – and a great deal that lay outside it. He was aware of his limitations, seldom pronouncing, for example, on French music; just occasionally he wasn't aware of them, and then he could come out with something outrageous – I remember a very private note, which I wish I'd kept, saying 'I never heard Tippett was a composer; I thought it was only words he couldn't write.' There spoke Britten's apostle, or maybe it was just a way of winding up an over-serious young man.

Long before his best and most famous broadcast (transcribed in 1975) he told me of his vow, taken at nineteen while still in Vienna and in the hands of the SS, "If I ever get out of this alive, I'll never again be in a bad mood".[3] So far as I could see, he was doing well by that vow.

At my quite unexpected interview before being recruited into William Glock's newly-reorganized BBC Radio Music empire, Hans was strongly present, Glock did most of the talking, and Hans's version broadcast to the world was that 'Mr. Black' had been typically 'grumpy' (a favourite word of his).

At an early stage of his time in charge of Chamber Music, Hans had the idea of a BBC Chamber Ensemble drawn from our Symphony Orchestra in London and giving concerts in places that couldn't afford existing groups. It ran aground on various administrative and musico-political grounds such as unfair competition, but he did succeed in persuading principals from the orchestra to rehearse the Mendelssohn Octet in their spare time, and I was privileged to produce an outstanding broadcast. The same group was soon prevailed on to prepare Schoenberg's *Verklärte Nacht* and then what proved a highly intelligible performance of the same composer's late and very difficult String Trio, which in view of its enormous demands on a mere handful of performers requires an acknowledgment here to Hugh Maguire, John Coulling and Alexander Kok. As the most passionate and knowledgeable of born-again Schoenbergians, Hans saw it as his duty to ensure that the great man no longer suffered from the syndrome the great man had summed up in the words "My music is not difficult to understand, it is merely badly played." His early exercise of initiative in asking Heather Harper to perform *The Book of the Hanging Gardens* is narrated in this book's essay on her. Hans's ambition that there should be no more bad broadcasts of Schoenberg came much closer to fulfilment than some of the others.

So far as performers were concerned, Hans strongly disapproved of the BBC's anonymous-audition system and refused to take part; while in charge of Chamber Music he got it agreed that members of the listening panel (auditions were heard live in those days) might if they wished go into the studio to check their impressions. Ironically, it was a performers' organization, the Incorporated Society of Musicians, that asked for this to be rescinded; to them anonymity and impartiality were indispensable to ensure fairness. There he was in a minority of not much more than one; certainly my sole incursion into an audition, hoping not to be noticed and not to disturb, proved very brief indeed. I still can't quite conceive of artists with so much at stake being happy to preface their performance with a detailed discussion of tempi, phrasing and so on, that being what Hans had in mind. He was happy arguing with anyone, but the converse didn't have to apply.

Another more successful innovation on his part, at least for a while, was a system of 'experimental recordings' designed specifically to cover cases where at an audition there had been one strongly enthusiastic opinion but two turn-downs, or where a producer had heard someone at a concert with no other 'evidence'. A programme would be set up by the panel member/producer, and treated like any other, i.e. recorded, basically, straight-through: the initial understanding, which soon went by the board, was 'no retakes whatever'. The recording was then heard, as if it were an audition, by three people including its producer; if it passed, the performers were paid and the programme broadcast. The crucial factor was the enthusiasm that went into its production, the feeling of *making a programme* rather than of being under assessment. Most of the early experimental recordings were broadcast in a monthly morning series of Hans's devising called *The Rising Generation*. The first was by a 'cellist named Dori Dawes, his discovery, not much heard of thereafter but someone who survived to become a priest in the West of England. I chipped in with Susan McGaw, who went on to do a fair bit better, and there were a few more. Other programmes in the same series were by people who'd simply passed auditions – I think of Norma Fisher, and definitely of John Shirley-Quirk. The programmes were of mixed standard, with John, near the late start of his singing career after some years as a chemistry teacher, outstanding. Sandy Goehr, the appointed producer, was away when the recording happened, so I was there instead and never looked back. With the swap of Chief Assistants, *The Rising Generation* lapsed, though debut broadcasts continued at much the same rate, while 'experimental recordings' still happened occasionally. The problem was that after a few years I was the only person who remembered what the idea had been, and they began to be used after auditions where there'd simply not been enough enthusiasm for a 'pass'. That was bound to mean that less 'interesting' (for better or worse) artists were involved – one authentication of another basically good Keller principle, that enthusiasm, which denotes a reaction, is sooner to be trusted than its opposite, which may merely show that there was no reaction. (All, that is, provided the ears are there in the first place, which in his time went without saying.)

Glock took it as part of his remit to cover both the manifestly worthwhile and the new though as-yet-unproven. Hans saw such professional gullibility as no part of his job description, a dichotomy that reached crisis point with the Piotr Zak hoax.[4] After a mere two years Hans ceased to be my immediate boss, but for his remaining seventeen years in the BBC we remained friends and quite close colleagues, his office being eminently visitable, whether with problems or with good things garnered from here, there and everywhere. I thus had little direct experience of his most productive BBC time, when his orchestral producers were generously funded to make enterprising and imaginative programmes; but he was ever-present, at meetings and in the corridor and at protracted lunch sessions in the Departmental canteen or at an Italian café just down Great Portland Street.

Throughout his BBC time he gave a certain amount of offence at Controllers' Meetings by ostentatiously working his way through his 'in-tray' while also participating fully in the proceedings. My one definite quarrel with him happened in the control cubicle of Studio I Maida Vale while I was producing the Invitation Concerts. He took the strongest interest in everything that happened at the BBC and was a welcome visitor to those concerts, not only while their producer's 'line manager' but also after his transfer to the orchestral group. One evening, however, his urge to deal with things got the better of him. I had worked out, from rehearsal timings, that the concert was likely to end a few minutes early, and had accordingly warned the continuity suite in Broadcasting House that they could expect to have two or three minutes to 'fill' with a record or a programme trail. Looking for the performer – I think it must have been the harpsichordist George Malcolm – to thank him, I found an empty space, and looking into the studio I saw that he had gone back on, instructed by Hans, to play an encore that would, of course, the expected under-run into an over-run of a minute or more. That was thought nothing in the context of the 1960s Third Programme, but I resented being made to confuse my colleagues in Broadcasting House, and the sheer cheek of his interference made me explode with "What the bloody hell do you think you're doing?!" He was amazed that his excellent initiative should have gone down so badly and that I should have been so public about my, to him, childishly possessive reaction. Next morning he was still adamant that he felt he'd acted rightly and would do it again in the same circumstances. We agreed to forget it and got on famously for a further decade and a half.

From 1971 onward BBC radio music was organized differently, according to a strategy known by the title of a notorious document setting it out, *Broadcasting in the Seventies*. Instead of a mixture of music and speech according to height of brow, the Home Service and Third/Music Programme, henceforth to be known as Radios 4 and 3, were to provide respectively all the 'serious' speech and 'serious' music; 'Light Music', including the BBC Concert

Orchestra, moved to Radio 2. Glock's time as Controller was nearing its end, and to streamline the music-production process the top managers decided to reinstate the post of Head of Music Programmes, Radio, abolished by him a decade earlier. By now Hans had made himself persona non grata after leading the revolt against the reorganization, which culminated in letters to the *Times* from 134 production staff in London and many in the regions. Letters of reprimand followed from the Managing Director, Radio, though even here, with clear breaches of contract a matter of record, nobody lost their job, not even the 'group of six' who had organized the revolt. Ian Trethowan called Hans in and told him "If this were the Gas Board you'd be sacked on the spot," to which Hans said "Then sack me, I don't want any favours".[5] In terms of long service and seniority the obvious person for Head was Peter Gould, who had long since succeeded Isaacs as my boss in the chamber music group. The Radio 3 Controller, Howard Newby, had a retentive memory and at one point observed to Hans that Peter lacked the slightest vestige of administrative ability, but the appointment proceeded.

Hans Keller's problems with Management during the 1970s – the second half of his BBC 'match', not to mention injury time – and his succession of posts have been well documented by Alison Garnham.[6] His 1938 vow must have become ever harder to keep, after the colossal row over *Broadcasting in the Seventies* and the onset of his motor neurone disease (which was kept a most closely-guarded secret). He spent more and more time away, not just on BBC work with the European Broadcasting Union, but lecturing and teaching, mostly in Canada and Israel. When at home, he was interested in everything. Though excluded from programme-making outside the field of talks, he found countless opportunities for action in both his final Chief Assistantships. He was genuinely in sympathy with any composer he thought had talent (which is not to say, as how could I, remembering that note about Tippett, that he always got it right), and untiring in his efforts to have new pieces objectively assessed and, if approved of, broadcast. One sign of his realistic thinking is that the 'readers' who assessed the constant stream of unsolicited new scores included not only major 'avant-garde' figures like Roberto Gerhard, but equally important if currently-neglected 'traditionalists' such as Edmund Rubbra. In coordinating 'new music' (where his writ still didn't run as far as the BBC's own commissions, something reserved to The Controller though eventually brought into the fiefdom by Hans's successor Stephen Plaistow), he pulled together a ramshackle collection of functions exercised by three different offices, mine among them. I was very relieved, since I had enough to do in a new role as Chief Producer, apart from which I found producers pretty uncooperative in accomodating works that had 'passed the panel'. If Hans did better there, it was another aspect of the syndrome summed up in my feeling that if I ever met a donkey with an extra hind leg it obviously never wanted, it would have been talking to Hans.

In John Reith's day the BBC had a very senior figure, Filson Young, go about the place with a watching brief to comment on things that could be done better, and things left undone that should be done. That, I felt, would have been a job for Hans at this late stage, perhaps in parallel to the Director of Programmes, Radio, with the title Questioner, Programmes, Radio – but no, an impracticable idea, for he would never have answered to 'QPR'.[7] Had he not totally identified with the BBC, I'm sure no money in the world could have persuaded him to stay till retirement age. Once retired, he still referred to the place as 'we' – seldom as 'you' and never as 'they'. He was above all an educator, and the BBC's traditional stance of leading its listeners upward was central to its appeal for him.

During the final years, more established producers as well as newer recruits were at times merely respectful of him, in a few cases very cautious indeed, or even downright hostile, intimidated perhaps by his formidable knowledge and invariable, ostentatious conviction of rightness. He vehemently refused to consider 'taste' or 'opinions' admissible criteria, and yet I remember seeing a note to him from Cormac Rigby, not yet a Reverend Father but Radio 3's formidable Presentation Editor, that began "You must not say 'I know' when you mean 'I think'". And in a sermon near the end of his amazing life Cormac put something in a nutshell which isn't totally irrelevant here: "The greatest enemy of the truth is the man who believes he has a monopoly of the truth."

There was also Hans's pseudo-aggressive manner, which in fact aimed simply to bring the other person out of himself and was meant in the kindest, most friendly way. The younger members of staff on levels junior to that of producer found such openness endlessly fascinating, and he was often to be seen as the centre of groups discussing all the important issues in life. A comparison with Socrates was hard to suppress, despite Hans's pronounced distaste for the 'Greek Keller'; he was, as Garnham tells, unusually upset when a senior manager called him a 'disruptive influence'. Hans and the Youth of Athens? They seemed to survive pretty uncorrupted.

All the same, his influence was waning, at least within the BBC, even if it maintained itself in Europe through his work with the European Broadcasting Union. The Concert Season was on principle broadcast Europe-wide, live, even by members who, given the opportunity to hold aloof, wouldn't have touched it with a barge-pole; and for all its high musical virtues it generated a certain amount of resistance among the 'lesser' members. In theory, all were equal, but everything depended on who got onto the working party, and there later 'European' priorities, namely the 'big' countries, prevailed. The volatile and personable Dragiša Savić of Yugoslav Radio was known to wax eloquent about centralization and dictation, and eventually instigated a rival scheme, *Let Us Know the Names*, which had various features the 'concert series' aimed to avoid, such as suggestions from particular countries rather than ideas put forward by the working party for local implementation.[8] That brought with it the other bogey, use of 'national' artists or composers simply on the grounds of their nationality – the exemplification of Buggins's Turn. Eleanor Warren came back from an EBU meeting during her brief time as Head of Music Progammes, Radio and told of these cross-currents, of Dragiša's outspokenness and of the mixed reception given to some of Hans's initiatives, summed up at the time in the observation "There *are* other singers than Jennifer Smith".

Despite rumours occasioned by his long absences in Canada and Israel, Hans stayed on, against both expectation and probably (in management circles) hope, until the official BBC retirement age of 60, which he reached in 1979. His ever-more-severe motor neurone disease was still a secret, though one or two of its manifestations were noticeable, such as an ever more laboured way of speaking which unfortunately gave, to me at least, the impression of bad temper (in him of all people, who'd taken that vow forty years before!).

Trying to assess the work Hans did in his various BBC positions, as distinct from his personal contributions and ideas, I sometimes find his opponents as well as his worshippers illuminating. It was Stephen Hearst's categorical opinion that, brilliant though Hans was, and likeable (Stephen's long-standing passion for Arsenal did not deter him from being a guest in Hans's inevitable taxi on their way to a number of Tottenham Hotspur's home matches), he should have remained a freelance and never joined a corporation. That, however, underestimates what he did during the pre-Hearst years in charge of orchestral music. Robert Ponsonby's 'not a corporate man' is not so wide of the mark: maybe there's a basic line to be drawn between those who haven't known military service and those who have – notably Ponsonby and Hearst, but Glock too had served in the war as an RAF flying control officer, a post demanding a fine sense of priorities when planes that might contain wounded men had to be allowed to land promptly. There were solid achievements while he had a 'real job', such as the initiation of a series called 'My Favourite Concertos', but though the 'short talks' and other innovations of the 1970s added spice, they were far too little if one thought what he'd done before ruling himself out of direct involvement with programmes. He was beyond doubt passionately involved with the Corporation, but what was un-corporate about him was in the first (or maybe second) place a basic rebelliousness based on what one may or may not be forgiven for calling a Talmudic tendency to argue about every bloody thing.[9] Nor might those with weighty matters on their minds find his jokiness any help in putting up with that: he once told me with relish that he had an interview with a high-up the next day, that the poor man was doubtless saying to his wife "Oh dear, I have to see that difficult Keller tomorrow", whereas he was saying "I shall go in and thoroughly enjoy myself". But in a rare moment of puzzlement he asked me once what it was that made management figures take so much against anything he suggested. I hadn't the heart to say "your exuberance".

More important still was his conviction that individual conscience must be supreme: not for him the Marxist argument that a single person's wisdom can never match the collected, collective wisdom of a party. He was to that degree not 'incorporable' in any system of cabinet government, where at times one has, because of one's position, to go along with decisions one disagrees with – which could have been why Glock found him such a difficult colleague.

Our relations during his remaining six years after leaving the BBC were intermittent and marked by a tendency to mutual misunderstanding that had already been creeping in during the 1970s. I'd get the odd letter about things badly done or left undone – but the watershed can probably be located much, much earlier, after the *Times* letter. Most of the 134 producers saw that they had to get on with it and make the best programmes they could under the new dispensation, while the hard core that had organized the whole thing went on agitating. Many of us, in effect, 'jumped ship' over questions like The Group's proposed reduction of music hours on Radio 3 to accommodate all the excellent speech programmes that our colleagues in those departments felt should be there. We had enough trouble over Radio 3, without setting out to persuade Radio 4 to re-define itself by resuming an output of music. Hans could be tetchy, I could be abrupt – but the mutual regard and admiration continued, and there were great times like the London Schmidt Festival in 1984. He was enormously active despite his illness, with a never-ending round of coaching at the Menuhin School and the Guildhall, writing in English and German, teaching privately and lecturing in universities and elsewhere.

His death in 1985 still came as a shock, even when I'd known for so long that he was desperately ill. The BBC agreed to the idea of a memorial concert, originally suggested by a violinist he greatly admired, Ida Haendel, and also by the clarinettist Thea King. The manager of the Wigmore Hall, William Lyne, saw it as a privilege when asked whether the concert could happen there, the Concert Hall of Broadcasting House being too small to accommodate the number of people expected, and it was a memorable occasion. It also conformed to long-standing tradition by 'over-running its slot' by at least a quarter of an hour, something Hans had always maintained need never happen given realistic planning!

The tone, but also the occasionally remarkable content, of our exchanges in those late years can be gathered from a correspondence after he left the BBC and while I was still there. A main part of my work for the preceding decade had been the importing and judging of recordings from overseas radio stations, which we might or might not then broadcast. In true Keller fashion he (literally) commented on my letter, which then went back and forth till the issue was, after a fashion, settled. (During his years in office these arguments might be initiated and continued on often badly-torn-off sheets of paper, or even on the backs of envelopes.) The end of the correspondence shows why such, on the face of it, irritating exchanges could turn out to be so fascinating. On 31 October 1983 he wrote:

Dear Leo

Not that it's urgent, but important, to my mind, it is. On Friday afternoon you put out a RIAS recording of the Zingara [piano] Trio's [Beethoven] Triple Concerto. With seeming disloyalty, I have to assure you that I would never have put out this performance – which I coached. I heard it live in Berlin, and again on Friday afternoon, thus able to confirm my impressions and my devastating criticisms, all of which I conveyed … and all of which were accepted without the slightest reservation. I don't want to bore you by going into detail, but let me say that I was absolutely honest to them, and that my concrete, specific, and essential criticisms were countless; I should say that so far as I remember, this was by far the worst performance I ever coached, and that they simply weren't ready to play the work in public. I cannot understand how the performance could have been passed; is any foreign tape welcome nowadays, in view of the financial aspect? … Yours ever [HK]

To which I replied (the asterisks mark the sites of Hans's marginalia (see below)):

Dear Hans,

Be reassured: the criterion for broadcasting a foreign tape, now as ever,* is that someone liked it. Since you didn't, there's something here within the spectrum between a disagreement and a misjudgement.** I will form my own opinion*** and give it to the someone in question, though not, as I know you'll understand, to you.****

Incidentally, if you are coaching outstanding youngsters who play abroad, it might be worth alerting them to what may be in the small print of their contract; since they believed soon after the concert that it hadn't gone well, the Trio might have tried to stop RIAS from distributing the tape. I can see that in their position they could well have been a) not fully informed, and b) anxious about offending those who'd booked them, but I think any civilized radio station would be sympathetic.***** Yours ever [LB]

Hans returned this with his comments on 4 November:

* NO. I well remember calling a meeting for that very purpose (before you came in), defining the difference between objective criteria and subjective pseudo-criticism.

** *Non sequitur.* My letter (needless to say, I hoped) confined itself to objective facts, unreservedly accepted not only by the trio, but by every musician who heard it, from Berlin's [?] to Josef Tal.

*** It isn't a question of opinion.

**** No. I operate quite differently, and educate our youth (at the Menuhin School and the Guildhall) likewise; there are no such secrets. (Opinions, yes; facts, no.)

***** Yes, important, thank you. The whole matter is far beneath discussion, for there are unalterable musical facts, such as –
  a. Every meaningful phrase has only one main accent. Where there's more than one, something has gone wrong with the composition, or the playing, or both.
  b. This principal accent makes sense of the rest of the phrase. Where it doesn't, it has been misplaced.
  c. At any given stage, there's a demonstrable and relatable difference between metre (background) and rhythm (foreground). Where metre replaces rhythm, meaning is, at the very least, interrupted.
  d. Not even in a triple c'to must str. intonation be, in all circumstances, 'well-tempered'; even in pno trios great composers think in terms of creative intonation – which is, invariably, harmonically demonstrable; there are motifs which can only be written for str., not for piano.†
  e. There are musicians – few, admittedly – who confine their negative criticisms, if they communicate them, to facts. As one gets to know them, one automatically trusts their verdicts. Examples in my life: Seiber, Cooke, Paul Hamburger, myself. (Not Britten, unless you forced him thus to confine himself.) You yourself may well be amongst them, but I've never heard enough from you to be able to judge.††

In sum, my answers to a (very) certain type of communication always 'spell it out', as a matter of principle, so forgive me if I carefully define obviosities (and invent nouns in the process). Which certain type of communication? In which a problem is *created*. Best, H.

To which I append a couple of comments of my own:

† This is a point I recall his making, apropos the Schubert piano trios, in a television programme on Schubert that never got as far as a broadcast, because in the view of the television bosses (Culshaw and Drummond, no less) it contained too many un-televisual faces and continental accents – that Schubert uses octaves in the piano in order to get motifs to work on that instrument which would otherwise have been far less effective than when first heard on the stringed instruments.

†† He had in fact had experience of my internal 'artists' reports' and at an early stage noted the one on Susan Bradshaw's experimental recording of the Brahms-Handel Variations, which made a large number of factual points.

After the lapse of many years, the most striking thing about that correspondence is its seamless transition from a grouse about a relatively minor matter to a classic statement of his philosophy. He had, of course, made those points about accent many, many times before.

He was a man I would for nothing in the world have missed.

NOTES

1   Among whom I can remember Hans having a good word to say only for Groucho, to whom through his walk and humour, not to mention his moustache, he sometimes seemed to be dedicating the sincerest form of flattery.
2   Grumpily arguing was something Leo Black was good at.
3   The story of Keller's arrest and escape from Nazified Austria was told in Radio 4's series *The Time of My Life*. It formed the first chapter of *1975 (1984 minus 9)* and is reprinted in Alison Garnham's *Hans Keller and Internment: The Development of an Émigré Musician*, London, Plumbago, 2010.
4   The Piotr Zak episode is discussed in the previous entry (on William Glock). I recently renewed my acquaintance with *Mobile* (thanks to YouTube) and now think that much of the fuss could have been avoided had Hans simply avoided characterizing it as 'not music'. Music is whatever musicians do, both he and Susan Bradshaw were undoubtedly musicians, and what they produced in the session was in fact their idea of a really bad avant-garde piece. Sheer musical instinct could not be circumvented, as the recording makes apparent; the badness of the work lies in its inadequate (because merely instinctive) striving after some sort of form and climax, its sheer tiresome length (all of seven minutes!) and a certain tentativeness apparent in the performance of two people who were, after all, not trained percussionists. Since *Mobile* there

has been enough improvisation within composed works to deprive the idea of uniqueness. But that we weren't to know in 1961, when Mátyás Seiber's Violin Sonata was the only obvious instance.

5   In fact the 'resistance' was led and coordinated by a group of six senior members of different departments: from Music Programmes there were Hans Keller, Bob Simpson and Deryck Cooke; from Drama the Assistant Head, Hallam Tennyson; the Head of Talks, Lord Archie Gordon, and Leslie Stokes, a crucial member of the Third Programme planning staff.

6   In conversation I heard him express strong opposition to the Welsh Arts Council's proposal for joint funding of the BBC Welsh Symphony, which the top BBC Management welcomed; his advice to the orchestra's managers, he said, was that it would lead to endless identical public concerts in awful halls up and down the Principality. I half-remember hearing from one or other HMPR that this unilateral contradiction of Management policy was what led to his discontinuance as CA-RSO, though Alison Garnham's research turned up nothing to confirm that.

7   Given, that is, Hans's fervent loyalty to Tottenham Hotspur. QPR (Queen's Park Rangers, another London team) nowadays languishes in the middle-to-upper regions of the Championship (= Second Division) but was strong enough to challenge for the old First Division title in the early 1970s. I lived near their ground and was at the crucial final match of the season in question when they were pipped to the post by Arsenal, and still remember the low moan from the crowd (pianissimo!) "WE ... WANT ... ONE!" which greatly amused Hans when I told him about it. That a football crowd could rise to such ironic humour, translating a normally triumphalist chant (WE ... WANT ... FIVE) into self-mockery, has never ceased to amaze me, the more so given the importance of the occasion.

8   Dragiša had a well-nigh infallible recipe for instant cordiality at international gatherings. He'd ask *"De quel pays êtes vous?"* (From what country do you come?), and whatever the reply he'd then throw his arms round the person concerned, crying *"Mon ami!"* (My friend!). He did it to me and it really worked. Hans was distinctly chary of physical contact, something that could well have gone back to the brutalities of 'the time of his life'. He was in any case short and thin whereas Dragiša was tall and solid, built rather on the lines of the leading Croatian tennis player of the time, Nikki Pilic.

9   Though compare Ian McIntyre's comment on the goy Alasdair Milne in a *Times* review of the latter's memoirs 1988, that the middle 1950s in television were a time 'when an instruction from your superiors was a basis for discussion'.

3   *Harry Croft-Jackson*

As well as Isaacs, Keller and Crossley-Holland there was one more Chief Assistant, a former Manchester cotton-broker named Harry Croft-Jackson, who tried, on the whole effectively but with a maximum of self-importance that went some way towards undoing his good work, to ensure order and consistency throughout the Department's dealings – as when Scriabin suddenly had to be 'billed' ("I Have Ruled") as Skryabin. The Dvořák symphonies changed their numbering around then, and there was never any lack of minutiae to go into the Music Division Book of Reference, colloquially known as Harry's Green Book. The total control freak, he had some success inducing other-worldly producers to do things consistently; one of his sayings was "Ye'd sign 'Shot at Dawn' if I put it front of ye". Harry had hopes of prospering under the new regime, possibly fostered by William or maybe not: the latter at one point observed to me and Hans Keller, "Harry's the sort of man who if you made him Controller, Music would want to be Director of Radio, and if you made him that he'd want to be Director General, and if he were DG he'd want to be Prime Minister". One of the important bits of 'Music Programme Organization' entrusted to Harry was the assessment of unsolicited musical scores. For new works, apart from those by the very-best-known composers and those specially commissioned by the Controller, mostly from the very-best-known composers, there was the Reading Panel, whose decisions caused many a grievance and gave rise to many a legend. The letters of acceptance or refusal came from Harry. I spent quite a lot of my first morning having departmental philosophy and procedures outlined by him, something that greatly amused Hans when I was finally released to go and report in.

Harry was jovial enough when not acting under the influence of ambition or self-importance; having been organist at Kirkwall in Orkney, he also had a comprehensive knowledge of the organ repertoire. William set no store whatever by finding a producer with that particular specialist knowledge, so Harry was happy to take over the weekly organ recital as his fiefdom, as private and undisturbed as the Music Talks output. With my growing enthusiasm for Franz Schmidt, I appreciated his readiness to include in the organ recital schedule regular performances of that composer's spectacular Toccata played by the resident Orcadian W. O. Minay.

Given his need to be always right and my chronic mood, which, except when producing artists, was edgy and brusque, we were bound to clash now and again. Harry it was who drew a clear line under that chapter; he had retired, I had just produced a Charles Ives programme that ended with the quiet and touching Third Symphony.[1] After its broadcast, heard at home on a Sunday afternoon, the phone rang and it was Harry, ringing from Orkney: "You and I, we've had our differences, Leo, but I had to say to you I found that a really beautiful programme." Give a good man long enough and he'll show himself.

NOTES

1   Not, of course, that I could possibly know him (I doubt whether even William did), but for a very short while in the middle 1960s, a bit before he began to be more generally in vogue, the American composer Charles Ives was a leitmotif in my work – not least because of his quotability, with dicta like the famous "Stand up and use your ears like a man!", or "Nobody but Mrs. Ives and Ralph D. Griggs likes ANY of my pieces except some of the weakest sisters: ARE MY EARS ON WRONG?!" I admired in him the 'clouded sound', dense, dark, active, like a natural process of great complexity with no necessarily communicable meaning. He was one master of it, Skalkottas another, Michael Tippett a third, while it strikes me that Schoenberg had it in him but was too intent on precision – like Coleridge, in fact, who, as Keats said, 'would let go by a fine isolated verisimilitude caught from the penetralium of mystery, from being incapable of remaining content with half-knowledge'. I was fascinated by resemblances between, for example, the opening of Ives's *Central Park in the Dark* and Alban Berg's first *Wozzeck* interlude, as by the natural-process quality of his climaxes – the terrific whirlpool of sound suddenly giving way unconcernedly to calm, as if it didn't matter but simply happened. (I have in mind things like 'The Housatonic at Stockbridge' from *Three Places in New England*, or *Central Park in the Dark*, or *Hallowe'en*.)

So far as programmes were concerned, short, effective pieces like the 'Alcotts' movement of the *Concord* Piano Sonata took their place alongside long and, as I now view it, ineffective monsters of impenetrability like the rest of that work. I pass over some of his versifying, as in –

> Where is the lady all in pink?
> Last year she waved to me, I think.
> Can she have died? Can that rot!
> She is present, but she sees me not.
>
> *The Circus Band*

Come back McGonagall, all is forgiven! Songs were among the easier pieces to programme. An American tenor, David Astor, came for an intriguing recital, accompanied by the up-to-anything Ernest Lush, which included *Charlie Rutlage* ('Another good cow-puncher/has gone to meet his fate,/I hope he'll find his resting place/within the golden gate, within the golden gate, etc.). At the end we decided the song would be all the better for including Ives's 'stage directions'; the innocent onlooker peering into the Concert Hall of Broadcasting House might have been amazed to see Astor, Black, the new young producer Martin Dalby who had come to eavesdrop, and the balancer, leaping up and down emitting bull-noises, whooping and shouting things like "Git along, little dogies". The resulting farrago was dubbed unobtrusively in behind the music at the editing session.

Memories of Ives at his noisiest re-surfaced during my first visit to Chicago in 1978 for the BBC's experimental live relay of a Thursday afternoon concert by the city's unsurpassable Symphony Orchestra. Easley Blackwood, composer of that concert's new work, was known to me from a programme he had made some years earlier with the equally formidable Chicago violinist, Esther Glazer. It had consisted of all four of Ives's violin sonatas. Not all are long, so it was a bit less intimidating than that might suggest, though tough enough in all conscience. The brief fourth one, subtitled *Children's Day at the Camp Meeting*, recalls childhood high spirits in the immortal tempo marking *allegro con slugarocko*. 'An American Dimension' tells of my crucial Blackwood experience with the Chicago subway – Ives would have loved it and realized that he did, after all, say things to people other than 'Mrs. Ives and Ralph D. Griggs'.

4   Robert Simpson

Robert Simpson, major composer and very experienced producer by the time I joined the BBC, was a fascinating colleague if not quite a friend. Ever since Oxford days I'd noticed his programmes, and his advocacy of Mozart's church music had lured me into a fatal error in my choice of research subject. As for his own music, his First Symphony had impressed me, as it had Durham University, which awarded him an honorary Doctorate of Music on the strength of it. His second impressed me less – I wrote at an early stage in my voluminous correspondence with my new friend Hugh Wood, "he must have *two* D. Mus.-es". Gradually I lost count and track, which is surely my still-remediable loss. Once I was in the publishing world he was kind to Dr. Kalmus's clever young man who tried to sell him Berg and Schoenberg. He let me take him to lunch at least once, not omitting the verdict that such music was anti-life. I soon became a new boy at the BBC, so there he was, gruffly amiable, able to hold his own in argument with the likes of Keller, but one of the odd men out since Glock's arrival. He coined as nickname for the blue-riband Invitation series, 'The Kippers and Custard Concerts', a conceit I enjoyed both before and after I became their producer. As a composer he clearly also had a life of his own and said he liked to watch wrestling on television while listening to Bruckner on his gramophone – it seemed curiously appropriate. One lunchtime he joined the happy throng round the Yalding canteen table and reported that the previous night he'd watched a European Cup soccer match from Austria, and amid the hubbub of the crowd had at one point distinctly caught the sound of a cornet playing "a Brucknerian variant of a noble old English melody" (viz. 'Colonel Bogey'). This I can only try to reproduce as –

BOL – LOCKS, A – HAND – THE SAME – TO – YOU

Despite his lack of sympathy with so much music that went so far back, he was by no means against all younger British composers, and at one point included Hugh Wood's quite recent Second Quartet in his series *Cross Section*, whose raison d'être was to present a variety of music composed in any given year. I think, however, that he had grave doubts as to the musical value of the newly fashionable 'Manchester School'. He respected Glock as a practical musician but was otherwise his stubborn opponent, nor had he any time for corporate hierarchies ("in the BBC the scum rises to the top"). Some of that was understandable, but there were things about him I could never sympathize with – not just his determination to see the entire symphonic oeuvre of Havergal Brian onto the air and his view of the Second Viennese School as a regrettable

Robert Simpson (I) (Milein Cosman)

anti-life diversion to the true course of music, but, notably, his total lack of interest in microphone presentation such as would have befitted his fascinating programme ideas. He did deign to introduce personally, and most effectively given his forthright manner, *The Innocent Ear*, which let music be heard without the listener's being told in advance whether it was by a 'major' or a 'minor' composer. But otherwise the cliché "I leave presentation to [whatever the script-writing unit happened to be called at the time]" was deemed acceptable. And yet his BBC Music Guide to Beethoven's symphonies is not only full of unique insights but also compellingly written in Bob's inimitable, earthy way.

Behind my attitude of mixed admiration and regret lay, of course, the fact that through some shortcoming in myself I never really came adequately to terms with his music, less because of any 'conservatism' – it was often complex and 'new' enough for most people with ears – than on the grounds of a certain excessively macho quality, a baring and beating of the breast that seemed to derive from the less likeable side of his idol Carl Nielsen, whom I also admired to the point of provoking Hans Keller's latent BBC-manager side. In Nielsen you have another composer to whom I had been won over through Bob's broadcasts. Bruckner I already loved, but came to understand better through things Bob had written, and I was touched when he presented me, one of 'Glock's lot', with a copy of his book on the Bruckner symphonies.

He was never less than a figure to respect immensely. One of my post-Schoenbergian enthusiasms was the Greek violinist-composer Nikos Skalkottas; when I organized a series with his music I gave it the euphoric and biographically justifiable title, *The Quiet Genius*. Programme billings reached a variety of people in the department, and soon enough I had a note in Bob's best up-market English, saying that perusal of my title had caused his eyebrows to become somewhat elevated. I am always rather impressed by moral fervour, of which Bob was rarely short, and asked my boss Peter Gould for advice. He advised me to stick with my hyperbole.

Bob's knowledge of Bruckner was unparalleled though not heedlessly uncritical – he described one point in the first movement of the Third Symphony as "stamping up and down in the mud". But composers' problems were his own problems, and their achievements something he knew he had it in him to follow, however modestly. Beethoven and key was another field on which he was immensely strong; at one point he proposed a series on Beethoven's works in B flat – material for *Private Eye*, had it then existed, but it would have been fascinating. For some administrative reason it didn't happen. His empathy with Beethoven extended as far as the great man's many arrangements of British folksongs for voices and piano trio, and I was impelled to try them in a programme. They struck me as exemplary and fully equal in musical and educative value to the Bach chorale harmonizations that rightly count as classics. So thank you, Bob, for that!

When in due course Peter Gould was put in charge of more-or-less the entire output, he needed two slightly senior people to help him, and posts of Chief Producer were advertised. After four years on the roof in London W11 translating Schoenberg I felt ready for a change back, Eleanor Warren was also in the running, and given Bob's eleven years of resolute scepticism about the whole 'new regime' and his manifest need for time to do what he did best of all – compose – I think he would have gone his way without troubling himself over things like promotion, despite the fact that in the pre-Glock days he'd enjoyed a measure of seniority as Third Programme Music Organizer. Peter Gould, however, seems to have wanted to show the Bosses what a keen lot his producers were, and prevailed on Bob to apply. When the outcome (Eleanor and myself) was known, he left the briefest of notes on my desk saying 'Congrats', but I gathered that he was rightly furious – less, surely, at being 'passed over' than at being manipulated like that. He had his real life in his composition, though, and any thoughts of resignation were suppressed until the big row in 1980 over Aubrey Singer's plan to rationalize the BBC's orchestras.

Bob's fierce appreciation of the natural world was an important part of him. One of my favourite Simpson remarks was "People who call me single-minded should watch my cat eating its dinner!". In Beethoven he sensed and reacted to an awed awareness of endless space that had in his own life prompted him to take up astronomy. And he once returned from a holiday in the north of Scotland, where Fingal's Cave had vastly impressed him, not least because "Mendelssohn got it absolutely right – that opening theme, it's exactly the feeling of being in the cave". And he could be generous in his tributes to artistry, as when he returned from a Bach competition in Bolzano enthusing about the newly-emerged talent of Maurizio Pollini, but above all paying tribute to John Ogdon: "I'm the least patriotic cuss you could find, but this man makes me proud to be British." I'd say the same of Simpson, whether or not I take to his music.

5 Leo Wurmser

The two finest practical musicians in the department during my time were the German, Peter Gellhorn, who broadcast as a solo pianist and then became director of the BBC Chorus at the point when they were re-named the BBC Singers, and the Austrian refugee Leo Wurmser, a former pupil of Franz Schmidt who during a spell as conductor of the BBC Midland Light Orchestra in Birmingham had introduced to this country his teacher's *Variations on a Theme of Beethoven* for left-hand-only piano and orchestra. In UE days I'd paid him a visit to try and sell him something from our orchestral catalogue, most of which he knew anyway; I think that in my innocence I even tried to persuade him to take an interest in this composer named Schmidt. When I flourished the latest light offering by our leading purveyor of such things, the handsome and prolific Gilbert Vinter, Leo went a bit sour, saying in effect "Gilbert seems to rule the roost here anyway, he really doesn't need a helping hand from me." He later moved to the opera unit in London. In that field he had a stunningly comprehensive knowledge; once, when Hans Keller was taking his time over an address to a Third Programme music meeting (maybe the speech that began "I have seven points in reply; you will not understand the first three"), Leo scribbled on a piece of paper, from memory, the relevant lines of the 'Chairman of the Council' in Pfitzner's *Palestrina*, to the effect that no delegate may speak for more than a quarter of an hour, and passed it to him.

The opera unit was very strong. After Peter Crossley-Holland's final departure Himalaya-bound it included not only Wurmser but also the Cambridge-trained scholar and conductor Lionel Salter, lately back from working in television. Salter, an immensely knowledgeable and many-sided man, modelled himself on his polymath teacher, Professor Edward Dent. He was outspoken, and at one point made the pages of a tabloid after adjudicating at a competitive music festival where he said what an awful piece of rubbish one of the set pieces was. That deeply offended many of the hard-working participants and their even harder-working families (music, like sport, having its 'tournament fathers and mothers'), and the paper splashed across its front page 'Parents Slam Judge at Festival of Tears'. When Salter moved up to succeed Gerald Abraham as Assistant Controller, his place was taken first by Brian Trowell, later to become King Edward Professor of Music at King's College London and Heather Professor of Music at Oxford, and then by the distinguished Verdi scholar, Julian Budden, who in the fullness of time produced the standard study of the composer's operas.

Leo Wurmser soon had a tempting offer from Glyndebourne, which might have transformed what one took from his demeanour to be a rather sad and solitary life, but Glock somehow induced him to stay at the BBC. Whatever was promised never materialized; Hans said to me of Leo after his death "We're dancing on his grave", and referred to an episode, naming no names, in the preface to his first book, *1975 (1984 minus 9)*. For Leo Wurmser I took on the English translation of Hindemith's opera *Cardillac*, over which he proved a hard taskmaster – but then, as Dent had said to him once, "You have the advantage of me, Mr. Wurmser; you learned English, I merely picked it up".

His final years were at least sweetened by the attentions of a formidable young secretary, who couldn't do too much for him – and that out of the sheer goodness of her heart. When she was first allotted to him, Leo was taken aback by the brash figure she cut, but soon learned to appreciate her all-important virtues and generosity. Jan Seddon in due course married the equally energetic Transcription Music Organizer, a former top balancer named James Burnett (the man who had survived Walter Legge's scrutiny when balancing the Schwarzkopf Invitation Concert), and later occupied an important position as manager to leading artists for the agents Harold Holt. It's good to have a redeeming feature to add to the rather sad story of a fine musician stranded out of the depths where he was at home.

6 Basil Lam

My uncle Bill (born Gamaliel), who was 'in handbags', always used to say "I always say, 'Ard Work Ain't Easy". Which I could cap with "Old Music? New It Ain't." Before the war there were things like a series of Bach Cantata broadcasts. With only one wavelength available to cater for all tastes, they were not universally popular; one orchestral player told the story of being picked up by a taxi, asked what his work was and summarily expelled from the vehicle after confessing that he was on his way to take part in another Bach cantata. The post-war Third Programme isolated its high culture from such unappreciative ears, and to considerable extent music from Bach's time and before could flourish. It was looked after by a producer on a par with all the others, deputed to see that it was suitably broadcast. A certain Basil Lam (St. John's, Oxford) had had a long spell as that producer before I joined, and the memorable, variously ruthless Denis Stevens also played a part still recalled with bated breath by those who had worked alongside him. Jimmy Burnett told the story of a Handel oratorio never really timed in rehearsal, so that the broadcast over-ran to a degree unacceptable even by Third Programme standards. Once it had been taken off the air, at a suitable juncture and doubtless with a broadcast apology, Dr. Stevens marched into the studio with the music in full tilt and simply stopped it in its tracks. Now Basil returned, the polymath supreme and the only member of the Department to have done the ton (on his motorbike, during the earliest days of the M1). Basil also maintained that in his youth he'd practised the pole vault. It was all part of the worthy old 'English amateur' idea; one great mate of Basil's was the clavichordist Michael Thomas, whose penchant was yet another symptom in the syndrome, vintage cars. To a considerable extent these muscular scholars shared the characteristics of many ordinary professional musicians, but had an originality and ability to think that compensated for shortcomings in sheer reliable technique.

The best of them knew their field forwards, backwards and sideways. Arnold Goldsbrough springs to mind, with his advocacy of the great Handel choral-and-orchestral works, and Henry Washington, whose Schola Polyphonica presented the masterpieces of Renaissance counterpoint. It was very impressive, despite the air of the English gentleman amateur that clung to a lot of it. 'Henry' was a true professional, but as with the greatest conductors his inspiration took over on the night, and the one sure thing when Schola Polyphonica went on the air live was that the rehearsal timing would change by several minutes: whether longer or shorter was in the lap of the Gods, or rather of Henry's own very special inner timekeeper. With their knowledge and integrity, these men were oak-trees, though other equally intriguing parts of the forest were less visited, those marked out by musicians of the calibre of Anthony Lewis and Anthony Bernard, who left on their gramophone records a treasure-trove of Baroque music superbly performed by instrumentalists and singers alike. Maybe with my mind on things far closer in time I simply didn't notice their presence, but so far as the Baroque was concerned the BBC's preference when I arrived was unmistakably 'Arnold'.

Basil presided over a lot of it, also finding time to edit his own edition of *Messiah*, which was duly recorded with an enviable cast of solo singers under Charles Mackerras. Time was something he always seemed to have, a good deal of it filled with telling comments based on a thorough knowledge of how harmony and counterpoint work. Other swathes were taken up by alarmingly well-informed disquisitions on culture and aesthetics; he had an all-embracing knowledge of the English Romantics and of Coleridge in particular, and his insistence on absolute standards could be a salutary reminder to a young man full of the joys of discovery. ("My Dear Fellow, if you elevate the Second-Rate you leave yourself no Vocabulary with which to celebrate the Supremely Fine" – somehow he attracts Johnsonian capitals.) A favourite form of dismissal when under-informed younger opinion-givers came under discussion was "These Swine", and "Treasonable Clerks" also figured in his vocabulary. All that of course made him the greatest time-waster, and I too often showed my impatience, but his breadth of culture matched (and hardly overlapped with!) that of even a Hans Keller, who found him very hard to take but wasn't above arguing endlessly with him and other heavyweights such as Deryck Cooke and Bob Simpson round a Yalding restaurant table at lunchtime. Many a time I'd arrive there quite late, well after one o'clock, to find Basil holding forth in front of an already empty plate; I'd enjoy a not unduly hurried lunch and return to my office with him still in full flow.

Basil laid no claim to distinction as a performer, but his own ensemble was considered of a standard to broadcast Baroque trio sonatas; the music deserved a hearing and they were there to give it one, on 'traditionally modified' instruments, i.e. those such as any other fiddler or 'cellist of the time used, with Basil at the harpsichord.

Given our lack of tape-playing office equipment, the system for spotting oversights in the editing of recordings consisted of two ladies in the Programme Reporting Unit of Recording Services who listened to our tapes and provided a detailed log that would help the Third Programme schedule clerks keep track of things like precise timings and cues. It also came in handy for the producer, were he or she inclined to recommend a programme for repeat in whole or part. Those 'programme reporters' were not musicians, and though they did wonderfully they couldn't be expected to spot everything in music which by its nature tends to stop and start. Where they could be a great help was over speech. After Basil had recorded two Bach 'cello suites played by Amaryllis Fleming, a lady of colourful vocabulary, he dropped in from the next office in a very jolly frame of mind to say he'd just been spared an embarrassment; a programme reporter had rung up and said in her sedatest tones "Mr. Lam, I've been listening to your 'cello programme and there's something which I think you might prefer not to have broadcast". He duly ordered a play-back: in a dance that began with a short upbeat Amaryllis had done something she hadn't liked, broken off, said in strict time "Oh FUCK!" and resumed in equally strict time. Used to her as he was, it had all seemed so natural to Basil that he hadn't even noticed.

All too soon the great changes in 'Old Music' began, as players and especially conducting scholars began to look more closely at just how music would have been played in its time, how the instruments would have been – at everything, in fact, except the ears that heard the music. Only seldom have the notes the composer wrote down purported to be a full and final statement of what he wanted. Around the end of Glock's BBC time, circa 1970, the penny dropped: almost all Western music since about 1600 had come to be performed in a way that had more to do with how life had gone meanwhile than with how it sounded in the first place. Scholarship shook off its winding-sheet, the Period Band was born, closely followed by that still more dubious category, the Period Singer. Eminently marketable, great for recording on various grounds, not too much strain on the technique apart from the learning of various mannerisms the musicologists could instruct one in, and fun for the brain. It also brought to the fore a new breed of conducting scholar, still with us. The BBC was in the van from the moment it began to turn into a bandwaggon, encouraging, supporting and turning a deaf ear to the imperfections of the moment in the hope of better things to come. They came, and how they came. There are, of course, people whose view is "Yes, but I hate how it sounds and the way radio's gone mad about it".

To be fair, sheer intuition can take one so far and no further, and anyone performing music would do well to know something of how it was meant to sound, what were the conventions and physical realities when it came into the world. One may, however, argue, asking modestly "what's the point of trying to recreate the exact sound of a period when there's no hope of recreating its exact listener?" Here's one of those pinpoints on which a multitude of angels can lurch about till kingdom come. Strings may have been made of gut, but what were ears made of? Not cloth, one hopes.

Once established, the category 'Old Music' took over like the Japanese guest saying "So sorry, this my garden now". Look upon this picture: after Klemperer, Kleiber *Vater*, Monteux, Furtwängler, Toscanini, the new great names were Hogwood, Norrington, Gardiner, Harnoncourt, Leonhardt, Kuijken, Goebel and the major recorder-player Frans Brüggen, who soon turned into a conductor. To read a major American scholar to the effect that

Sir Roger Norrington was the next great Beethoven conductor, in the line of Toscanini, was like reading Dr. Johnson on the 'thirteenth stroke of the clock' – not just palpable nonsense in itself but also throwing doubt on everything that went before. But Beethoven has become one more branch of 'old music'. I wonder what he would have had to say about that.

Basil now found himself complemented, to put it mildly, by a new generation of 'Old Music' producers with knowledge but a different education and culture. The one who inherited his humanist mantle and some of his breadth of taste was Nicholas Anderson, whose programmes, if not written in his heart's blood, at least seemed to bear his signature. Basil felt isolated as never before, and took his second departure. As a contributor he returned to complete, with infinite slowness, intricacy and displays of temperament, a vast project like those in the early days of the Third Programme, a survey that acquired the working title 'From Chant to 1600', though I seem to remember that when broadcast it was called something else. 'After 1600' was clearly the new boys' territory, and off limits to old fogies. So much the worse for it and them, but that's the way of the world.

Deryck Cooke (Milein Cosman)

7 Deryck Cooke

Deryck Cooke has become a cult figure among students of musical analysis, and in view of his mammoth efforts completing Mahler's Tenth Symphony, then getting round the intolerant and intolerable Alma Mahler of the huge violet handwriting, nobody should argue with that, not even those who, like me, dissent from the general view that his completion sounds at all times so like Mahler as to be above criticism. He already had a BBC history when I joined, and was then in charge of providing notes and scripts for the announcers to use or read. That, of course, was the least of him. He was a genial, outspoken man, little more enamoured of the new avant-garde or the 'Glock regime' than was Robert Simpson. He did, however, get on famously with Hans, who admired him a great deal since they could and did argue about everything, particularly the detailed analysis of works they both knew well.

Deryck at one point devised a spoof worthy to stand alongside Howard Hartog's best. Part of his work as 'information assistant' was to provide the *Radio Times* with a weekly selection of music broadcasts by foreign radio stations. I owed valuable parts of my education, such as the post-war relays from Bayreuth, to such broadcasts, so it was a useful job to be doing; but it could be pretty tedious, and for several weeks Deryck included excerpts from a fictitious 'Levantine Mass'. Details of the excerpt for the week were invented at a Greek restaurant named Ttokos on the corner of Clipstone and Cleveland Streets, a hundred yards from Yalding, and so far as I know nobody ever wrote in to complain that they'd tried to find Ttokos's *Levantine Mass* at the specified time and wavelength and been disappointed. But then foreign broadcasts were pretty elusive at the best of times.

8   Ralph Usherwood

This is a strange one, about someone I never actually met. The Art Editor of the *Radio Times* used to endear himself to those producers who commanded the English language by approaching them every so often to write a 250-word piece about a programme of theirs that was about to be broadcast. We knew little more about him than that, and I only discovered much later that his widely-ranging brief included the commissioning of the striking covers with which in those days *Radio Times* made itself prominent on the news stands. It covered only BBC programmes, and Mr. Usherwood was clearly in contact with leading artists and graphic designers, for names like Leonard Rosoman, John Minton and Ronald Searle appear in the list of men who designed covers. Our 250-word contributions were modest by comparison, but they were a chance to draw attention to our programmes, and a good training ground for potential writers on music.

There was almost an incident after my fellow-producer Alan Walker, later a professor and already a prominent analyst of music, turned out a piece whose gravamen was that you couldn't really write about music: it began 'when the editor asked me …' and ended 'if you could [convert people by writing about music], Arnold Stravinskovich would be everyone's favourite composer.' Coming from someone who was taking money for doing just that, I found the piece glib, and happening to have one in hand for the Invitation Concert the following week I sent it up rotten, in a tone generally reminiscent of Groucho Marx, starting with the same words and invoking the age-old chestnut that ends "I only came to read the meter". Mr. Usherwood was genuinely puzzled and offended that I should drag private disagreements into the bright light of his periodical, and told me so in no uncertain terms – I'd in effect been saying he should have spotted that the Walker article was below par and weighed in at that point. As I wouldn't for the world have offended him, I re-wrote my piece in a more conciliatory vein and it duly appeared. I'm sure Alan Walker hadn't the least idea any of that was going on.

When not provoked into self-defence he was the most courteous of men, and each time he'd received one's 250 words he sent a note saying 'I am so pleased you could do this for us'. In my bright way I once wrote to him that I, of course, always knew how pleased he was, so that he could save himself the trouble in my case. That went down less than well; I had clearly been tempting him to do something that clashed with his 100% considerate nature.

At one point I wrote a piece for the *Radio Times* of 4 November 1965 suggesting that in his 'Mannheim' violin sonatas Mozart had in effect split himself in two, then come together again. In due course I received a message, typically scribbled on a torn-out sheet of the *Radio Times* for the day of the broadcast in question, from Hans, who wrote 'Having been critical (tho' not critical enough) of a recent Haydn note of yours, I feel it is my duty to give you my opinion of this article – which I think is a little masterpiece, absolutely outstanding'.

Thus encouraged, I returned to the charge a few months later with another on the same subject:

> Haydn to Leopold Mozart: 'Your son is the greatest composer known to me … He has taste and moreover the most profound knowledge of composition'. And from a lost diary of Schubert's, remembered by a friend: 'The magic sounds of Mozart's music haunt me still … Amid the darkness of this life they show us a far-off brightness, clarity and beauty … How infinitely many such comforting intimations of a brighter and better life you have brought'.
>
> Schubert's words, though a young man's, are not idle, unless one's reactions to 'intimations' is the easy "you must be mad". Once in a lifetime they may appear incarnate – as Aloysia Weber did to the twenty-one-year-old Mozart in the 'anything-can-happen' period when his genius finally burst into flame. Mostly, though, they have to be 'sublimated' (ugly, question-begging word), identified wheresoever, while the worldly rest of it becomes a matter of staying upright on the high wire between despair and self-deception. Take, centrally, Mozart's marriage to Aloysia's prosaic sister; while his 'most profound knowledge of composition' produced several splendid arias for the grown Aloysia (a cold, hard woman but a magnificent singer), the marriage to Constanze continually demonstrated that compulsive tenderness of an ever-giving nature – perhaps part of what Haydn meant by 'taste', and something Schubert, the fellow-genius poised on his own high wire, was uniquely placed to sense.

A first reaction was another message from Hans: 'Impressed … your style has improved'. Translated, that meant 'You have, thank goodness, at last stopped trying to sound like me'. But then a letter arrived from a sane and sensible lady in Brighouse, Yorks., Mrs. Dorothy Eyles, asking in a puzzled though not hostile way what on earth a lot of it meant. I realized that, not for the first time, Mr. Usherwood's limit had forced me to cram too many thoughts into too few words and to elide links that would have made me intelligible to a sane and sensible Yorkshire lady. Two further letters resolved the matter. In the first I expanded the article and spelt out those links, complete with an erudite footnote. The second, again from Mrs. Eyles, ran:

I find what you say refreshing, penetrating and heartening and I think you should write a book developed from the ideas in this one paragraph, though whether it would turn out to be a book on music, philosophy or the springs of personality, I don't know. Perhaps you have already written such a book and I haven't heard of it … Thank you again for your patience and generosity in explaining these insights to me.

And all because Ush always said '250 words'. The spirit moves in mysterious ways, though not yet so mysterious as to have produced such a book. If it ever happens, I'll know whose memory to dedicate it to.

9   *Paul Hamburger*

Paul Hamburger was just one of many Austrian Jewish musicians by whom our musical life was for half-a-century enriched, or hijacked, depending on your viewpoint, when they found refuge in this country after the events of 1938. Alongside established figures like the composer-scholars Hans Gal and Egon Wellesz and the conductor Karl Rankl, some were students in their late teens with their education still to complete, such as the three upper members of the later Amadeus Quartet, or the musical analyst and polymath Hans Keller. Paul Hamburger was not the least among them.

Once he was in England, aged seventeen, the obligatory spell in an internment camp was followed by studies at the Royal College of Music with Frank Merrick and Ralph Vaughan Williams. He later profited from work with major singing teachers, acquiring a comprehensive knowledge of the physiology of the voice. Hans Keller remembered how when the internees in his Westmoreland camp were finally told they'd been diagnosed as friend not foe and were free to venture forth in search of their fortune, Paul was so upset that he staged a one-man sit-down strike and refused to go. In a letter to me very near the end of his life he remembered the army's providing them with 'warm food and good beds'. He sensed security in any hard-and-fast system, a character trait that later helped him to do valuable work at Glyndebourne and for the BBC; I remain eternally grateful that it was not tested to destruction as it would have been had he stayed in Vienna.

Not the least remarkable aspect of the Hamburger generation was the degree to which, by their late teens, they had already acquired from somewhere a rock-solid technical and philosophical basis for life in music at the highest level. He soon became known as an inspired coach, working with the English Opera Group and broadcasting as accompanist on BBC Radio. During this part of his life he was obsessed with chess and a constant visitor to the Gambit Chess Rooms in the City of London; eventually he realized he was wasting so much time there that he had to beg the organizers to ban him from the premises. Years later I played one game against him but it was no contest. "Ah, very aggressive!" he remarked as he mopped up my rashly-advanced pieces. In the 1950s he was on the music staff at Glyndebourne and made a reputation as a vocal consultant whose advice world-ranking singers were not too proud to seek. He worked with artists of the calibre of Elisabeth Söderström, Janet Baker and Heather Harper, and often with the baritone Thomas Hemsley, sometimes in costume as Schubert (which was Nature's type-casting), Hemsley embodying the composer's singer friend Vogl.

Regular musical partners were the singer and folksong collector Esther Salaman, with whom he toured to the Forces, Austria and South Africa, and whom he married in 1948; the pianist Helen Pyke, and after her death Liza Fuchsova, in four-hand piano duets; the violinist Suzanne Rozsa and the 'cellist Eleanor Warren, with whom he gave the first performance of Britten's 'Cello Sonata by British artists; and in the Benvenuto Duo the soprano Clare Walmesley and mezzo-soprano Laura Sarti. He worked with an immense range of other artists. Not all of them, he felt, knew what they were about; those he learned "to soft-soap", though he once told me, during his BBC time, that he'd spent much of a recording with a greatly overrated singer writing his resignation letter in his head. Like others of its kind, it remained unposted. When a partner wanted to learn, he was an unfailing fount of wisdom, laying great stress on character and drama.

He seems to have been a fixture throughout my mature life, but I didn't in fact meet him till the end of the 1950s when he was already nearly forty and I in my late twenties, during my time with the Kalmus office in London. A home-from-home during those years of aspiration was the Austrian Cultural Institute in Rutland Gate, which under the kindly eye of Otto Ritschl promoted regular concerts. A later director used to say, all too accurately, that after the music we should have "A SMALL glass of vine", but in Otto's time the Grüner Veltliner still flowed freely. At one concert I was roped in to turn the pages for the pianist in Schoenberg's *Pierrot lunaire*; in the best Philip Larkin manner, Paul afterwards didn't congratulate me on my tact and brilliant timing, nor say "There, had we the gift to see ahead"; it was, however, a start.

A mere year or so on, as a very new BBC music producer, I experienced his gifts and temperament as accompanist to one or other singer or instrumentalist. My immediate boss, Hans Keller, regaled me with anecdotes of his friend's eccentricity. Paul's bedrock of profound knowledge and analysis impressed me like no-one else's save Hans's: each thought the other a genius and it was on Hans's initiative, during his time in charge of chamber music and recitals, that Paul became an official BBC staff accompanist. There were those who after half-listening maintained that he forced his own ideas on the artists with whom he worked. I very much suspect that it only happened where there was already a manifest willingness to learn: the thought of a Janet Baker browbeaten into doing things she didn't believe in strikes me as unrealistic, and Paul was the BBC accompanist she most willingly worked with.

As a Schubertian I profited by his understanding of that great composer. Quite early on in our BBC time, at a recording of piano duets with Liza Fuchsova, he suddenly exclaimed "Ah, now I know what Leo loves about Schubert – his numinous side!" He too was well aware of the deeply religious element in Schubert's musical character, as of the links between Schubert and a still greater idol, Bruckner. His perfect German helped me avoid one or two pitfalls; when I first wrote a note on Schubert's song *An Schwager Kronos* I alleged that in its poem Goethe 'addresses Time in the most familiar terms, like a brother-in-law': I didn't know the word Schwager's other meaning ('postilion', which my fifty-year-old German dictionary already classified as obsolete – sorry Goethe). Paul always liked to see what was to be said, and (to use a catch-phrase of a fellow-immigré, the comedian Vic Oliver) 'laffed his blooming head orf'. (The two meanings are in fact related.)

When Eleanor Warren became a BBC music producer later in the 1960s she persuaded her line manager that apart from being a much-valued contributor, a staff accompanist and her duo-partner, Paul had it in him to be a producer. His contract allowed him to go on performing over the air; his meticulous mind kept the most precise record of every such engagement, and twenty years later, when the Corporation's internal accounting would have been at a total loss, he could tell a producer whether or not a repeat fee was due for a second hearing of any performance, and if so how much, to the nearest penny. He brought to BBC internal matters a totally reliable succession of value judgements based on accurate hearing and long experience; there, as elsewhere, he was absolutely intolerant of froth and cliché, but always generous about real achievement and independent thought, even when it contradicted his own ideas. In that respect I would place his integrity even above Hans Keller's. On Eleanor's promotion to be head of the department he succeeded her as Chief Producer, Artists; her tradition of showing aspiring performers that, whatever the Corporation's immediate verdict on their offerings, it was on their side and wished them well, was in safe hands.

BBC producers in the 1970s spent a good deal of time assessing overseas radio recordings for possible broadcast. Paul's perceptiveness and vast experience made him an utterly reliable if sometimes over-voluble reporter with absolute standards going way back, as when he recommended a Mozart recording with "tuck it away somewhere, or use Bruno Walter". He was prepared to acknowledge insight, new or old, when he ran across it, but also to write off pseudo-insight, however hallowed. He felt things had improved, by and large, down the decades when he'd worked to precisely that end, and after I introduced a programme on comparative interpretations of Schumann's *Frauenliebe und -leben* he wrote listing the ones he'd liked – Sheila Armstrong, Elly Ameling – and those he'd found 'rubbish' – Lotte Lehmann, Elisabeth Schumann! He was never afraid to give offence in the cause of musical values, and even dared criticize iconic figures in French song such as Maggie Teyte and Charles Panzéra.

Like many of the BBC's best musicians he was uninterested in matters technical; once he commented on a curiously muffled sound to an otherwise excellent recording. On examination I was able to reassure him that it came merely from the fact that he'd been given a tape whose recorded oxide layer was left facing outwards, so that he'd heard it through the backing, as if through a thick pair of socks. That was a measure of his non-involvement with technology, though also a fair example of the half-sighted leading the blind. Always generous towards achievement, he retained the sharpest eye and ear for the manifold idiocies of the musical world, as exemplified in the corner-cutting and unmusicality of many a so-called great 'cellist. In a broadcast talk on that subject he allowed a glowing exception, Pierre Fournier.

Vienna was for ages a love-hate relationship. Asked in a Radio 4 broadcast during the 1970s what he'd say to a young musician about to transfer there, he replied, in his eminently imitable accent, "I vould say, vy do you vant to go to zet DUMP!?"; nor did I ever hear him speak a good word for the Viennese celebrities of his boyhood and after. The name Erik Werba, in particular, could always raise his hackles. A letter he wrote in 1980 from his office as Chief Producer, Artists, to a young Japanese singer who had sent him a tape went so far beyond the call of duty as to make that the faintest echo on the wind, and showed a fine selection of his virtues (the excerpts that follow have been translated into English from the German that Paul naturally wrote to a Vienna-based Oriental):

Dear Miss T –

… Yes, you have fine vocal material and during your five years in Vienna you have obviously tried hard to learn more. But what have these tourist-trade music bureaucrats made of you! In the first place your voice, which is certainly good and well-supported, is still stuck in your throat, where it does battle with the pharynx. You need to practise separately support, breast, nasal and head registers, then put them together, and from there on learn all the varied mixtures. (In '*Er ist's*', but only there, you already show a subtle imposto-presence – a good sign.)

Secondly, my dear – and I hope that my fault-finding won't be too burdensome but will rather give you a new direction – just everything is musically topsy-turvy. A chocolate sauce has been poured over your expressive intentions. I know you are a soubrette (to go, at least, by your choice of songs on the tape), and am not one of those who simply cannot stand the teasing and gallant at any price – but it has to be correctly applied. With you, however, nothing happens when a change of character, a variation of the voice or a different rhythmic movement ought to be on show; but when there is nothing to underline, or something very subtle, suddenly all manner of things go on, for example abrupt changes of tempo, flattening-out of the sound, big rubati that break up the form and whose function would be far better conveyed by phrasing and colouring of the voice – which is to say, four fifths of it all is superficiality.

Don't be cross with me for being so frank, but the current level of Lieder-singing here in England is higher, since singing teachers and accompanists like myself (an old Viennese), but also many of my English colleagues, have tried for years to root out old slovenly ways and superficialities, replacing them with fresh life and gripping theatre.

But I mustn't work off my bad temper on you, the least guilty party in all that. My advice to you is, find yourself a new singing teacher with sound Italian training (hard to come by, alas), and also new repetiteurs with independent views; also trust your own musicality more than you do at the moment – but not just in a vague general way but checking everything bar by bar …

P.S. I must congratulate your accompanist, Herrn [Erwin] Ortner; to be sure, he has taken over one or two silly threadbare tricks, but he is musical and can play the piano. And how!

In his final years he overcame a long-standing fear of flying and rediscovered his affection for Vienna, finding new friends and pupils. Despite ill-health he continued to coach young singers and pianists at courses and summer schools, and was still teaching at London's Guildhall School of Music and Drama a few months before his end. After the death of his second wife, Clare Walmesley, in 1987, and when not globe-trotting, he was given a home in Somerset by her sister Cecily Shouldham, who lovingly cared for him in his last years.

He approached the piano as a master-craftsman not disdainful of adventitious aids. Sharing a recorded broadcast with the fleet-fingered Valerie Tryon, who played solo pieces by Skalkottas, he was thunderstruck to see her perform immensely complex music without having written in a single fingering. His own copies were studded with markings for every note, and the more experienced BBC Music Library issue clerks knew better than to let anyone else borrow a volume of songs with Paul's fingerings, in case they rubbed them out. There had been scenes … He was adamant that, so far from the fingerings 'tying him down', they were the very basis for freedom in performance. By the same token, after a St. John's Smith Square concert by my wife Felicity (a fine rather than 'great' 'cellist), he wrote to us, 'I know in retrospect that every fingering and bowing was precisely worked out, yet the effect was one of total spontaneity'. Good order and discipline again. He could be heavy-handed, or rather heavy-fingered and 'note-y', and in broadcasts he at times relied unduly on the balancer's ability to sort things out; nor was three-against-four his strongest suit. But his playing at its best had what Schoenberg called 'that strict matter-of-factness which is the hallmark of everything truly individual'.

There were, of course, things on which we had to agree to differ. He was of the generation to whom smoking came as second nature, and was forever slipping out of the studio during breaks to enjoy his cigarette wherever the smoke wouldn't percolate through to the singer he was working with; I'd once started, found nothing in it, stopped. And yet when told after a serious heart attack that he simply must give it up, he succeeded remarkably, and astonished his colleagues by going on to live for years. My infatuation with Viennese operetta, serious enough at one time, had run its course by the end of my twenties, whereas any postcard Paul sent us from there during his final years would say what he'd been to and enjoyed at the Volksoper. His equally Viennese *Kaffee-mit-Schlag*/chocolate-cake regimen I could metabolize, if he twisted my arm, but I seldom yielded to it; conversely, my love of sport and tendency to lapse into exercise remained a mystery to him, and after I reported on the first of various strenuous walking tours undertaken with Felicity his expression for that was a 'goyim nachez' – something only Gentiles would like. I think he could have been the origin of Benny in the old Viennese-Jewish joke, who on his return from holiday was asked, first, "What did you do in Gastein?", then "What, you never went for a walk in the woods?" and replied "Bin ich a Reh?" (What am I, a deer?).

He left invaluable contributions to the assessment of major musicians, and the sheer range of his interests and knowledge was a wonder. The Viennese classics and the mandatory Britten were by no means the end of it; he seems, for example, to have been the first person to moot the idea that some kind of mystical experience might lie behind certain outstanding post-war music by Edmund Rubbra. One treasured his profound reflection on his subject, his intimate knowledge of its detail, and a mastery of the English language which meant he knew words most British people had forgotten if they'd ever learned them. His broadcast talks were equally imaginative; I recall in particular a daring reconstruction of Brahms's creative processes while composing the Double Concerto ("I've used that theme already? I can't have done, I need it now!").

Weaving its way through all my own broadcasting work there was, I at last realize, a thread running athwart many prevailing orthodoxies: an insistence on music as sheer sound, with a corresponding undervaluation of the things that go to make up its context. Immediately after retiring in 1982, Paul wrote me a marvellous letter that summed up what he saw in me:

Du bist vielleicht der einzige in diesem Ziegelkästchen genannt Yalding ("in questo deserto che chiamano Parigi," wie es Violetta in einem ziemlich anderen aber nicht völlig unähnlichen Zusammenhang ausdrückt), der eine konsequente künstlerische Politik wirklich innehat und verfolgt. Die andern Kollegen, so liebenswert sie auch sind – und ich schliesse mich

da in meiner gehabten Funktion keineswegs aus – erinnern mich sehr
an die Haltung des K. u. K. Ministerpräsidenten Taffee [sic], der 1888
im Parlament erklärte, das Grundprinzip der österreichischen Politik
sei das Fortwursteln. Als diese Äusserung einen Proteststurm hervorrief,
sagte er ein paar Wochen später indigniert vor den Abgeordneten, er
sei missverstanden worden; das eigentliche Prinzip der österreichischen
Politik sei nicht das Fortwursteln, sondern das Durchg'fretten.

Na dann, wobei bleibts nach der Neu-Organization der BBC
Musikabteilung; beim 'slogging on' oder beim 'muddling through'?

(You are perhaps the only one in this box of building bricks called
Yalding ("this desert they call Paris," as Violetta puts it in a pretty
different but not totally dissimilar context) who really has in him and
pursues a consistent artistic policy. The other colleagues, lovable though
they are (and I by no means exclude myself in the position I occupied),
remind me very much of the Imperial and Royal Prime Minister
[Eduard, Graf von] Taaffe, who in 1888 declared in Parliament that the
basic principle in Austrian politics was to muddle through. When this
remark provoked a storm of protest, he indignantly told the members a
few weeks later that he had been misunderstood; the basic principle in
Austrian politics wasn't to muddle through, it was to slog on.

Well, then: how are things after the reorganization of the BBC's
Music Department; are you slogging on, or muddling through?)

I was never aware of anything in myself so consistent or conscious as
an 'artistic policy', but I'm sure that part of what Paul had in mind was my
dependence on, and vulnerability to, sheer sound – in all its parameters,
needless to say, for over a period of too many years it was another of my
intolerant and intolerable maxims that the only valid form of hearing is
structural hearing. How that undervalues things like colour and beauty in
performance, not to mention drama and expression! And yet it has a kernel of
truth, and is a challenge to the listening ear, one that perhaps only the fittest
will be in a state to survive.

My favourite visual recollection of Paul is from a holiday when Felicity
and I hired Cecily's holiday flat in Somerset; he lived there in the Old Bakery
when not working from a flat in London, and came down for a day or two.
We both recall him vividly, seated in the vegetable garden in a floppy hat,
picking things for the evening meal and looking for all the world like my idea
of one of his favourite characters in one of our favourite authors, Heimito
von Doderer – Amtsrat (Substantive Counsellor) Julius Zihal, a retired civil
servant whose views on 'good order and discipline, Imperial and Royal style'
he had long before rendered into English and shown me.

I saw him for the last time when he visited our house a few months before he died, to hear Felicity and her pianist play for friends and neighbours the programme of an impending concert. Delivered by his faithful London lady taxi-driver, he struggled down the path to the house's side entrance on his suffering feet, and listened with the utmost concentration. His postcard afterwards was grateful not only for the 'fine performances' but for the chance to be 'exceptionally, among a group of music-lovers': he had felt 'warm and comforted'.

He was a great man, whose like we shall not see again.

10   Susan Bradshaw

The pianist-writer Susan Bradshaw was never a BBC staff member, but played so crucial a role in my recruitment that I include her here rather than elsewhere. In search of his new radical-minded young producers, Glock got Hans Keller to ask around, and one person he talked to was Susan. She'd become prominent in the budding London avant-garde after studies with Messiaen in Paris, and was already active in both her fields. Placed as I was at the Kalmus office, I came into contact with her, and she was moreover the flatmate of her fellow-pianist Susan McGaw, who had married Hugh Wood a few months before I entered into my long-term tie with the Corporation. Asked about me, she was, in Hans's words 'very positive and very specific'. Her 'specific' musical evidence must remain one of those mysteries; perhaps I'd turned the pages in the right place when she played the piano part in *Pierrot lunaire*, though I remember doing so only for Paul Hamburger.

I soon paid off my debt to her in the strangest way. After a few months in charge of Chamber Music and Recitals, Hans instituted 'experimental recordings', and it so happened that Susan made one, of the Brahms Handel Variations. I was one of the people asked to listen to it. Knowing the work by heart from playing it, I heard all manner of things I couldn't take, both musical and technical, and was, like her, 'specific'. The only criticism I can any longer remember was my first, namely that the long-term structure lost some of its firm basis if a pianist immediately upped the tempo as early as the first variation. Hans, a lifelong disapprover of confidentiality, not only passed on the reservations but said who they came from, and reported Susan as saying "Ah, now *that's* the sort of criticism I approve of." We were very unworldly, innocent people, I think. She did soon pass an audition, and broadcast both as solo pianist (notably with the Bach Two-part Inventions) and in two trios, the Mabillon with the outstanding flautist William Bennett and oboist Philip Jones, and the Voice and Viola Trio, in which her partners were the delightful Maureen Lehane and a viola player named Victor Manton. My producer-contact with Susan, once established, lasted down to her accompaniment of Jennifer Smith at the 1987 Keller Memorial Concert.

She was a total admirer of Pierre Boulez, enormously well-informed about all the latest developments, but healthily sceptical about some of them, hence her collaboration with Hans in the Piotr Zak hoax described earlier in the essays on Glock and Keller. Susan was a model of musical integrity and intensely loyal, both to everything she believed in and to anyone she felt was a friend. The course of my life after 1960 would have been vastly different without her intervention – indeed I prefer not to speculate.

11   Stephen Hearst

My middle BBC years, the 1970s, were enlivened by the presence and active intervention of a new Controller running the new Radio 3 as successor to the Third Programme's urbane Howard Newby. The choice fell on an abrasive Viennese-born ex-television-executive named Stephen Hearst (originally Stefan Hirsch), yet another of the post-Anschluss intake. Coming out of internment alongside Norbert Brainin and Siegmund Nissel, Hearst had for six years served his new country in the Pioneer (later Royal Pioneer) Corps, ending his army time as a Captain in charge of Italian prisoners-of-war in Gaza (Palestine). He went on to study history at Brasenose College, Oxford. Mention of the baritone singer Thomas Hemsley usually elicited the reminiscence that the two of them had regularly received each other's mail in the 'H' pigeon-hole of the BNC (Brasenose) lodge. There followed a glittering career in television, making series with contributors of the stature of Jacob Bronowski and Alastair Cooke. This, then, was the counterpart of the other new Controller, the one for Music, namely Robert Ponsonby (Eton and the Guards). Unlike William after his initial rush of blood to the head, Ponsonby wanted to be involved in day-to-day decisions; Hearst for his part detected that one of the first things he must do was try and bring music production staff down to earth, just a little nearer the 'real world'. Trying to satisfy two such men must have been a nightmare; certainly Peter Gould in his capacity as Head of Music Programmes used to come back from meetings in Broadcasting House shorn of his natural bonhomie and clearly at a loss. To do the splits week in, week out, was asking too much of anyone, yet he stuck at it for five years.

The decade since the start of the Music Programme had seen me, first, as a more-than-full time producer, then for four years as part-time producer spending the rest of my time translating words by or about Arnold Schoenberg, and as from the middle of 1971 doing a new job, that of joint-assistant-head, with the title Chief Producer. In the latter capacity I had a good deal of contact with the new Controller.

A certain type of high functionary seems to think the most despicable form of argument is not the notorious personal one, the 'argumentum ad hominem', but something I call the 'argumentum ad onion'. It means one actually knows, intimately and comprehensively, the material about which one is laying down the law. Stephen Hearst was never given to that. He respected real knowledge and achievement in any field, even if he did alarm Music Division with his outspokenness and insistence on programmes that listeners would understand and not switch off. Not for nothing did someone like me, who liked him, nickname him 'Siegfried', and he felt obliged to refer more than once to his 'feud with Yalding', which could take on the most trivial forms.[1] The potential for conflict, inherent in the whole age-old Planning and Supply system, now turned into real opposition.[2]

At the outset I detected in him an obsession with big, glamorous names and a tendency to think adjectives rather than content; it was good if programmes came out 'lively', of course, but it didn't do to start with that in mind. However, any minute trace of friction between us vanished almost overnight; he admired what I did in programme-making, even if he sometimes cautioned me, "Leo, you can't spend your whole life with The Eternal Verities," and I think he appreciated my eventual efforts to smooth relations between Network and Department. At the back of it all lay a love of music deeper than that of his predecessor, and absent in his immediate successor. As a boy in pre-war Vienna he had developed fairly traditional musical tastes, and he was by training a historian; much of what the Glock hierarchy had been doing and continued to do was Greek to him, but he would have been the first to point out that it was Music Division's job, not his, to produce the music; he simply made air-time for it and tried to ensure that the network retained some listeners. That was never easy to check, since the Radio 3 audience was sub-minute by the standards of the statisticians who had to interpret Listener Research figures: that 0.1% of the population meant a programme could have been heard by 50,000 people was hard to take on board, and it must have been harder still to admit that it could, strictly speaking, have been represented by a dash in the table and still have been heard by 49,999. "No-one listened" would be the automatic and fallacious conclusion of managers seeing that dash; the Audience Research people themselves begged us not to take the results of such minimal sampling in any sense literally, it was just that a figure of 0.2% probably meant a programme had been heard by more people than if it registered 0.1%. The injunction, I think, fell on deaf ears in the upper echelons of Management.

One other recommendation: looking back to that time, I realize that not even in his earliest days, fresh out of television, did I ever hear Stephen refer to the Radio 3 audience as 'viewers'. Would I could say the same of all television pundits who divagated into radio.

From my eyrie at least halfway up Yalding's ivory tower, clutching those eternal verities to my heart, I came to admire immensely Stephen's firm foundation in the 'real world' where politics and economics ruled. He was afraid of no-one; when the young fellow producing a gramophone series called *Man of Action* had the bad luck to somehow play in the wrong record during an edition with the General Electric magnate Sir Arnold Weinstock going on about his life, Stephen had the future Lord on the phone within minutes demanding that the man be sacked. He wasn't: Stephen could, I think, have stood up to Robert Maxwell if necessary. We shared a disruptive sense of humour, and at his weekly planning meetings it was even possible to produce a tape from up one's sleeve and offer a little treat, as I did when we had a foreign recording of Helen Donath singing Mozart's '*Nehmt meinen Dank*'. At Test Match-time some attention would be paid to the TV monitor if Geoffrey Boycott was batting: Stephen greatly admired his bloody-mindedness. Speaking of treats, the drinks cupboard was briefly visited at Christmas.

In the early 1970s Hans Keller was instrumental in recruiting as producer a clever young musical analyst named Misha Donat, who was also a connoisseur of the film and its music – something that must have taken Hans way back to the days when he and Donald Mitchell had included regular criticism of film music in *Music Survey*.[3] I never quite knew why the appointment of Misha, who clearly knew his stuff, became such an issue, first with Peter Gould and then with Stephen Hearst – maybe it had in Peter's case to do with the BBC's recruitment procedures, for I vividly recalled the confusion a decade earlier over my apparent reluctance to join the permanent staff. In Misha Donat's case there was even an extraordinary get-together between him, Hans and Hearst, with the aim of showing Controller, Radio 3 what an excellent young man the new recruit or recruit-in-spe was. In fact Controller asked Recruit sharply "How old are you, and what do you know about broadcasting?" and the party wasn't judged a success. Misha nonetheless arrived and remained a faithful Keller disciple, both in his emphasis on the educative side of broadcasting and through his penchant for analysing music. The two combined notoriously in a Haydn String Quartet series broadcast during Hearst's time, when what with introduction, analysis and musical illustrations the first actual quartet began twenty-three minutes into the programme. Two decades later Stephen is still known to mouth eloquently about that and his impotence to stop it – the sort of unbelievable thing about which, in a favourite phrase of his, "no-one says moo". But his other favourite saying to us was "In this job I learn something every day".

The ethos of the Hearst years was never better exemplified than on 13 September 1974, the centenary of Schoenberg's birth. The musical revelations in Controller, Radio 3's early Viennese years came from figures like the charismatic soprano Maria Jeritza, and few composers were further from his sympathies than the founder of twelve-note music. But I made out a case for Schoenberg as historic figure and major composer, and it wasn't difficult to persuade Stephen to dedicate a day to him. It happened to include the penultimate night of the Proms, which by long-standing tradition provided one supreme masterpiece, Beethoven's Choral Symphony, and Robert Ponsonby planned in the string-orchestra version of *Verklärte Nacht* as the first half. A good deal of Schoenberg was heard that day, beginning at the very beginning (in two senses, biographical and 7.05 in the morning) with his 1897 String Quartet in D major. *This Week's Composer*, conveniently, was Brahms, so that the Schoenberg orchestration of the G minor Piano Quartet found a place, followed by a very unusual item, a portion of his 1931 Frankfurt Radio lecture on the Orchestral Variations, read by Peter Barker in my translation, with sizeable excerpts from a recording of the composer's original broadcast delivered in his strong Viennese accent. (For some reason that I never fathomed, a tape of the talk was in the BBC's radio archives.) And so it went on, with the orchestral broadcast either side of the one o'clock news consisting of the *Gurrelieder*; after a short break, the master was back at three in an offering from a concert series with music by Schoenberg and his pupil Roberto Gerhard performed by the London Sinfonietta. In the interval of the Prom a talk was commissioned, as intellectual climax of the day, from the Guru Himself, George Steiner, with the impressive title *The Necessity of Music*. I greatly offended Stephen after it had been broadcast by declaring that I'd hoped for philosophy and had been offered mere sociology.

'Programmatic days' were altogether Stephen's style; for the very first, a weekend of French culture, he asked me to be the coordinator, but I explained that I had a rather skimpy background for the job, having concentrated all my life on things German and particularly Viennese. Having long since concluded that much of Music Division constituted a 'Viennese Conspiracy', he took my point, and the job was eventually done in style by the newly-arrived Elaine Padmore. Stephen naturally had more success involving me in a Viennese day overseen by the Manchester talks producer Michael Green, who later became Controller of Radio 4. One favourite thing I managed to sneak in as a fill-up was a disc of the great Viennese actor-comedian Hans Moser: his sketch of a typically obstructive 'Dienstmann' or porter wreaking havoc on the luggage of a couple from out of town. It may not have pleased everyone, for when I played the record to Suzanne Rosza, violinist wife of the Amadeus Quartet's 'cellist Martin Lovett and duo-partner of Paul Hamburger, she simply said it made her glad she didn't live in Vienna.

During Hans Keller's final BBC period he gave two remarkable series of lectures at the Royal Northern College of Music, which BBC North's enterprising Ann Stangar recorded and had broadcast on Radio 3. The first was on the four Schoenberg string quartets, the second a series of four talks on the different movements and aspects of a single great work, Beethoven's String Quartet in B flat, op. 130 (with its alternative finales, the Grosse Fuge and its replacement).[4] Once again Stephen showed his open-mindedness; despite everything, he appreciated Hans's first Schoenberg programme, which treated the (still just) tonal D minor quartet, roundly declaring that he'd enjoyed it very much. He had, as ever, learned something.[5]

But where he felt those involved had forgotten about the facts of broadcasting life he could be scathing. Elisabeth Lutyens had an opera staged at Sadler's Wells, the nature of which may be deduced from its triply trendy title *Time Off? Not the Ghost of a Chance!*, and after the broadcast Stephen made it clear that for him English music had no sacred cows: as an offering to the radio listener it had been less than nothing.

After several years in Radio 3, Stephen was moved upstairs to become one of the rather mysterious 'special assistants' who adorned the Management floors, his new job being to advise Radio's Managing Director, David Hatch. It was part of a re-shuffle designed to give the then Controller of Radio 4, Ian McIntyre, who'd come in for a lot of flak when he tried to enliven that notoriously conservative channel, a more congenial post. Stephen and I were more or less out of contact for the rest of our BBC time, though when I planned a *This Week's Composer* series featuring Karl Goldmark and found an aria recorded by Jeritza, I remembered that she had been Stephen's boyhood idol and notified him of the programme. He was touched. After we both left, we carried on a regular correspondence, a delight for me since he was so easy to provoke into remonstration and reminiscence, especially on the subject of his native Austria. It was, for instance, a mischievous pleasure, given his love-hate relationship with a certain Hans Non Sachs, to be able to report back to him a declaration by no less an eminence than the Austrian Ambassador that his country would remain immensely proud of the troika of cultural figures it had expelled to England in 1938 – Esslin, Hearst and Keller.[6]

I did one freelance job for Stephen in his post-retirement role as an independent television producer, but the work involved was out of proportion to the money, and there was nothing more of the kind. I did, however, discover various surprising things about him, such as his lifelong fascination with the Arsenal football team. That went back to his boyhood, and I got an amazing picture of young Hirsch following the fortunes of players like Der Hapgood, Der Bastin and perhaps even my own ultimate idol (cricketing rather than footballing) Der Compton, even as young Keller was rejoicing in the power of the great side that represented the famous Jewish sports organization, Hakoah. Even then they'd have been at loggerheads …

One manifestation of Stephen's humanity came the evening the Department's Current Planning Assistant, Julian Hogg, played in the final of the BBC Club (London) table-tennis tournament. He had studied clarinet and singing at the Royal College of Music and was the practical, humorous Englishman, though during the 1970s he fell more and more under Hans Keller's spell (he is now Chair of the Cosman Keller Art and Music Trust). Julian was also an extremely well-coordinated sportsman, county-standard hockey-player and good enough at table tennis to jump straight back into the game at my instigation and start beating all and sundry with his age-old pimpled bat, so threadbare and unpredictable as to be technically illegal. I rate it as one of Stephen's great 'mitzvahs' that he came to watch Julian; what other Controller would even have considered giving up an evening to watch a distant subordinate play a game?

His "I learn something every day in this job" is the vital clue to Stephen: how many of us on the other, 'right' side of Great Portland Street could have said as much?

NOTES

1   At other times I followed Beethoven and called him 'King Stephen'.

2   He wasn't totally uncritical of the talks output either, summing it up more than once to us as 'Whither Marxism?'.

3   Hans's writings on the screen were later published as: *Hans Keller, Film Music and Beyond: Writings on Music and the Screen, 1946-59*, ed. Christopher Wintle, London, Plumbago, 2006.

4   These lectures have been transcribed by Alison Garnham as an appendix to her doctoral dissertation: A. M. Garnham, *Hans Keller and the BBC*, University of London (Goldsmiths' College).

5   I thought at the time that Hans missed one point in discussing the background 'against which' the *alla tedesca* movement of Beethoven's Op. 130 is composed. He came to no conclusion, and certainly none of the obvious forms – sonata, variation, binary, ternary – really fits the bill. It struck me that the 'sequence of dances' was in its time a form favoured by great composers, if mostly for its money-making possibilities, and that the similarities and differences between the *tedesca*'s opening theme and its sequel made that a strong candidate. I never had a chance to put this idea to Hans.

6   Martin Esslin (Julius Pereszlenyi) was born in Budapest in 1918 and became a refugee from Vienna in 1938. He was a world authority on the Theatre of the Absurd, and Head of BBC Radio Drama, 1963-77. He died in 2002. The Ambassador, Dr. Alexander Christiani, made the remark during a speech at the Freud Museum in Hampstead to mark the launch of Hans Keller's *Music and Pschology*, ed. Christopher Wintle, London, Plumbago, 2003 (the speech appears on www.plumbago.co.uk).

Part Three

Luigi Dallapiccola (I) (Milein Cosman)

Composers

1 Luigi Dallapiccola

The senior living composers who made the greatest impression on me in my early BBC years were the exiled Spaniard Roberto Gerhard, who lived in Cambridge, and the Italian Luigi Dallapiccola. After the vapidity of Nono, and Berio's trendy good humour, I found in Dallapiccola something true and lasting. I was first in touch with him as early as the end of 1960, when William Glock had heard he was starting work on an opera about Ulysses and asked me to find out more. I received a sizeable letter (in French) telling of the opera's genesis. When he was about six he had seen an experimental silent film made in colour, with a scene where Ulysses pointed to his forehead to tell his comrades that Polyphemus must be blinded: '*Je n'ai jamais oublié le 'geste' d'Ulisse*' (I have never forgotten Ulysses's gesture). One evening in Florence, a quarter of a century later,

> *J'ai eu la vision de l'Opéra. Un instant. Ma il m'a fallu seize ans d'attente avant d'écrire mon livret … Il me faudra <u>des longues années</u> de travail. D'ailleurs je ne suis pas pressé.*

> (I had the idea of the Opera. In a flash. But I had to wait sixteen years before writing my libretto … it would take me <u>long years</u> of labour. Besides, I was in no hurry.)

For 1964 I was keen to present a programme with some of his important early works and wrote to him again. He replied with the history of his *Musica per tre pianoforti*. Its violence had caused protests in various Italian cities during the 1930s, though one critic who didn't know him had understood what he was attempting to do, right down to his 're-creation of the Gabrielis' spatial stereophony'. He also alerted me to the need for a small chorus rather than solo voices in the second set of Michelangelo choruses:

> *N'oubliez pas que, en 1935, en Italie il n'y avait pratiquement pas des choeurs … Avez-vous vu que, si possible, je demande des voix de garçons? Rêves d'un compositeur … hélas.*

Luigi Dallapiccola (II) (Milein Cosman)

(Don't forget that, in 1935, there were practically no choirs in Italy ... Have you taken on board that, if possible, I am asking for boys' voices? Ah, the dreams of a composer ...)

He duly had his dream realized when we recorded the piece with the Wandsworth Boys' Choir. He also named a couple of days when he could be available to play the second piano in *Musica*, and it duly happened, with Celia Arieli and Peter Wallfisch as the other two pianists. There were two such programmes a year or two apart; in the other he played for Mary Thomas in the *Quattro liriche di Antonio Machado*, for Yfrah Neaman in the Two Studies for Violin and Piano, and for John Noble in *Rencesvals*. Mary's typical comment when I asked if I might broadcast a little of a rehearsal we'd recorded was "Yes, but I hope they don't think Who's That Awful Stupid Woman!?".

His *Preghiere* was due to feature in an Invitation Concert, and the same letter continued:

> *Très reconnaissant pour les "Preghiere"; j'espère avec l'inoubliable J. Shirley-Quirk et sous le direction de mon cher, intelligent, excessivement doué John Carewe.*

> (Very grateful for the *Preghiere* [Prayers]; I hope with the unforgettable [John] Shirley-Quirk and under the direction of my dear, intelligent, excessively gifted John Carewe.)

(John Shirley-Quirk, the baritone soloist in that performance, was delighted with the sound of the word '*inoubliable*'!)

Safely home after taking part in the programme, Dallapiccola wrote me a worried letter confessing that when he'd arrived nobody had asked the purpose of his visit, so that his passport had been stamped with the wrong kind of visa, and what was to be done?! I was able to write back, after due consultation with the Music Bookings Manager, reassuring him that however tough those people might be (but hadn't been!) when a foreigner arrived, after he left they couldn't care less what he'd got up to, so long as it had been legal, nor would it have any effect on the payment of his fee (which, typically, he hadn't even mentioned).

A postcard in 1966 says '*le travail m'écrase*' (work crushes me) – *Ulisse* was under way – and a letter two years later still speaks of working on the opera ten hours a day. For *The Listener* of 4 January 1968 I wrote an appreciation of his work, which he liked and of which he said '*J'aimerais bien d'être véritablement semblable au portrait que vous avez fait de moi*' (I'd very much like to be able to live up to the portrait you've done of me).

Dallapiccola was very small and would look up at you as if in respect, which he indeed felt for everyone in whom he sensed music. Entirely free from egoism, he talked in the most natural way about his life and art, in a halting but endearing English which used the word 'oo-ords' (as in *parole*) a good deal. He was emphatic in some of his opinions, describing his first publishers, Carisch, as 'thieves and robbers', but had a lovely sense of humour. Speaking of his impending retirement from the Cherubini Conservatoire in Florence, he said, "My colleagues, they fear retiring, because they know they will be at home all day with their terrible wife. But me, I HAVE A NICE WIFE!" His famous identification of a twelve-note row in the Commendatore's music from *Don Giovanni* occurred to me when I detected something similar in the Fauré song 'O mort, poussière d'étoiles' at the end of the cycle *La Chanson d'Eve*, but when I alerted Dallapiccola to this he didn't take it too seriously, writing back that he'd always thought Czerny the second dodecaphonist on the basis of a chromatic scale in one of his studies.

In the opening decade of the third millennium we hear too little of Dallapiccola, far less than during my BBC time. Hugh Wood summed up his magic in a seventieth-birthday tribute:

> Lyricism, the singing line, on the one hand, and the most skilful of contrapuntal devices on the other are, the pair of them, bosom friends who are there to help each other. They are not sworn enemies who have to be reconciled.[1]

It goes for Bach, it goes for Mozart, and it goes for Luigi Dallapiccola. Magic such as that is too precious to be the victim of fashion – may his time come again.

NOTES

1   *Tempo*, No. 8, March 1974, p. 17. Reprinted in: Hugh Wood, *Staking Out the Territory and Other Writings on Music*, ed. Christopher Wintle, London, Plumbago, 2008.

2   *Hanns Eisler (not forgetting Mary Thomas)*

Hanns Eisler, son of a painter, studied with Schoenberg in Vienna just after the end of the First World War. His left-wing political views didn't endear him to his teacher, who wrote at one point that he'd like to put him over his knee and give him six of the best; on the other hand, when it was a matter of comparative talent Schoenberg was known to place him on a level with Berg and Webern. The standards inculcated by Schoenberg (who scrupulously avoided teaching the twelve-note technique) remained with Eisler, so that at all stages he was a supreme craftsman. His communism was more to the taste of one of Schoenberg's slightly later Berlin pupils, the conductor Walter Goehr, who would have passed on knowledge of Eisler to his son Alexander (Sandy). Already a well-regarded composer, Sandy became another of the young producers recruited into the BBC by Glock. One of his weightiest contributions was to initiate the first British performance of a major Eisler work, the *Deutsche Sinfonie*. I knew virtually nothing of Eisler then, my close involvement with Schoenberg's writings having yet to start, and though I had on Sandy's initiative provided some substitute lyrics to go into a stage production of Brecht's *Schweyk in the Second World War* with incidental music by Eisler, I still had little idea what to expect. Given Sandy's background I knew such a symphony might well turn out left-wing, not to say propagandist. In fact, as conducted by Lawrence Leonard it proved mightily impressive, a perfect mixture of approachable and thought-provoking, with some of the solidity of Mahler – who had, after all been on the right, or rather left, side in an anecdote narrated by Egon Wellesz: Mahler and Pfitzner met at a Vienna hotel, Mahler euphoric at having run across a workers' procession, which had seemed to him like a collection of all his brothers – only for Pfitzner to arrive very late and very grumpy at having been held up by a repulsive throng of grim-faced, threatening men. Eisler, I decided, was someone to look into.

My interest once aroused, I sought out his most lyrical, least propagandist music. There were chamber works based on endlessly ingenious film scores from his exile years in Hollywood, notably *Fourteen Ways of Describing Rain* and *Septets* (based on American children's songs and on music for a film about a circus); but above all there were songs, which I mostly had sung by a delightful Welsh soprano named Mary Thomas. She'd emerged from the anonymity of the Ambrosian Singers, and was making a name as the singer with Peter Maxwell Davies's new-music ensemble The Pierrot Players, later The Fires of London. (The Ambrosian Singers were an incredibly varied collection of on-their-way soloists with more or less every great name of the future in their ranks, marshalled by a supreme organizer, the tenor John McCarthy, who was sometimes known on the grounds of his general manner as Father McCarthy.) Mary helped turn Max's *Eight Songs for a Mad King* into something of a cult work and gave outstandingly musical performances of the vocal part in Schoenberg's *Pierrot lunaire*, which I preferred to anyone else's, past or present. Eisler she sang as to the manner born, more sympathetically, or so I thought, than 'accredited' performers such as Roswitha Trexler from the German Democratic Republic. She understood, for example, his not infrequent marking *'höflich'* – politely. Her accompanist was always Paul Hamburger, who on occasion rose to the challenge of partnering her at the harmonium in *Der Pflaumenbaum* (the urban plum-tree, behind railings, not a hope of fruit, but a plum tree for all that, look at its leaves!) and on a fiendish contraption known as the jangle-box in *Lied von der Tünche* (Whitewash Song, a Brecht recipe for social renewal 'before the whole pigsty falls in').

Eisler chose to live in the DDR on his return from exile in the USA and his output of good communist Agitprop made him required reading there – so much so that the great East German baritone Siegfried Lorenz once told me he'd become so thoroughly sick of having him shoved down his throat that he avoided singing his music, until persuaded for a Berlin recital some years after the 1989 'Wende' and a few decades after Eisler's death. My sedulous de-politicization of Eisler in my broadcasts irritated his faithful pupil David Blake, who took issue with an expression I used in one of those 250-word Usherwood pieces, 'Dreaded Marxist-type marching music': the Goon show had been with us for years but can't have penetrated to the fastnesses of York University. David Blake sent a reproving letter from there, saying how consoled and uplifted he and his comrades were when they could foregather in his room and sing the 'Solidarity Song'. To which there was no answer: in the fullness of time I was to learn all too well how maddening it is to see someone apparently less qualified muscle in on a subject one knows backwards.

Mary became a feature of my programmes. Her versatility extended from recent music, such as Lukas Foss's *Time Cycle*, back into the Viennese classics. With its slightly girlish timbre, hers was not a voice I would have cast in many Schubert songs, but by the same token it was unforgettable in the forlorn *Mignon-Lieder*. She had a sharp eye for the world's follies and a nice sense of humour, once reporting that she'd accepted a recital engagement in the deepest recesses of The Principality, and been asked to make do with the resident accompanist about the place: "they said, 'Oh, she's very good – got a Madam, she 'ave'!" One of her later recordings came about after Jacques-Louis Monod rang me at some unearthly hour of the night in a state of great excitement – "Léo, Léo, I 'ave found Ze One Good Piece of Krenek!" (who was by then up to about Opus 1000). It was a cantata, *Durch die Nacht*, for solo voice and chamber ensemble, to poems by Karl Kraus. I took Jacques-Louis's word, and didn't regret it, for the theme of a sleepless night and renewed hope at daybreak had opened up an unwonted vein of geniality in the sombrely

Protean Meister; I was also delighted to find it ending with a poem – Flieder (Lilac) – I already knew well as the text of one of 'my' Eisler songs (mostly sung by Mary, though one I also gave to Elizabeth Harwood), *Printemps allemand*.[1]

NOTES

1   Music is bound to have its fashions, its ups and downs, and by the same token equally important composers such as Edmund Rubbra now stand a chance (though no more) of retrieving some of the esteem so rightly accorded them before 1959 and our temporary worship of anything post-Schoenbergian: but neglect of any major talent is a pity, and men such as Eisler, Gerhard and Skalkottas should be heard. I have included an account of Skalkottas and my work for him at the BBC as Appendix 1.

3   Roberto Gerhard

The tear-jerking moments in life come most unpredictably. One of mine was prompted when, during a documentary on Alexander Schneider, the violinist quoted Pablo Casals as using about and to him the single word 'Hombre!' (Man). The comprehensiveness of that appreciation was too much for me: and I would apply the same encapsulation of masculinity to Schoenberg's Catalan pupil Roberto Gerhard, who after a spell as Music Librarian to the Madrid court left Spain for good with the advent of Franco and fascism. He settled in Cambridge, supported himself through his skill as a composer of incidental music, and continued to work out an intensely personal style until his death in 1970. While everything post-Schoenbergian had been shrouded in unfavourable rumour, which is to say until Glock's appointment to the BBC, 'Roberto' remained a fairly unknown quantity, and a still less-known quality. David Drew tried valiantly in that extended survey of his music in *The Score* of 1956, but even a UE-alumnus such as I remained ignorant of what it truly had to offer. My induction into Invitation Concert production changed that for good: Glock included in my first two seasons *Concert for 8*, which I summed up for Mr. Usherwood as 'Pierrot in the Sawmill', *Hymnody* and the Second String Quartet.

My mind moved by due process from ignorance to cliché: twelve-note Schoenberg plus local Spanish colour – well put, that man! – so I outlined to him an idea for a programme in a new series, *The Composer Develops*, to trace the growth of the 'Spanish Schoenberg'. The letter 'Roberto' sent back could scarcely have been a more forceful instruction to push off in a different direction:

> As far as my Spanishness is concerned I can honestly say that *other people* are far more aware of it than I myself. Not only has there never been any complacency about it on my part, any conscious display, nay, any consciousness at all of the thing. The period where Catalan folk-song had influenced my music was long past – relatively long – in 1923. Incidentally, it was the very first question Schbrg. fired at me on our first interview: "Are you in favour of musical nationalism?" and like a pistol-shot I answered: "No!" – and the point is: I had never asked myself the question or thought about it. I simply knew that I knew ... I think I became constitutionally – if we may couple the two words – allergic to nationalism the day I saw how stupid it was to be a Catalan separatist, allergic to every kind of nationalism, that is ... The Sardanas are all *pièces d'occasion*. 'Alegrias' was expressly commissioned as a *flamenco* piece, these are examples of colour-display on commission,

not on authentic impulse … You might quote some pages of the Violin Concerto as contradicting what I am saying here. Maybe, I'm not a slave to consistency: in addition the work became intensely autobiographical … I simply could not avoid the past resuscitating in every one of its dim fleeting fases [sic] and faces. Incidentally, the 12-note episodes are '*memories*, not anticipations', the Scherzo goes back to ideas from 1928 – the Largo, on the other hand, *is* contemporary (1941 or 2 or 3, I forget) …

Talking of 'influences' I think you might find in Haiku some trace of my admiration for Strwsky's [sic] *Japanese Lyrics*, et *pour cause*!! – they represent the nearest approximation between him and the Schoenberg school – Webern is almost 'quoted' – a more authentic proximity than anything later in Strwsky, to my mind. I must tell you that in 1923 I think I knew *Pierrot* fairly well, technically, [though] the spirit was still foreign to me. Webern I knew not at all. The [Wind] Quintet is of course unthinkable without a true acquaintance with Schbrg's Quintet – on influences and divergencies you'd find more than you'd have time for … The score of the Nonet has just been issued … the true *development* here is in the rhythmic domain – *don't* compare with Messiaen, it would have to be to his detriment! There's no influence, our conceptions are diametrically opposed.

Antal Doráti gave the premiere of Roberto's Concerto for Orchestra in Boston during his spell as Chief Conductor of the BBC Symphony Orchestra. When William included it in his South Bank season of public concerts, I was asked to write the programme note and accepted the more eagerly since the companion work in the concert was Mahler's Sixth Symphony, about which for various reasons I was well-nigh neurotically enthusiastic at the time – all the hammer-blows of fate, all the cowbells bespeaking man's existential loneliness … that was me, then. (Nowadays I take those cowbells as a reminder that life, work and solidarity endure even in the most rarefied and inhospitable conditions. Sorry, Maestro.) I listened and listened to the tape of the New York performance, and came up with something that Roberto pronounced the best thing ever written about a work of his (unaccustomed as I am to public boasting …).[1] Maybe it had something to do with the fact that for some reason or other I'd had no sight of a score and had had to trust my ears, something I always preferred to do anyway. Paper analysis can be the death-knell of musical appreciation, and the super-analyst Keller always insisted that one should only set about works whose sound one knew intimately.

Roberto was a man who spoke his mind – I had one brief clash with him as producer, and there was a more noticeable degree of tension between him and his Invitation Concert conductor, Jacques-Louis Monod, narrated elsewhere. But he sticks in my mind as the 'hombre' he always was. Hugh Wood once summed up his magic in the simple words "everything dances". I treasure the thought that I knew him, even slightly.

NOTES

1   My programme note for Roberto Gerhard's Concerto for Orchestra (1965) played at a South Bank Concert given by the BBC Symphony Orchestra on 2 February 1966 appears as Appendix 2.

4   In absentia: *Franz Schmidt*

Some composers creep up on you. This one must count as an 'absent friend', for I could scarcely have known someone who died in Vienna early in 1939. To follow briefly the pattern of Philip Larkin's *I Remember, I Remember*, it was in Oxford that I first didn't hear of Franz Schmidt. Studies with the Viennese émigré Egon Wellesz covered most of the major personalities of his time there, with never a mention of the city's leading teacher during the 1930s, the man who had played the second 'cello part in the 1903 premiere of *Verklärte Nacht* by Wellesz's teacher Schoenberg. For heaven's sake, the Oxford curriculum steered well clear of even that still-living and not-yet-understood figure, without going into dead minor contemporaries.

Vienna it was that first opened my ears to the missing link, again in a negative way that smartly closed them again. The pianist Paul Wittgenstein, brother of Ludwig and scion of an immensely rich industrial family, revisited his native city to perform one of the left-hand-only works he'd commissioned from leading composers – Richard Strauss, Ravel, Prokofiev, the young Benjamin Britten and Hindemith, whose work he disliked so intensely that he refused to play it. What he performed when I heard him was by none of those, but by the Austro-Hungarian composer Franz Schmidt, born the same year as Schoenberg, 1874, along with Gustav Holst, Charles Ives, and Josef Suk. Wittgenstein had lost his right arm in the First World War, but relentless willpower saw him through a creditable career using his remaining hand. Had not Brahms, after all, transcribed Bach's violin Chaconne as an exercise for the left hand? Unfortunately, by 1956 Wittgenstein was nearing the end, and the playing, which had always been forceful (the idea was to make as much sound with one hand as other pianists with two), was now brutal. It was a distasteful experience, and as an Adagio wended its weary way I found myself thinking "If they take a wrong turning, we could all still be sitting here tomorrow morning". I also thought "this must have been Fritz Kreisler's harmony teacher". I was to learn better.

But how? Soon after – *post hoc non propter hoc*, I wouldn't blame Wittgenstein – I fell ill with a mysterious low fever and was carted off to the outskirts of the city and the commodious Wilhelminenspital. There I lay for many weeks, not getting any better, but intrigued by a piece of music that kept sounding over the tannoy in the ward: had the Viennese been conversant with the name Alberto Mantovani and his over-luscious string sound, I'd have said that was what I was hearing. It was both exciting and beautiful, and turned out to be by the very same Franz Schmidt who had so bored me at the concert. The Intermezzo from the first of his two operas, *Notre Dame*, had entered my life, and with it Schmidt's amazing gypsy strain.

A chance to think on from that better impression came when I'd returned to England and was working for the publishing firm that had tried to train me in Vienna. The crucial moments came after I'd found in the office cupboard a record of Schmidt's Fourth Symphony. It was, clearly, music of stature and poignancy, and I never looked back. When I read that Schmidt had described its opening trumpet tune as 'the last music heard on earth by a man who has spent his entire life under its sign', my curious hospital experiences came flooding back, and I resolved that here was the music I wanted to see me over to the other side when the time came.

Then there was Hans Keller. Having known Schmidt as a boy, he was pleased when off my own bat I discovered his idol's music. He never referred to him in my hearing as a great composer, but clearly saw Schmidt, composer, pianist, 'cellist and unparalleled musical memory, as the most complete musician imaginable, and I shall be eternally grateful that one of our last contacts was when he helped to plan a Schmidt Festival in London. At the BBC he'd done what he could, both importing recordings from Austrian Radio and inspiring a most unusual concert in Manchester at which Sir Charles Groves conducted Schoenberg's Orchestral Variations Op. 31 and a set by Schmidt on a 'Hussar's Song'. Incomparably easier to listen to, the Schmidt nevertheless came off second-best when during the interval the audience voted for the work they wanted to hear again. They breed 'em tough in Manchester.

I've mentioned the contribution Maurice Cole made to my knowledge of Schmidt, and when I took over the supervision of foreign recordings I made sure we overlooked no halfway-plausible offering of his works – we did, after all, have the option of not broadcasting what had been listened to and judged inadequate.[1] But probably the major break-through was in 1974, when amid the plethora of offerings featuring all five centenarians, we actually made our own recording of that same A major Quintet through which the decaying Wittgenstein had bashed and crashed his way two decades earlier. The guiding spirit was the clarinettist Thea King, long a closet Schmidt fanatic, and by great good luck her piano partner at the time was Clifford Benson, a young man sensitive far beyond his years. Thea was able to recruit an able English Chamber Orchestra colleague, José Luis García, to 'lead' the ensemble (a strange one, since there is no second violin in the quintet, instead of which the clarinet vies with first violin and melodic left-hand piano in a unique triumvirate of melody instruments. That was a scoring Schmidt adopted for the last two of his three Wittgenstein quintets). The A major contains one of his extremely rare featured solo passages for the 'cello, and we were blessed in that the beautifully talented Thomas Igloi was still around to play it – he died just two years later. The violist was Ruşen Güneş, also from the ECO. Knowing no better, I let the ensemble play both the Adagio I'd heard in Vienna and the alternative slow movement (a solo intermezzo Jörg Demus had played for me ten years before). Neither Thea nor I had any idea that the two were supposed to be alternatives, Wittgenstein having taken against the idea of a movement for solo piano in a work for five instruments and insisted that Schmidt write him a 'normal' slow movement.

The Book with Seven Seals, Schmidt's last masterpiece, is an oratorio based on the Book of Revelation. During my early BBC years there were two performances of it, one with Leo Wurmser conducting his old teacher's great work, the other in public with an enterprising but broad-brush conductor named Bryan Fairfax. Both used an English translation: the press being what it is, the greatly superior Wurmser performance was totally overlooked (it was 'only on the radio', where up to a hundred thousand people might have heard it, whereas the Fairfax, a public concert before a few hundred, was reviewed, if to no great effect). Recordings of the work came our way from the Austrian Radio from time to time, and, shortly before I left, a Viennese string quartet actually offered the first of Schmidt's two string quartets, the one in A major, which I naturally snapped up for a studio recording.

The major event of my final BBC years so far as Schmidt was concerned was a Festival promoted jointly by the BBC and Austrian Cultural Institute in 1984, with Hans's vigorous participation – he'd retired five years before and had any amount of time and energy to pursue worthwhile schemes. The main events included an orchestral concert in the Maida Vale studios at which the BBC Symphony Orchestra's Chief Conductor, Sir John Pritchard, conducted a not very good performance of the Fourth Symphony, also the Carnival Music and Intermezzo from *Notre Dame*, which he positively disliked. He'd wanted to do the Second Symphony but the concert formed part of a broadcast series and that work was on the way from Vienna already. Harold Truscott's book on Schmidt's orchestral music was launched during the Festival by Sir John, who told how his mentor in Vienna forty years before had told him "You must conduct Schmidt". We were all too polite to ask why, given the enormous power that had meanwhile accrued to him, he'd waited so long. At a discussion, the old chestnut that Schmidt as a 'typical Austrian' must ipso facto have been a Nazi was trotted out by a visiting professor, and Hans was able to quote back at him the composer's words: "One can only make music with gypsies, and only make friends with Jews." Finally, there was a very long concert in a Kensington church, at which Thea, Clifford and three of the Allegri Quartet's members played no fewer than three major Schmidt chamber works – the B flat and A major quintets and the A major string quartet. That gluttonous idea naturally came from Hans; I 'had me doubts', but as it turned out the whole thing was a striking success.

A year after our 'Festival' I was able to visit Vienna and tell a Schmidt conference about his performance history in Great Britain. After I left, I was invited to the Vienna Philharmonic's 1990 'sesquicentenary' junketings, where I delivered a paper based on Schmidt's unconventional views about the piano (he detested it for its instantly decaying sound, but played it like hardly anyone else in the world) and its place in 'organology'. That more or less concluded my Schmidt activities, but I left in the hope that I'd been able to satisfy existing interest, which there undoubtedly was (Stephen Hearst used to hear regularly from a VIP named Dipak Nandy, who'd complain that we were neglecting Schmidt AGAIN), and to arouse interest in those who'd so far not come across him. With the Welleszes of this world concentrating their minds elsewhere, that section of the public was too numerous. But I tried. Hans may or may not have reckoned him a 'great composer'; I for one am less picky about my language and certainly wouldn't be without him. At the very least, the days may be over when people, on the analogy of "Goldmark? Oh, you mean Korngold," would say to me "Franz Schmidt? Oh, you mean, Florent Schmitt".

NOTES

1   We once received a tape of a particularly prestigious gala concert at the Vienna State Opera that included Richard Strauss's enormously complex choral piece *An den Baum Daphne* (a party-piece of the excellent BBC Singers), sung with truly ghastly wobble and uncertainty by the State Opera Chorus. After it had been listened to, as all overseas recordings were, there was no question of broadcasting it, but rather than lose the other excellent pieces on the tape, I rang up ORF's Head of Music, Gottfried Kraus, to ask humbly whether he thought that in this case we might make an exception. (A similar approach through the normal Foreign Relations channels would surely not have worked, for Conditions of Use were Conditions of Use). Gottfried laughed like a drain, said "*Es war ein Skan-DAAL!*"!" and that was the end of it. We certainly used to junk the enormous opening litany of announcements in various languages listing every overseas radio station that had ordered an Austrian festival tape – '*Hier ist das Salzburger Studio der Österreichischen Rundfunk, angeschlossen die British Broadcasting Corporation, Westdeutscher Rundfunk, Sender Freies Berlin …*' and so on for several minutes: I nicknamed that routine the '*Angeschlossens*', on the analogy of the Bible's 'begats', but the only time our listeners ever heard it was if we took a Salzburg concert live, which happened once in a blue moon.

5   *Hugh Wood, Composer and Friend*

The most important friendship of my life dates from 1954. By then I had achieved, from my base at Wadham College, the first of two music degrees at Oxford University, whereas a young History student at New College had, as he felt it, painfully little to do with the Music Faculty's doings. His only available option was to eavesdrop on a couple of lecture courses and receive such advice as the kindlier tutors would dispense. Not that the music students lived in each others' pockets, but we were all after a certain expertise and were at least being taught it, whereas a student with a passionate desire to be part of the musical world, but not the preliminary training to study it, could and did feel very left out. Hugh Wood had heard enough music in the course of a civilized upbringing not far from the twin Lancashire musical centres, Manchester and Liverpool, and his own music was already stirring within him, but in an inchoate and tantalizingly distant fashion. He took every opportunity to write incidental music, whose impact he summed up with:

> One returns to the reproaches of one's tutors ("I can't think why you haven't had time to write me a decent essay this week"), the merciless kindness of one's friends ("Never mind: next time you'll write something really good!").[1]

Hugh began 'reading' History at Oxford in 1951, after the two years of National Service then still expected of our young men; one could ask, as many of us did, to have it deferred till after our degrees, but he quite wisely got it over first, so ensuring that he was two years more mature on arrival. One aspiring composition unconnected with college dramatics was a set of part-songs for mixed chorus and piano, *Songs for Springtime*,[2] which were included in the University Musical Club and Union's annual composers' concert of February 1954. It should be added, the Faculty's 'gloomy palace of ice'[3] notwithstanding, that many of the leading student musicians in fact studied other subjects; some of them, such as the oboist Neil Black, would go on to achieve major distinction as performers. The composers at the 1954 concert were Anthony Hedges (Faculty, later Lecturer at Hull University), and Hugh Wood. It was reviewed in the student periodical *Isis* by a certain Leo Black, whose often intemperate remarks, sometimes compounded by personal animus, pro or con, were a matter for concern, likewise the occasional spikiness of his own music – for he too composed but had nothing in that particular concert, at which he instead accompanied the future Purcell authority Franklin B. Zimmerman in the piano part of Hindemith's Horn Sonata. Something about Hugh Wood's 'amateur' effort evidently got through to him, for he commented in his review that though their technical level was way below that of Hedges's work, his songs had much charm, not least through their 'unselfconsciousness'. He then did his best to spoil the treat by adding 'any composer who is to progress must be or become self-conscious'. End of sermon.

And that could have been that, save for the strong impression the review made on an aspirant to composerdom accustomed to being at best ignored and at worst snubbed by fellow-students who were studying music. Within days a letter arrived thanking his critic for so unexpected a review, and frankly expressing Hugh's uncertainties and problems in deciding what to do next about his unrequited love for music. It proved the start of a truly voluminous correspondence, and more immediately of an article by him as part of a series commissioned by me as that term's music editor for *Isis*, entitled *The Composer's World*. The above quotation formed part of that piece.

The friendship went through many stages: at first, Hugh was 'down from' Oxford while I, aiming in vain to write a dissertation (which in those days we still called a thesis), remained there. As I was studying for a 'composition degree' in my final year, Hugh had found private teaching in London, at first with a very sound and kind minor composer named William Lloyd Webber. The immediate aim was to graduate to the dominant seventh … By the time I took myself off to learn the publishing business in Vienna, I had completed a porridgey string quartet that drained every last ounce of creativity from me and presumably would have justified my calling myself a composer, or at least a 'Bachelor of Music' (how appropriate …) while Hugh was still methodically mastering all the steps up to and beyond that famous dominant seventh. Life's little ironies, for look at us now!

Supply-teaching, music copying and whatever musical work he could garner were the economic foundation for Hugh's first post-Oxford years. For a while he taught at Morley College. Further study took him far enough on for his own compositions to begin acquiring the 'self-consciousness' postulated by his Oxford critic. Two works from those years were heard within the space of five days in July 1959. The earlier of them, a first essay in string quartet form, was played by the Amici String Quartet at a Cheltenham Festival concert of the Society for the Promotion of New Music on the eleventh, having been preceded on the seventh by the premiere of music from rather later. By then he was so immeasurably far on from the dominant seventh as to know how twelve-note rows can be handled to the mutual satisfaction of composer and listener, and had produced a set of variations for viola and piano. They were given their first public performance at the Wigmore Hall, London, by a leading violist of the day, Cecil Aronowitz, and a prominent interpreter of recent piano music, Margaret Kitchin. About the time of the composition of the Variations Hugh became engaged to the pianist Susan McGaw, who had studied at the Royal Academy of Music in London and then with Yvonne Lefébure in Paris.

I was meanwhile back from Vienna and embarked on my star-crossed attempt at a publishing career. One very energetic, more-senior though still-young member of the firm was Stephan Harpner, son of a noted Austrian-refugee lawyer who had helped found the Anglo-Austrian Music Society here. In the autumn of 1959 I wrote Stephan a business-like letter to Vienna, where there would soon be a meeting to decide the firm's next production schedule. By that time the Manchester School, notably Maxwell Davies, Birtwistle and Goehr ('Max, Harry and Sandy'), were beginning to be talked about, with 'Max' already well connected to Schott's. The letter to Harpner mentioned Hugh Wood's Variations, saying:

> I've thought for several years that some day he is going to write really good music. This is a view that is now shared by people like Seiber, Milner and Iain Hamilton – in fact they might put the prospect a bit nearer than I would. He still has an enormous amount to learn, because he started late; but what he learns, he learns for good. I think that in perhaps five years he will be writing really good music, not so advanced as to put everybody off, and with real 'content' (because he's a real personality, not just a clever note-spinner with the right connections). And by then the coming avant-garde vogue will be over and done with [!], and the people who matter will quite possibly be wanting the sort of music he will be writing … I think Hugh is going to be a composer to take seriously, after the present race of bright boys have gone out of fashion. I don't mean I'm against taking, for example, Marc Wilkinson, only that, if we do, we should be clear about why we are taking them, i.e. for our sake and not for theirs. Whereas Hugh Wood is, in the long run, someone to take more seriously.[4]

Stephan clearly pulled some weight with his Viennese directors Alfred Kalmus, Alfred Schlee and Ernst Hartmann, for in due course the minutes of the Production Meeting arrived in the London office and registered agreement to publish both a Birtwistle piece, *Monody for Corpus Christi*, and the Wood Variations, which thus became their composers' 'Opus 1'. A great day. Hugh followed them up with a Trio for flute, viola and piano in 1961, and Three Piano Pieces in 1963, the latter written for and given their first performance by Susan McGaw, who was by then his wife (they married at the start of 1960).

With us both living in London for a few years our correspondence dropped off, but it was to revive as Hugh moved on to university jobs in Glasgow, Liverpool and Cambridge. His immense conscientiousness about all work he undertook meant that time for composition was limited, but a succession of pieces established him as an important figure with an individual voice. The Cheltenham Festival performed his first mature string quartet, BBC commissions followed for a work with soprano and tenor solist and orchestra (*Scenes from Comus*), and then a 'cello concerto, and by the end of the decade he was up to Opus 15. About the end of the sixties he overcame his scepticism about current ideas on 'free form', and tried out something of that kind in a further string quartet. Breaking the habits of a lifetime, he sought my advice about his sketches for the work; what I saw looked eminently viable and I told him so. Once completed, the quartet (his second) was dedicated to me.

The next step along what must have seemed anything but a clearly-marked-out road came when in 1973 *The Listener* carried an introduction to the premiere of his Violin Concerto, and *The Musical Times* soon afterwards commissioned the first lengthy article to be written about his music. In both cases I was the author.

As from the later 1970s until he turned 67 in 1999, Hugh was a fellow of Churchill College Cambridge, appointed on the initiative of the new Professor of Music, my boyhood friend Alexander Goehr in yet another guise. The authoritative analytical book on Hugh's music by Ed Venn published in 2007 makes clear that 'Sandy' was not merely an employer but a serious influence on certain aspects of Hugh Wood's mature musical thinking. That thinking has never ceased to deepen and develop up to the time of writing (early 2009).

In June 1982 he turned fifty, one month and one day before I was due to do the same. I went to the party given by him and Susan in Dartmouth Park Road, Kentish Town, London NW5, and there engaged in a lively conversation, mostly about jogging, swimming and table tennis rather than our shared profession of music, with a younger and bewitching lady who at the time was coming up to a divorce from the conductor Andrew (now Sir Andrew) Davis. As a great advocate of Hugh's works, he had been at the party but had already left, to the relief of his about-to-be-ex-wife Felicity. In the fullness of time she became my wife, by which time we'd moved into a detached house just round the corner from the Woods. We're still there, though Hugh has moved a few metres at 90 degrees to Dartmouth Park Road, so now he's just round two corners. Thank you for all that, Hugh and Susan.

Two things happened close together in September 1988. I was made redundant by the BBC, and Jenny Wood, the luminously lovely 26-year-old daughter of Hugh and Susan, was murdered by a mental patient on day-release while she was on holiday in Bavaria. The impact of my 'blow' was mimimal if complex; that of the Woods' horrendous, so I took it as a tremendous sign of long friendship that they could summon up the courage to emerge from their mourning and be part of a small dinner-party given in Broadcasting House to mark what we euphemistically called my retirement.

Hugh Wood is a man of wide culture, almost vociferously loyal to all causes in which he believes; most have been artistic, and documented in typically thorough and eloquent articles such as 'A Photograph of Brahms' (first published in the *Cambridge Companion to Brahms*). The full extent of his sympathies and wisdom can be gathered from his recent selected essays.[5] Being of the generation that salutes Kingsley Amis and Philip Larkin, he is capable of considerable scepticism about more recent and trendy cultural products; anger has always been a strong suit, provoked by a predictable variety of subjects from lackadaisical and lazy students to sloppy writing and frivolous composing methods. When Most Distinguished Cambridge Colleague George Steiner rebuked him for reading like Kingsley Amis in that Brahms piece, he was delighted.

He is also a man of intense principle, in the political field as well as the cultural-professional. The post-war realization that communism was, at best, a system believing in the pre-emptive strike against its enemies has remained with him; my Jewish background pushes my political template still further back, to the necessity of fending off all that tends towards Fascism, and the 1945 euphoria at the thought that Nazism had been wiped out at Nuremberg has given way to a recognition that it and capitalism share certain underlying methods and aims (something my father told me sixty years ago, but at the wrong time for me to believe it). We have nothing better to offer, but don't for that reason have to approve. Hence my sympathy with a great writer like the ex-DDR novelist Hermann Kant, beneath whose pyrotechnics and court jester humour lies that primal post-war resolve in the further part of Germany that the country must be prevented from ever again wreaking the havoc of the years between 1933 and 1945. The odd attempt to interest Hugh in Kant was met with the straightest and broadest of dead bats.

His joy in the world's offerings has extended in its time to a systematic attempt to take in the dying repertoire of the great London music halls as they closed down during the 1960s (our correspondence is full of lines like 'I don't wish to know that' and 'Kindly leave the stage!'). He is altogether a great laugher, notably at the Marx Brothers; I have seen him literally rolling in the aisle when watching the twin Grouchos at the mirror, or Mr. Whitmore's Florida call – though he once sent me a classic Alexandrine couplet of Hölderlin's, *Die Scherzhaften* (The Jokers):

> *Immer lacht ihr und scherzt? Ihr musst! O Freunde! Mir geht dies*
> *In die Seele, denn dies müssen Verzweifelte nur.*

> (Are you always playing and joking? You must! O friends,
> That goes to my heart, for only men in despair must do this.)

And if things don't go as he would have wished, a certain Eeyore side can come to the fore.

He values people, going to endless trouble to keep in touch with and help them. In my life he has played somewhat the role attributed by F. Scott Fitzgerald in *The Crack-up* to Edmund Wilson – that of conscience, just as others have been super-ego (Hans Keller), brain (Paul Hamburger) or incorporation of the gentler virtues (citation suppressed). He also has a superb English style that must have rubbed off on the way I write. So I am in many ways in his debt.

Ed Venn's exhaustive analytical book on Hugh's music appeared in 2007, when its subject was already 75. Its author found excellent words to sum up the music's attraction for him:

> The emotionalism ... to be found in much of Wood's music ... is a vital part of the resistance against the mechanical, artificial and dehumanized world in which we live. The evocations of love and loss and the elevation of individual over collective experience to be found throughout Wood's oeuvre speak eloquently of the importance of keeping us human.[6]

I cannot improve on that, and rejoice to see that what I have felt since the early 1960s a young academic of the third millennium likewise feels in his rather different time. Another point made by Dr. Venn is that the Music Industry's treatment of Hugh Wood down the decades needs to be added to the already-lengthy list of injustices brought about by fashion and commercial interests:

> The Hugh Wood problem, then, is how one is to engage critically with a substantial body of music that, for all its passion and conviction, remains on the margin of the contemporary canon for largely political reasons.[7]

No other names are named, but that of Edmund Rubbra springs immediately to mind (my mind at least, though I could be regarded as partial), and of Franz Schmidt and ... and ... yes, the line *will* stretch out to the crack of doom. Other people must, like me, find it a scandalous indication of the anomalous values enshrined in the British honours system that Hugh Wood should never in his 77 years have been offered any recognition of that kind. His mastery of composition and the warmth of his articulate and explosive personality must make up for that – and do.

NOTES

1   'Viewpoint', *Isis*, 5 May 1954, p. 20.
2   Curiously, it appears to be the only very early work overlooked or deliberately not mentioned by Edward Venn in his comprehensive *The Music of Hugh Wood*, Aldershot, Ashgate, 2007.
3   'Viewpoint', ibid.
4   My slightly snide comment harmed Marc Wilkinson not at all. A most talented composer of incidental music, he went on to a vastly successful career at the National Theatre, on Broadway and in films. He did, in fact, have a piece, *Variants of Glass*, published by UE around the time in question.
5   Hugh Wood: *Staking Out the Territory and Other Writings on Music*, ed. Christopher Wintle, London, Plumbago, 2008. This includes a reprint of the Brahms essay.
6   Venn, 2007, p. 226-27.
7   Ibid., p. xii.

Luigi Dallapiccola (III) (Milein Cosman)

Part Four

Janet Baker (Milein Cosman)

Performers

1 Walter Goehr

The war years in Amersham brought our family into quite close contact with a number of German and Austrian refugees such as a large, very sombre German communist named Bertha Heimberg. For a while she was our housekeeper, whose unavailability to attend the school play on the grounds that it was the anniversary of 'our leader's death' I only fully understood half a century later, when I found the name Ernst Thälmann attached to every main street in towns that had formed part of the lately-defunct German Democratic Republic. I've often wondered how Miss Heimberg fared once her party had its way after the war and the Soviet occupation.

The conductor Walter Goehr lived less than half a mile away from us, just the other side of the Metropolitan railway line. He'd studied in Schoenberg's composition master-class in Berlin, fled like his teacher in 1933 and settled in Amersham. He noted my precocious musicality; later, Hans Keller was to maintain, with how much accuracy I cannot judge, that for a long time Walter had undervalued the at-least-equal-but-different talent of his own son Peter Alexander, a fortnight younger than me and universally known as Sandy. The Goehrs we 'for the duration' knew well. Walter was nut-brown and wrinkled and altogether fascinating. Of course I knew nothing of either his studies with Schoenberg or his legendary predatoriness with women, but his instinctive musicality made a strong impression. Mrs. (Laelia) was just as striking, a blonde lady most vividly remembered for her appearances on the scene with several very lively poodles whose leads would gradually weave around her what one had to call a dog's-cradle. An early Intimation of Immorality came as I overheard her playing a boogie-woogie piece by Monia Liter; but it was Schoenberg's Op. 19 piano piecelets that I eventually copied out at the Goehrs'.

Significantly, of our two left-wing fathers, Walter went by the golden rule that he who fails to survive fails altogether and so sent Sandy to the nearest minor public school, Berkhamsted; whereas my Fabian Socialist father stuck to egalitarian principles, which dictated state education – the best, obviously, since I was in the top decile, and the Left's literal egalitarianism and anti-elitism of the 1960s and after was still twenty years away.

My first live experience of Walter as practical musician was a war-time concert at the Aeolian Hall in Bond Street, during the interregnum between blitz and buzz-bombs, with one of the earliest performances of Britten's *Les Illuminations*, sung not by its dedicatee, the Swiss soprano Sophie Wyss, but by Peter Pears. My recollections of that are mostly of Rimbaud's texts translated in the programme – 'first a thigh, then another thigh': that I found mysterious in a stomach-tightening way. Another occasion I recall is the first performance of the Monteverdi Vespers as reconstructed by Hans Redlich, conducted by Walter, and impresario'd I suppose by Michael Tippett, whose Morley College Choir took part. That happened in Central Hall Westminster soon after the war ended, and my only specific memory of it is of the long wobbly vocal decorations in pieces like '*Nigra Sum*' and '*Duo Seraphim*'. What I do remember is asking my parents afterwards, in my horribly self-satisfied way, "I suppose not many of the boys at school would have been able to understand that?". I was earnestly reassured. Tippett's published letters make it abundantly clear that he valued Walter Goehr above anyone else in England for his helpfulness and insight.[1]

My last contact with Walter came another decade later, during my time with Universal Edition in London. He'd prepared a performing edition of Monteverdi's *L'incoronazione di Poppea*, for which a piano score was needed, and Dr. Kalmus suggested that I find time to do it. Knowing me well, Walter was happy, and I spent a lot of time with him and his second wife Jean (a former BBC secretary from the days when he'd conducted the Corporation's light-music *Orchestre Raymonde* under the pseudonym George Walter) at their house in Putney. Walter's re-creation of Monteverdi at the piano had great intensity, and I produced what I still find a rather well-sounding piano version of it. He also found the alluringly under-dressed picture for the cover; that drew a shocked response from UE Vienna's Dr. Wagner, who was also German co-translator of the libretto – '*hier gibt's ein Gesetz gegen Schmutz und Schund, und das soll auf das Kuvert*?!' (We have a law against filth and trash, and that's to go on the cover?!) But of course Walter got his way, and very pretty the cover is too. At one point there was a hope that a different Walter, 'Felsenstein' (to me a new name!), might produce the opera in Berlin, which would have been a wonderful closing of the circle. Our Walter was ecstatic for other reasons too – "he'll have her naked!" – but it never happened. As for this country, Raymond Leppard's Brown Windsor, wall-to-wall-strings version muscled in on Glyndebourne and that was that.

During the same period Sandy's studies with Richard Hall in Manchester and Olivier Messiaen and Yvonne Loriod in Paris had culminated in the composition of a cantata for two soloists and eight instruments, *The Deluge*, which the BBC asked Walter to conduct in a programme of new works. I recall his saying something mildly quizzical as he told me that, but of course he did conduct it, and Sandy never looked back. Very soon after, Sandy became one of three young musicians recruited to liven up BBC radio music – I was another. He went on to become Professor of Music at Leeds, so pre-empting the title

John Black, Alexander Goehr and Leo Black in the 1940s (Laelia Goehr)

(half-mocking, half-affectionate) given me by schoolmates, and then the same at Cambridge; when my life's-work on Schubert finally appeared, its first review was on the opposite page to one of a collection of essays about Sandy on his seventieth birthday. Strange, the way certain people shadow you through life.

Walter knew his limitations. Despite all his years in this country and his openness to talents such as Tippett's, he hadn't transmuted into an English musician. During the *Poppea* time, Universal were seeking a suitably prestigious first performance for a set of orchestral variations by Anthony Milner. Having seemingly got nowhere with the Hallé Orchestra and Sir John Barbirolli (who did eventually give the premiere), I showed the score to Walter. He found that it 'looked like music of Hroobhra'. That clearly didn't make it his cup of tea, for all his versatility.

Walter died quite suddenly of a heart attack, not very long after the *Poppea* vocal score appeared. He's still one of my yardsticks for musical intelligence and vitality.

NOTES

1   On pp. 196-97 of his *Staking Out the Territory*, London, Plumbago, 2008, Hugh Wood quotes a letter to Sir Steuart Wilson of 4 April 1950 in which Tippett expressed his deep indebtedness:

> Goehr has treated the music with as much care and responsible consideration as for any composer dead or alive. I must say honestly that, apart from Continental thoroughness and courtesy (which I am slowly getting used to!), from Goehr alone in this country have I received, without asking for it, just this unfailing effort and pains.

2   *Heather Harper*

Few singers dominated their field in the early 1960s as did the soprano Heather Harper. I first became aware of her earlier, near the end of my Oxford time; Jack Westrup had cast his annual opera production, hitting upon this quite young and almost-unknown singer for Verdi's Lady Macbeth, and as a friend of the opera's undergraduate producer, Howard Baker, I had the briefest of meetings with her in the street. By the time I joined the BBC she was well established and, given her versatility, she was working hard and variously. The cleanness and flexibility of her voice made her a natural for what in those days of innocence we still referred to as the 'pre-classical repertoire', and she was certainly a favourite with Arnold Goldsbrough, who conducted most of the major Handel programmes Glock planned into the Invitation Concerts. It wasn't exactly mutual admiration; she once vowed to me that she'd never again work with Goldsbrough, because he couldn't take a decision as to how something went and not have changed his mind between rehearsal and performance. They had, however, collaborated unforgettably in music like Handel's barbaric psalm setting *Dixit Dominus*, a work that prompted me to uncover a surprising lacuna in the BBC's Sound Archives. I'd hoped to make a microphone 'trail' that would juxtapose Handel's rhythmic chanting at the words '*conquassabit capita*' (he hath banged their heads together) with the very similar sounds made by an English football crowd reacting dismissively to some egregious foul by one of the visiting team: "OFF, OFF, OFF …". It turned out that the otherwise omnivorous Archives had never put on record that most English of noises.

One of Hans Keller's early initiatives during his couple of years in charge of Chamber Music and Recitals was to ask Heather to perform Schoenberg's difficult song-cycle *The Book of the Hanging Gardens*, first for a studio recording and later at an Invitation Concert in Belfast.[1] Although one or two of the lowest-lying passages didn't suit her voice ideally (we had to wait a year or two for Margaret Price, with her unique 'mezzo extension'), Heather's supreme musicianship and scrupulous preparation paid off. She was also an excellent pianist, able to do a lot of preliminary study at the keyboard; nevertheless, Hans suggested that when he sat in on a rehearsal to contribute ideas, I should play. She agreed, and we spent a few fascinating hours at her house in Lancaster Grove, London NW3, working on that intricate piece. Later, apropos of Roger Smalley, Hans called his Schoenberg interpretations "the most musical I have encountered, apart, in intention, from yours when accompanying Heather Harper in *The Book of the Hanging Gardens*". Which was good enough for me. The soprano solo in the finale of Schoenberg's Second String Quartet was a natural follow-up, with the Dartington Quartet entering my professional life and staying for many years; and throughout the 1960s Heather gave regular recitals with songs I'd mostly chosen. I still rate her delivery of Schubert's *Die Allmacht* as hors concours, but she eventually found she was only happy with an orchestra behind her and the recitals dried up. I was a pretty unconditional admirer, even warming to her Arabella at Covent Garden, which had been criticized for lacking glamour (well, try following Lisa della Casa!). I found that intelligence went a hell of a long way.

Among artists with whom I worked in those earliest days, she was the best of colleagues and never less than memorable as a performer. Nobody received 'suggestions' (meaning a degree at least of implicit criticism) with more equanimity – "Tell me precisely what you want me to do differently." If one didn't know precisely, one would have been better advised to keep one's mouth shut. Another Invitation Concert idea for her was the original, often bitonal version of Hindemith's *Das Marienleben*. Heather and Ernest Lush made out the strongest possible case for it.

My friendship with Heather and her first husband Leonard Buck was reflected in a trip to Cornwall, where she was to sing the principal soprano role in a production of Monteverdi's *Poppea* at a very early incarnation of the Prussia Cove Summer School. When the organizers realized that the course had among its listeners the man who'd compiled the vocal score of the Goehr edition, they prevailed on me to deliver an impromptu lecture about the work. My strongest memory of the visit is, however, that wherever one strayed in the grounds and gardens one came across yet another group rehearsing Schubert's Octet.

Once in charge of the Invitation Concerts, I travelled to Coventry for the one that formed part of the celebrations round the opening of the new Cathedral. Heather played a crucial role, both in the major concert and in my own more modest enterprise. At the time the spotlight naturally fell on the world premiere of Britten's *War Requiem*, as on the politicking that led to the last-minute withdrawal (transitive verb!) of the soprano Galina Vishnevskaya, and her replacement by Heather. Predictably, come the recording Mrs. Rostropovich's exit permit from the Soviet Union was miraculously restored: foreign currency ruled, OK. Our concert was a more modest affair, but with fascinating music that included Richard Rodney Bennett's Fantasy for Piano (a BBC commission played by Liza Fuchsova), Beethoven's divinely consolatory *Elegischer Gesang* for four singers and string quartet, Mozart's Nocturnes with basset horns (so that at least three of the four singers – Heather, Janet Baker, John Mitchinson and John Shirley-Quirk – would have more to do, the Beethoven taking up all of eight minutes for its two performances) and Webern's curious quartet with saxophone. I wondered then and for a long time after whether Webern had ever even heard a saxophone, and if so, how come: certainly the part he wrote for it seemed equally suited or unsuited to any other instrument.[2] An indelible recollection is of the final note in a Mendelssohn duet, when it was quite impossible to tell whether one or two voices were singing, so perfectly did Heather and Janet match their sound in unison. The Hamburger-Fuchsova duo ended the concert with Stravinsky's Concerto for Two Pianos.

In the 1970s the Corporation began to take an interest in issuing more records of its better productions, the public having previously been able to get its hands on only a minimal selection of admittedly choice items such as Ludwig Koch, one of the truly classic voices from my boyhood, on British birds. Music came into it only marginally, for money held centre stage, but one of my chores was to attend a committee every so often and discuss ideas. The collectable item at such meetings was a deferential young man from Marketing who invariably addressed Douglas Muggeridge (a network Controller in charge of the meeting) as 'Chair'. There was for a very short while a label called BBC Artium, brainchild of Roy Tempest, the one really enterprising character in BBC Enterprises, the side of the Corporation whose job it was to make money from marketing. He accepted one or two ideas from me, or rather us: Heather made a Lieder record at my suggestion, Edith Vogel was by consensus the departmental recommendation to make a piano record, some Viennese sonatas played by Norbert Brainin with Lamar Crowson and Lili Kraus were issued, and after Michala Petri's first broadcast here, a record of her made in Denmark was taken into the catalogue.

After I left I made friends with the very senior record producer Christopher Raeburn; each of us regarded the other as the best in his line, without actually approving very much of the product. There were what I call 'non-interlocking criteria': he heard a few of my programmes, most of them with the best singers who'd been available, and I think he found I simply hadn't worked with good enough people, while I, who had produced precisely one record, that not very adequate representation of Heather, distrusted the whole ethos of record making and marketing. Given her talents and temperament, the record was the equivalent of 'once round Lil, twice round the gasworks'; a lot of takes, retakes and editing led to a finished product detectably less inspiring than a live broadcast would have been.

With Heather's withdrawal from the field of piano-accompanied Lieder our contact diminished, but having mentioned one husband I should pay tribute to the second, a personable Argentinian named Eduardo Benarroch. He was also fearless, having the guts to stand up at a television discussion during the Falklands war to put the other side of the matter. We played tennis for while. Friendships such as those with Heather, as with Liz Harwood and Janet Baker, were an enormously important part of my very work-orientated life during those years – a steadying influence on which I can look back with immense joy.

NOTES

1   Such duplication of effort and expense was found completely acceptable on artistic grounds. In the 1970s the BBC would often go in for studio recordings of Baroque music the same performers were due to record commercially. To my mind there wasn't in that case the same difference in the nature of the performance, and it dragged the departmental level of pernickety tape-editing up to an all-time record level that had, if the truth were known, very little to do with music-making.

2   Much later I discovered that Adolf Loos, anti-ornament architect and major spiritual figure in the Vienna of Webern's time, had, when in mufti, been fascinated by jazz and had played Webern records that featured the instrument. Somehow the spirit hadn't quite taken, or so it seemed to me. We did, however, secure the services of Mr. Saxophone of those days, Michael Krein himself, for what little there was to play.

3   John Shirley-Quirk, Michael Langdon

That first *Rising Generation* recording with John Shirley-Quirk led to twenty years of intermittent collaboration, during almost all of which his pianist was Martin Isepp. They covered for me great swathes of the Lied repertoire: I can still hear him singing the beginning of Pfitzner's *Über ein Stündlein*, and his openness to that much-undervalued composer was an invaluable follow-up to my first experience of Pfitzner songs, thanks to the amazing elderly German baritone Robert Titze. I treasured John's directness of expression and warmth of feeling, coupled with a 'speaking' baritone voice that stayed in the memory once heard. (When the admirable Thomas Quasthoff appeared on the scene during the 1990s, something in his timbre and delivery reminded me irresistibly of John.) He looked you straight in the eye when talking to you, a challenge to which I had to respond with some idea or other. He has been known to maintain that he learned from me everything he knows about Lieder, and I can only hope that in Martin's presence he is equally generous about *him*, for theirs was a great partnership.

Another male singer who helped with my education during those early years was the bass Michael Langdon. He was one of the great performers as Baron Ochs in *Der Rosenkavalier*, but turned out to have an interesting song repertoire too, introducing me to Carl Loewe, to Strauss curiosities such as *Im Spätboot* and above all to Schubert's *basso* songs, among which I took greatly to *Grenzen der Menschheit* and *Auf der Donau*. When I came to plan in Schoenberg songs he proved cooperative, giving more than one splendid performance of things like the very early *Dank* from the composer's Op. 1 – a heavyweight, not to say ponderous, counterpart to Strauss's *Zueignung*. His transposition from baritone to bass demanded a bottom F from the piano, a note not found on the Steinway but present on the largest Bösendorfers concealed under a flap to avoid disturbing the pianist's orientation in pieces that go no lower than the customary A. He eventually appeared in the BBC's first series of recitals on the South Bank, and I was amazed to see the hesitant, almost sheepish, platform presence of this great actor of arrogant roles like Ochs and Osmin. He simply didn't do it often enough! But there was nothing wrong with the singing. He was one of the madcap crew who succeeded in humanizing the Royal Opera's new and initially arrogant Music Director, Sir Georg Solti, to the point where he was willing to suffer as well as play practical jokes. Later he became an outstanding director of the National Opera Studio.

4 'Liz and Janet' (Elizabeth Harwood and Janet Baker, not to mention Jacques-Louis Monod)

My working life, and for that matter my pre-working life, has been beautified by a succession of soprano goddesses. In childhood and boyhood there were those Elisabeth Schumann records; and in adolescence I was transfixed by post-war 78s of the young Victoria de los Angeles, which were an epiphany seeming to promise things I never found at any future point in the 'real world' and should have been better advised not to look for.[1]

A BBC music producer's job was very far from a nine-till-five affair. We were not quite 'on call' every hour of the day or night, but programmes had to be made when artists were available, not to mention the live early-morning recitals in my very first years, one of which featured a newly-prominent young soprano, Elizabeth Harwood. As for the numerically predominant recordings, performers tended to dislike early hours and to be free and raring to go in the evenings and at the weekend. That made for a disorganized or vestigial private life, so that friendships made along the way became an important offshoot of the production work. Major performers tend in any case to be original and outgoing characters, a tonic to the brooding introverts whose talent lies in making programmes out of music rather than performing it.

I didn't 'discover' Elizabeth Harwood – that kind of discovery tends to be a myth concealing an ego-trip – for by the time of our first contact she had already begun to broadcast. She came through in the early 1960s like the sun on a dull morning; one day, having worked late the previous night, I stayed at home and turned on the early Home Service recital, to hear an unknown soprano voice pouring forth a stream of utterly delightful sounds. The remarkable Jennifer Vyvyan was my ideal of the English soprano, and as I took in this new one I thought, quite unsuitably, that here was her successor, another in the same mould. Recitals were produced week in, week out, so there was soon a chance to offer work to the new paragon: first, she shared a Schubert programme with the tenor Alexander Young, and I still remember her total relaxation and pleasure in being there. When it was his turn to sing she didn't retire to nourish her ego in the stalls of Broadcasting House's Concert Hall but perched on the announcer's table, listening intently. A measure of socialising – coffee or pub, depending on the time of day – was the norm after such broadcasts, but with her it had to be a pleasure deferred, since her immediate need was to go and find her bubble-car, which had been towed away after she'd parked it in the wrong place.

Other broadcasts soon followed, still in the morning, and she turned out to be one of the very few singers to whom it meant nothing to meet a half-past-eight deadline for the necessary balance test. She then lived in Ladbroke

Grove, less than a mile away from the Maida Vale studios, and despite that first experience, parking had not yet become the nightmare it now is. She was making a reputation as a new star of the Sadlers Wells Opera, soon to become the English National, where an early triumph was as Zerbinetta in *Ariadne auf Naxos*: with outstanding coloratura and natural warmth she was a born Richard Strauss singer.

I lived even nearer the studios, and so not far from her, and one way and another we became friends. Once or twice I took her out for a meal after stage appearances, for like any other performer she needed to unwind. Her immense good nature and bubbling manner were based on a shrewd eye for the world – I recall her once saying "Because I look like this," (stunningly blonde and fullish of figure, with an enchanting smile) "men expect me to do things that simply aren't me." She was at that time basically unattached, though for one recital she turned up with a very minor composer in tow, who complained about the BBC that "nobody would ever give ye a plain tale". Her Yorkshireness came across as warm and positive. Eventually, on a train to sing with the Welsh National Opera in Cardiff, she found herself sharing a compartment (for trains still had compartments then) with a young man, one of three brothers who ran a well-known greetings-card company. Their conversation developed into a romance, and before very long she married him. I had kept from UE days a photocopy of the manuscript of Richard Strauss's song *Morgen*, which, with its message of sunshine and happiness tomorrow as today, seemed the perfect wedding gift for such a couple.

Janet Baker I first heard about from Walter Goehr, who prophesied a great future for her at a time when Kathleen Ferrier was still a vivid memory and the obvious thought was 'who's the next in line?' It didn't turn out quite that way – it never does if one looks for 'the second' of anyone; what comes along is always 'the first and only', a quite new model. For a start, Ferrier was a true contralto, while Janet Baker's voice lay securely and splendidly in the middle between that and soprano, with the depth of the one and the lightness of the other. The correct designation was 'mezzo-soprano', but mezzo means 'half', and neither the singer nor her formidable agent, Mrs. Emmie Tillett, were having that. So she was marketed as a contralto.

Elizabeth and Janet became a memorable Fiordiligi and Dorabella in Scottish Opera's *Così fan tutte*. Another great piece for Liz was the set of luscious Baudelaire songs by Debussy, whose sensuality I once underlined by dubbing in some of the poems from a record made by the great French actor, Pierre Blanchar. His voice and delivery were calculated to send either sex into a paroxysm. She sang Schubert, too, with total sympathy. To travel out to Hadley Wood to look at a new piece with her was a major pleasure in life, and the hospitality (her mother Connie being a great standby) was always generous. She had a good critical ear; once, thinking I knew the opening of one of Richard Strauss's *Four Last Songs* by heart, I played its opening bars, made some slight mistake over the harmonies and immediately she chipped in with "Ah, we have a new version of Strauss, have we, Mr. Black?"

Liz was the charmer supreme but free from any trace of mere surface gloss. Handel, Debussy, Schubert, they all sounded equally right, and she sang the other Strauss (the one known to the few who didn't get it as 'If-Strauss-then-Johann, if-Richard-then-Wagner') like an angel. She was a stalwart of her opera house and one of the best Zerbinettas there's been. The difficulties of coloratura meant nothing to her: she co-starred on an antipodean tour with Joan Sutherland, and yet she always kept that amazing warmth. Perhaps her biggest public success was when Karajan took her up and she recorded for him Hanna Glawari and Musetta. Was it ever quite the same after that, and if not, why not? What is this effect of superman conductors on the artists they deign to 'use'?

She was versatile and prepared for challenges. One set of Dallapiccola's ensemble songs, the *Sex carmina Alcaei*, is based on and opens with an unusually euphonious line containing one appearance of each of the twelve notes of the chromatic scale; as a good pupil of a great lyric soprano, Lina Pagliughi, Liz knew how to give an Italian composer's melody its due, even when it was a twelve-note row, and she did glowing justice to the work in a studio-recorded programme where the chamber orchestra was directed by the French conductor Jacques-Louis Monod (no relation of the Nobel-Prize-winning scientist). He usually had a few pithy words to sum up a situation, which could on occasion greatly offend, as when, in the presence of the Melos Ensemble with whom he was preparing a twelve-note Schoenberg chamber work for an early Invitation Concert, he said "I do not understand zis dees-honest music-making"; a request from Roberto Gerhard for a more percussive minor second from the piano in his *Hymnody* prompted the comment "But Roberto, it weel sound like a kick erp ze arse!". The composer flushed and said that was a new musical concept for him; they were already on uneasy terms because Jacques-Louis had had a portion of the previous new work, *Concert for 8*, re-barred in the hope of getting the ensemble to follow a regular beat, rather than expecting them to adjust to constant changes from five to three to seven and so on, ad infinitum. (This was well before the days of the London Sinfonietta, which would come to do such things as if sleepwalking.) I was drawn in, sharing the very urgent task of re-writing, and duly received an ironic phone call from Roberto thanking me for my efforts in improving his piece. Being a brusque young man, I simply said "It was that or no parts"; despite being a brusque elderly man, he didn't hold it against me.

While in charge of Chamber Music, Hans Keller tried to ensure a 100% accurate performance of Schoenberg's *Ode to Napoleon* with Peter Pears and the Allegri String Quartet by having Jacques-Louis as the pianist. Monod certainly knew his Schoenberg – one might say 'basically, in retrograde, inverted and in retrograde inversion' and, as Hans put it, down to the smallest misprint – but with the *Ode* the partnership ran aground on his somewhat dictatorial manner. I was not involved but heard what happened. The quartet's 'cellist, William Pleeth, soon to achieve the limelight as Jacqueline du Pré's lucky mentor, proclaimed that with them democracy ruled. J.-L. M. was incredulous, and Hans had eventually to dispense with him. The arguments and ill temper upset the ultra-civil and sensitive Peter Pears, who softly and silently vanished away. Hans completed a remarkable double by not only sacking his pianist but also recruiting his senior announcer: Alvar Lidell spoke the arrogant Byron text as if it had been written for him, and the performance went all right, not least because the ever-reliable Susan Bradshaw, who had stepped in at the piano, exercised a watchful ear. Over Liz, however, Jacques-Louis was in sovereign good humour: he appreciated her voice, her scrupulous musicianship and her equanimity, adding "And you know, Léo, it never 'urt to 'ave a pretty girl around".

But she was much, much more than that: a peacemaker. I heard from Margaret Price her story of 'guesting' in Cologne and getting into a tremendous row with Lucia Popp. Margaret took off for her next stint in a terrible tizz, and the Cologne Opera Intendant found it prudent to ring Hamburg – "Miss Price is on her way – I should warn you that she's very upset: you'll have a rough ride." To which the other end (I imagine it was that very remarkable human being Rolf Liebermann) said, "Most considerate, but I think we have a secret weapon that can deal with it". In the words of Our Diva, "I got to Hamburg, stepped off the train and who did I see waiting for me? LIZ HARWOOD!". A couple of hours of girlish giggles, and difficult colleagues were the faintest memory.

Jacques could indeed be appreciative. During rehearsals for a similar programme with Janet Baker, he said "When she open 'er mouth, I couldn' believe what was going on be'ind me. Odder singer sing one not in ze 'ead, anodder in de chest, anodder in ze back of ze neck: but Janet, she don' sing not', SHE PERFORM A PIECE." I place this alongside Stephen Hearst's tribute, years later, that whereas not one living English politician could command his respect, it was an honour to be alive in the same country and at the same time as Janet Baker. She too was eminently prepared to take on unusual repertoire, and after a few carefully chosen early Schoenberg songs and an all-Strauss recital, in which I compiled a sequence matching the stages of Schumann's *Frauenliebe und -leben*, I sprang on her the idea of an all-Schoenberg recital. That meant, of course, including the rather mysterious Three Songs Opus 48 from early in his twelve-note period. Those she sang quite naturally, bearing out the composer's observation that once a really musical singer came to terms with his twelve-note vocal music, he or she automatically 'fell into' the underlying note-row. Meanwhile EMI had snitched the Strauss-cycle idea, but missing out a crucial song.

A Schubert recital by her in the mid-1960s afforded a rare glimpse of William Glock's feet of clay. It had been sensational. The announcer John Spurling gave me a lift home afterwards in his Morgan, so carried away by what he'd been hearing that he went straight through a red light, and had The Law been on hand he might have entered the Guinness Book of Records as the only person ever convicted of Driving Under The Influence of Janet Baker. And yet, after the week of the recital's transmission, William, who had nourished his love of Schubert at the feet of Artur Schnabel, complained to his regular Liaison Meeting (which I was far too junior to attend) that nothing interesting had been heard. For a while I carried on a substantial correspondence with her, setting the world to rights and introducing her to the less extreme works of Henry Miller; when I had to go into hospital in 1963 she wrote, "Please hurry up and get quite well again – the BBC has few enough nice faces about and we really can't spare yours … come back to us in splendid form *very* soon". She herself had had a serious illness not so long before, one which briefly made us fear that we should lose 'the second Ferrier' so soon as found – so I treasured those words all the more deeply.

I've been able now and then to hear again how those two were singing in the 1960s, and never have the slightest feeling that my enthusiasm was anything but totally justified. Janet in particular comes over as having not merely a perfect vocal technique (even my intolerant father acknowledged that), but also a unique comprehension of every issue presented by the music she sang. She herself summed it up in a newspaper interview, unwittingly shaming the 'masters of colour' such as the Divine Schwarzkopf, by saying she only had to think of the emotion the words expressed to find the right vocal colour. And both she and Liz could communicate joy, which is the rarest thing in musical performance. Among later singers I met it only in Doris Soffel.

Liz's later illness and tragically early death fall outside the scope of these memoirs. She and Janet were irreplaceable colleagues and friends figuring high on my list of the good things that came out of my 28 years at the BBC.

NOTES

1   My one actual contact with Victoria de los Angeles was unhappy. She came to record on a bad off day, and instead of broadcasting the result as a 'GTS Recital' I eventually hid away the usable bits in a programme whose much more successful element was Liszt piano music played by the magisterial David Wilde. From that afternoon with her I remember most distinctly Gerald Moore, not, alas, for his musical contribution (which was predictably impeccable) but for his intervention midway through the session: he stomped up the stairs to the control cubicle and told me "Young man, I've been listening to what your announcer's been saying and I've heard my name precisely once. That's not good enough!". Shun the great …

5 *Fernande Kaeser*

The encomium 'made in Switzerland' comes my way but rarely, implying as it does the perfect execution of a Martina Hingis or a Roger Federer. Very early in my BBC time William Glock asked me to look in on the Festival Hall rehearsal of an American conductor who'd written to him, and say what I thought. I arrived while an orchestral work was being rehearsed (even a week later I couldn't have told you what it was, though I seem to remember that the second half consisted of Beethoven's Seventh Symphony). Things changed drastically for the better when a small, dark-haired young woman walked on, sat down at the keyboard, and conjured up the opening chords of Beethoven's Fourth Piano Concerto. The rest of the morning was magic. I'd seldom or never heard piano-playing of such concentrated beauty and communicative power; the passion with which this apparent Swiss mouse delivered the fortissimo version of the chords at the first movement's recapitulation is with me still. For Fernande Kaeser music was, in the immortal words of another William (Bill Shankly, Manager Liverpool FC), "not a matter of life and death but more important than that".[1]

Here, clearly, was an artist I just had to work with. She went on to continue a reasonable career on both sides of the Atlantic, but in the course of time it became a career teaching rather than performing. I discovered much later, after dropping some dismissive remark about competitions, that in the early 1950s she'd won the top piano prize at the Geneva International, one of the relatively few such contests which really counted, long before the time when you absolutely have to have won somewhere, and preferably somewhere else too. That she'd been in good company emerged even later during a brief acquaintanceship with Jennifer Vyvyan's son: he dug out a programme that showed Fernande as the year's successful pianist, alongside two major singers, his mother and the American soprano Teresa Stich-Randall. They'd shared the top vocal prize (which must have been too small to reward suitably two such talents): I still remember hearing about it at the time, and the way in which the name Jennifer Vyvyan immediately became one to watch out for. She was in fact one of the greatest singers Britain has produced, and I regret having worked with her only once, in a programme of French songs. Not being British, the piano-prizewinner didn't get the same attention here. Fernande was the last pupil of Dinu Lipatti and had in her tenderest years received memorable advice from Clara Haskil; but despite Geneva the top agents weren't interested, which even then was an inhibitor of really widespread success.

Our BBC collaborations were few and far between, for she spent a lot of her time teaching in the USA, but they always produced something of lasting interest. The pearl among them was a programme with two sets of fairly obscure variations, Bach's *Aria variata alla maniera Italiana* and Mozart's on a theme by Duport. I count that as the most beautiful programme for which I was responsible in my twenty-eight BBC years. Basil Lam summed up her special quality when I played him something she'd recorded, saying "Well, it isn't fair is it, you give her a better piano than anyone else". Certainly her ability to find the poetry in any given instrument was phenomenal; it came partly from careful preparation, sometimes involving all the spare studio time available for a couple of days before the show, as well as a pianistic talent of rare quality.

Fernande's career was never glamorous, which is in part attributable to her own total distaste for the kind of 'glamour' that attracts attention regardless of talent, and also, perhaps, to that responsible attitude to preparation. On her one and only visit to our house, near the end of her life, she told of playing chamber music with a group. It was a pleasant enough evening, but one that ended in bathos when the chaps said "Right, the concert's in a fortnight's time." "Not with me it isn't," said Fernande, and that was the end of the matter.

There was certainly nothing missing on the musical side, as I realized when I discovered in the Austrian Radio's index of recordings a performance by her of the notoriously difficult Tippett Piano Concerto. Its designated first performer had withdrawn, declaring it unplayable; the veteran virtuoso Louis Kentner had then stepped in and proved him wrong; and here was five-foot-two Fernande taking it on! Poor health meant an early end to her work, and she died too young: I count her one of the great musicians in my life.

NOTES

1   I met the conductor at a congress some forty years later, and he still remembered Fernande's concerto with pleasure.

6   *Teresa Berganza*

A total delight in my early years was contact with Teresa Berganza, whom I first heard in a concert performance of *Figaro* broadcast from the Festival Hall. I can still hear the way she moulded Cherubino's '*Voi che sapete*'. When she returned to give a recital of Spanish songs, also on the South Bank, I looked after the BBC's recording of it, and her easy manner and total charm have stayed with me ever since. The fact that she had hay fever at the time seemed to make not the slightest difference to her singing, which was impeccable, and the Spanish repertoire was something I'd loved ever since Victoria de los Angeles's revelatory just-post-war 78 records of it.

Berganza's personality and approach to the concert and the people around her stood at the furthermost extreme from those of the great Moore or the great Schwarzkopf. My next and final contact with her was a recital she gave 'live' in the Concert Hall of Broadcasting House, when she ventured into unaccustomed repertoire: Schubert and Wolf were coloured and phrased in the most natural and musical way possible, though at one point in Schubert's *Dass sie hier gewesen*, at the words '*Düfte tun es und Tränen kund*' (perfumes and tears make it known), she took a breath after '*tun*', so separating a verb from its object. It was a minor misdemeanour, but enough to deter me from having the broadcast repeated. Of course, I listened a lot to her records and was delighted that she kept her quality to so late a stage; she seemed to have discovered the secret of eternal youth. But nobody keeps it for ever, and finally, when she appeared at the Wigmore Hall not far short of forty years after I'd first been thrilled by her singing, it became clear that enough was enough: we went home and so, I suppose, did she. A wonderful career, a wonderful singer.

7   Robert Tear

Not long after he arrived, Stephen Plaistow recorded a Cambridge contemporary of his and asked me to listen to the tape. I found the tenor singer somewhat dry of voice, and remarked in my secretary's hearing "that was like a mouthful of shredded wheat without milk" – at which (having noted my overreaction to the Berganzas of this world) she snarled "yes, it was a man's voice, wasn't it?" As a performer, however, the man was very interesting indeed, so I could understand Stephen's enthusiasm. The singer in question was Robert Tear, and I soon began to work with him. The parallels between his voice and artistry and those of Peter Pears were then too clear to miss, and it's ironic that he should have taken away so negative an impression of his spell in Aldeburgh, enduring the strange ways of the genius loci (a period in his life narrated in hilarious detail in his first book, *Tear Here*). My main interest in vocal music being the Lied, that was what Bob began to sing for me, working with the extraordinarily sensitive and musical Viola Tunnard. Our respective appreciations of her are down in black and white in Janet Anderson's 2001 book, *Playing with Courage*, though if I really delivered some of the encomia there attributed to me I can only say, like Beethoven once, "Did I say all that? I must have gone into a Rapture!"

The Tear-Tunnard partnership performed wonders like Schubert's 20-minute song *Einsamkeit*, which memorably traces a man's passage from novice to veteran and ends with some of the composer's most bewitching nature music, or a haunting programme of Schubert and Schumann songs and duets with April Cantelo. One thing eluded me, a rumbustious Richard Strauss song entitled *In der Campagna*, which I'd read but never heard and was keen to include in a Strauss group with Bob; Viola, then in the early stages of her terminal illness, rang me and pleaded that she simply couldn't get round the piano part, so we dropped it. Half a century later I was to hear a record of Gerald Moore not making much of a fist of it either, and Fischer-Dieskau still less of one, but that had probably been quick study. Bob found Viola's inspirational quality unique, and invaluable when he recorded for me; he was the singer in that fated recording of Brahms's *Abenddämmerung*. But for public appearances, he said, he needed someone whose own sensitivity was less of a weight on her shoulders – someone, in short, who'd be more support. That he found in Philip Ledger, harpsichordist, future Principal of the Royal Scottish Academy of Music and future Sir; after one experience of his playing I longed for something more expansive and romantic, not to say pianistic – someone like Ernest Lush, in fact – and Bob was, as ever, accommodating. The Tear-Lush team's major achievement for me was the complete Brahms *Die schöne Magelone*, which they recorded not once but twice, the Recordings

Library having somehow managed to lose the first tape. That didn't happen often, and artists always found it in themselves to be very forbearing when it did.

For one of his later programmes Bob learned a curious piece by a very old German composer named Wilhelm Rettich, along with songs by Rettich's former teacher Max Reger and by Schoenberg. *Der Cellospieler* set to music a charming fantasy by Carl Zuckmayer comparing the stages of life to the four successively higher strings of the 'cello, with a part for that instrument played by a newcomer, Emma Ferrand. The brunt of the programme was borne by the Reger and Schoenberg songs. Bob had the power and the kind of abruptness to give us Reger's macho side very convincingly. At one point he did something that was eminently Bob rather than (to my ears) eminently Reger; I asked Mr. Rettich what he thought his teacher's reaction might have been, but he simply beamed and said with great conviction "*Reger hat keinen solchen Tenor gehabt!*" (Reger never had a tenor like that!). It was from Rettich, a vigorous ninety-year-old who travelled from Amsterdam to London to hear his piece recorded, that I heard about Reger's fund of lewd stories, with which he would regale his students, having first sent the very young Georg Szell out of the room.

For a while Bob and I lived just round the corner from each other in London W11 and spent the latter part of many a Sunday morning over a quiet drink in a local pub, where he had an amazing way of sensing a fruit machine's readiness to discharge its accumulated coins. He'd bustle to the spot to make sure he and no one else was the beneficiary. It was also the time when a boyhood fascination with table tennis had re-awakened in me and I'd bought a table to go in my large kitchen-cum-front-room. Bob and I used it a good deal, and I had his measure, but never came remotely near his major sporting achievement – playing in a charity cricket match against a side that included Bully Botham and dropping a thunderbolt of a catch hit at him by the great man. My very occasional cricket was on a far less exalted level and I rarely 'troubled the scorers', as the saying used to go. At least Bob and I watched England win the 1966 football World Cup, on the Tears' television, I having not yet penetrated so far into the modern world as to acquire a set of my own. That Final made my mind up, and, like most of the male nation now over fifty, I spent the next forty years waiting for it to happen again. Finally Kelly Holmes provided a distraction to keep me happy to the end of my days, with a booster from Jessica Ennis in 2009.

Bob also featured in one of a number of happenings which, without our knowing it, brought me and my future wife together, when he was the tenor soloist in one of the best performances of Hugh Wood's *Scenes from Comus*. This was at the Festival Hall, during her marriage to its conductor, Andrew Davis; I was, all unbeknown, also there. Another such occasion, a good few

Hilary and Robert Tear

years earlier, was the recording of the Mendelssohn Octet by that group of Symphony Orchestra principals, by then known as the London Octet; she was at the time a student at the Royal Academy of Music, lodging with Hugh Maguire who led the ensemble, and she came to the recording. It's a small world, when not frustratingly large and over-populated.

8   Alfredo Campoli, André Tchaikowsky

So many of my BBC memories are of singers and pianists that it's good also to recall people like the violinist Alfredo Campoli, who was London-Italian at its grandest and most genial. Nothing could throw him, not firemen nor bucket-swinging cleaners walking through the Camden Theatre (later upgraded to Camden Palace but degraded in 2004 to the live-music venue 'Koko'!) while he was playing, nor even the tendency of that memorable studio's piano to edge its way downstage towards the stalls as the broadcast progressed. He had total confidence; asked once about nerves, he said, "Were I to permit myself to become nervous I couldn't display my talents to the full." One favourite saying, to his accompanists, was, "Leave me time for my twiddly bits!"

The opposite extreme as regards nerves was occupied by the Polish-born pianist André Tchaikowsky, who had them and was going to enjoy them. Before his one Invitation Concert appearance he vanished into the toilet and was only extracted with seconds to spare before he was due on to play the Goldberg Variations. It would indeed have been embarrassing to be caught short halfway through that particular work, even when playing it without the repeats. He was the nearest to a genius of all the performers I worked with, Benjamin Britten obviously excepted, and had a comparable composer's insight. For him, playing great music was a creative act. Just as Bob Simpson seemed inside a composer's creative mind, so did André as performer – hence, probably, his unique attitude to balance tests: before the broadcast he was perfectly prepared to let us hear anything from the piano's repertoire, so long as it wasn't the piece he was about to perform. That he wanted to spring out fresh as the dawn, which isn't to deny that we occasionally re-took one or other passage. He sang quite loudly as he played, setting balancers a problem which some solved better than others.

He was one of a small clutch of pianists encouraged by the perceptive Peter Gould during his earliest years in charge of the chamber music group – another was a young American, Stephen Bishop, who has since adopted the surname Kovacevich but has remained a master of musical design and texture. André was definitely one of the great eccentrics; my favourite saying of his concerned the 'improving machine' which he insisted the BBC must have somewhere on the premises – "I come and make these awful recordings, you put them in the improving machine for a few months and they come out sounding wonderful!" The other great André-ism should ring a bell with any honest pianist confronted by a passage marked 'espr.': "I did not play it very well, but I pulled a very expressive face." He also maintained that during one concert tour he'd walked on to play Beethoven's Fourth Piano Concerto in G, sat down, and landed on the chord of A flat. A composer's improvisatory talent

Alfredo Campoli (Milein Cosman)

had enabled him to get back to somewhere musically arguable during the six bars till the orchestra were due to enter with their B major chord. We were friends until his far too early death from colon cancer, and even played piano duets once (my list of piano-duet partners is short but quite distinguished: Hugh Wood, April Cantelo, Lili Kraus, André, Thea King, Michael Gielen – once, at someone's party after he'd conducted the Berg Chamber Concerto at an Invitation Concert – Paul Hamburger, that's about it). André's death was a great blow, and a loss to everyone except the Royal Shakespeare Company, to whom he left his skull so that he could tell his fellow-residents in one or other posthumous Hall of Residence, "I've appeared in *Hamlet*".

9   *Lili Kraus*

Another pianist who made a profound impression on me in my early BBC years was Lili Kraus. I'd grown up with her ten-inch 78 disc of Mozart's A minor Rondo K. 511, but knew little else about her, though by then I'd probably picked up her history of having been caught in the Far East (Java) when Japan entered the war, and her years in a prison camp. Audrey Hurst, from her agents Ibbs & Tillett, offered me recital suggestions not so long after I joined, and when I met Lili, she made an immediate impression of authority and inner strength. She was, to put no finer point on it, a battle-axe, but one of the best. I've thought since that I recognized a comparable latent power in a few people with a similar build – purely from television, the tennis player Monica Seles, and purely from photographs, the still-very-young English violinist Chloë Hanslip. It need not have to do with artistic validity, but in Lili's case it certainly had. She was well aware of her powers. I once commented on the 'beautiful sound' of a certain BBC piano and was immediately squashed as she drew herself up to her full five-foot-four and said "I make the beautiful sound". At one of those early recordings she told me what she read into the opening of Schubert's late C minor Impromptu: she played its resounding opening triple-octave G and said "It's like, My God, what Have I Done!!?" – hence the crushed pianissimo of the first melody, hiding its head in the shame of a single unaccompanied line.

She'd worked with the 'greats' and pseudo-greats of British music and didn't hold back with her opinions, as when Sir Malcolm Sargent's name came up, to be dismissed as "this BLOOODY Flash Harry". She also kept abreast of the best new artists, and once asked me, out of the blue, about the progress of the American pianist Ann Schein, whose great admirer I happened to be. (There you have another case of non-discovery: I'd been totally convinced by Ann from the opening minutes of the Wigmore Hall recital when I first heard her, but by then she'd already played at the White House and toured this country with the BBC Symphony Orchestra. She is a great and underrated pianist. We spent a good deal of time together, both making programmes in the BBC's studios, and also on the lower ground floor of Jacques Samuel Pianos in the Edgware Road, with me playing on a second piano the orchestral parts of concertos she was preparing.)

The great moments with Lili came when she and the leader of the Amadeus Quartet, Norbert Brainin, recorded for me many of Mozart's violin sonatas. Norbert had already made two programmes of three sonatas each with an ideal chamber music pianist, the emigré American Lamar Crowson; with Lamar moved on further to South Africa, Norbert wanted to work with Lili, as she with him. They committed to tape not only the majority of the remaining sonatas, but also one of Beethoven's three Opus 30s, and all three Schubert Sonatinas.[1] The Mozart in particular – most of them far too seldom played – were a revelation to me: I still regard those programmes as among the best things I achieved during my BBC time, and they were heard over and over again. (The BBC's pittance of a fee was augmented by such repeats, since half the amount was paid again each time a programme went out, and even augmented for inflation as time went by. The sonatas proved priceless material, since at around that time an item-repeat agreement was negotiated, which meant that having paid the 50% for repeating any part of the programme, the rest could be heard again in other programmes without any further payment. It complicated the paperwork, since Accounts had always to be told whether a fee was payable or not after any given repeat, and what with other producers chipping in to use such 'offcuts' the picture could become very confused – but it made for fascinating programming.) A later Head of Music Programmes, Ernest Warburton, complained to me that by now he'd heard the sonatas so often he knew when the mistakes were coming! And when in the late 1970s some senior members of the department made a valiant attempt to move on from mere producer-enthusiasm, with all the imbalances that could produce, towards 'output planning' (Hans Keller and Stephen Plaistow were the prime movers, though I was also keen in principle), the attempt to sort out a 'core repertoire' deserving regular broadcasts ran aground on things like my insistence, when asked to specify a few of the post-1778 Mozart violin sonatas to include, that the answer must be 'all of them'. By the same token, Nicholas Anderson would doubtless have said, as he did to me at one point when I was so naive as to ask, that there were no weak Bach church cantatas.

Lili lived in England for a time, before her final years spent in the States. Her daughter had a house somewhere along the endless Caledonian Road, where I once spent an evening. Before we played Schubert piano duets she served what one might call a modest repast – cold ham and bread and butter – on plates from which I did my best to remove a thickish film of dust without her noticing: Lili did not, I think, entertain much. The duets, however, were memorable for the right reasons. I'd recorded Schubert's B minor variations with the Hamburger-Fuchsova duo, and in those years to have a piece in my mind was much the same as having it in my fingers, provided it wasn't of the complexity of, say, Rachmaninov. Lili and I played the variations, which have some intricate running passages in the Secondo part, and she said at the end "Of course you've played that often before", to which I replied that it had been the first time ever. "*Ça n'existe pas!*" (That doesn't happen!) was her response. A good decade later, when she had settled in North Carolina and embarked on her final project, a recording of many of Mozart's piano concertos, she wrote to me about a proposed visit and said we should renew our duet-playing. I had to write back that, what with pressure of work and the need to find some contrasting relaxation, my hands were by then more adept at managing a table-tennis bat than a piano keyboard. She in turn wrote back "you say you are not *en forme* – I do not believe it!" So far as I recall, the visit never happened.

Lili's direct way of meeting worldly needs was illustrated the evening she and Norbert recorded the Schubert sonatinas. I heard about it from Eleanor Warren, who stood in for me as producer during my 1963 sick-leave. The BBC's Maida Vale studios were primarily, or from a numerical point of view, the home of the BBC Symphony Orchestra, and its restaurant's evening opening hours paid most attention to whether they were working or not; less numerous mortals using the remaining four studios had a lower priority, something which in the fullness of time I realized and worked out ways of circumventing, but (as remarked) a young producer was told nothing. Finding the place unstaffed, Lili had had no trouble unearthing a kettle and a toaster and preparing all that was needed to keep them going; if a manageress became involved, then Lili used her charm to keep things friendly. Charm she surely had, but given how she played she could have prospered as well without it.

NOTES

1   I was pleased when the briefly active BBC Artium record company agreed to issue an LP with sonatas chosen from those programmes.

10   Margaret Price

Peter Gould wasn't above coming up with the occasional striking idea, as when Margaret Price hove into view. She'd already broadcast, from Wales, Arthur Bliss's *Seven American Poems*, and Alvar Lidell, himself a singer, prophesied to me that here was someone bound for the very top. I soon afterwards began to offer her modest dates, a quarter of an hour's music at a time: the daytime Music Programme was by then going and there was all the more scope. I still remember her very first recital, shared with the flautist Colin Chambers, and the way she moulded the sinuous phrases of Obradors's *Del cabello más sutil*. Not much later came a session with a group of Britten's folksong arrangements recorded in the never-to-be forgotten Farringdon Theatre, pausing from time to time to let the noise of passing trains into Cannon Street station die away. Everyone involved knew that recording somehow represented a significant step forward in Margaret's artistic development. With not a lot to do under her Covent Garden contract, she was eminently 'available' and had the strictest possible advice and coaching from her accompanist, James Lockhart.[1] I, however, would never have come up with the bold idea that occurred to Peter: she was clearly in line to inherit the Heather Harper mantle as a Schoenberg singer, but what he proposed was that in one and the same programme she should perform *The Book of the Hanging Gardens*, which is for voice and piano, and (with harpsichord and 'cello continuo) Handel's great solo cantata *Lucrezia*. My scepticism got me nowhere; the session duly happened and yielded a fascinating programme, with me producing.

There were many stages in my producer-singer relationship with Margaret: evening meals with her and Jimmy played their part, at the flat in Marylebone High Street, previous owner Richard Rodney Bennett, chairs from Whiteley's by courtesy of Mr. Black. Another major step forward was when the Vienna Konzerthaus invited them to give an all-Schubert recital. She'd learned a lot of Schubert for me and was glad of a little advice over the best content and order for such a prestigious date. In the end her colossal worldwide success in opera meant she became less available for recital work, not least because even the parsimonious BBC had to some extent to acknowledge her level and standing in terms of the fee it paid her. Quite early in my time as a producer of broadcast song recitals I identified opera as the great enemy, not only because it demanded a quite different way of singing and projection, but also because opera houses were given to insisting on their pound of flesh and made it very hard for a singer to negotiate an irrevocably-agreed free day long enough in advance. Glyndebourne, in most other respects a summer paradise for a gifted singer, was particularly liable to throw that kind of spanner in the works.

NOTES

1   How many people still remember their disappointment on turning up at
     Covent Garden in the early 1960s to read that, 'owing to the indisposition of
     Madame Teresa Berganza the role of Cherubino will be sung tonight by Miss
     Margaret Price'. Miss WHO?!

Margaret Neville (top) and Elixabeth Harwood (bottom)

11 *Sheila Armstrong, Margaret Neville*

Had I to name a pair of artists who stood for the best in my 'second BBC period' from the mid-1960s onward, they must surely be the sopranos Sheila Armstrong and Margaret Neville, joint winners of the Mozart Prize from the London Mozart Players in 1965, the year Sheila also won the even more prestigious Kathleen Ferrier Award. For a quarter of a century they offered whoever had ears to hear the pure pleasure of musical purposefulness unpolluted by the star singer's ego.

Rilke would have said that Sheila sang 'along the grain' of the music. It could be simple, it could be complex: whichever way, it came out spot-on, and she was at home in a great range from Handel to our own time. The inspired performer needn't intellectualize about a piece to get to its heart. She and I worked on many projects from the middle '60s onward, for I valued her gift of cutting through the dross and homing in on the music's emotional truth.

That kind of remorseless honesty was never more in evidence than when she took on Fauré's quite obscure but beautiful late cycle, *Le Jardin clos*, full of half-lights and regretful thoughts that brought out the best in her exquisite middle register. Hardly anyone sings those songs, and Sheila must have thought her colleagues knew something she didn't, for not long before the recording was due she rang me to say she was getting nowhere with them – there seemed to be nothing there to perform – and wondered whether I shouldn't find someone else. I said, in effect, "No, it's you I want because it's right for you and vice versa," tacking on some version of Noel Coward's invaluable "Speak clearly, don't bump into the scenery". The recording went ahead, and yet again she did a great composer full justice in a performance that will, presumably, never be heard of again, that not being the kind of programme immortalized on labels such as BBC Classics (many of which merely reproduce other institutions' productions at which the BBC was no more than the sound-carrier). Elegiac final songs are a feature of more than one late Fauré cycle, and the one in *Le Jardin clos* could not have been more touching than when Sheila delivered it. Emotional truthfulness is a necessity, but a real challenge in the great song repertoire. For that matter, she once said to me that all recital work was terribly difficult, for where in an opera you had to play one part, in a song recital you had to find an instant way into innumerable worlds, one after another. (The memoirs of the supreme German coloratura soprano Erna Berger show her aware of the same challenge.) The instantaneous communication of a composer's world is something to treasure when one meets it; from my very limited experience as a 'juror', I remember when it was achieved by a young soprano named Ann (Jinks-)Sheridan competing in 1995 for a small study grant awarded by the Yamaha Company.

Any fine soprano is likely to be a born Strauss singer, and Sheila was no exception; the darker, more regretful emotions suited her, quite in contrast to her persona in the 'real world', and she could find something truly touching in a rather heavy, repetitive song such as *Geduld* from the early set, Op. 10. The way she sang certain other-worldly Schubert songs – *Die Götter Griechenlands* and above all *Die Mutter Erde* – likewise showed that here was someone who thought and felt deeply before opening her mouth. Duparc, too, suited her down to the ground: I've heard no one sing the tender *Phidylé* more affectingly. Among her later broadcasts for me were three recitals of Schumann, Brahms and Strauss, recorded at yearly intervals. The Schumann was beset with troubles; she had yet to perform his great female cycle *Frauenliebe und -leben*, and so far in her life she had remained childless. Suddenly she was pregnant, happy as never before, and we looked forward all the more to the programme. Then came the news that she had lost the baby. I would have understood perfectly had she withdrawn or at least asked to change the programme, but as a true professional she stuck with it and somehow found the inner strength to get through the session successfully. I never admired her more, and was delighted when not so long after she made a gramophone record of the songs.

With Margaret Neville, the sunniest of personalities, I worked – for the only time during my BBC employment – regularly on repertoire before she performed it. Someone so truthful and free from mannerisms was easy to accompany and indeed to anticipate; she would say "You know what I'm going to do before I do!". At the time she was enjoying deserved success as Gretel in a renowned production of *Hansel and Gretel* at Sadler's Wells, but she found time for a good deal of recital broadcasting in songs ranging from Mozart to the German composer-pianist Heinz Schröter, who came and recorded his charming *Liederspiel* with Margaret and the golden-voiced Ian Partridge, another stalwart of those blissful years. (When an Ian Partridge programme was broadcast during working hours a procession of secretaries could be seen swooning all the way down the corridors of Yalding House.) There was something of Elizabeth Harwood's radiant good nature about Maggie Neville and her singing, coupled with an ability to bring off unusually slow tempi: I had heard of an 'adagio dancer', while having no idea what that might be, and Maggie was beyond doubt an adagio singer as well as a sparkling soubrette. Curiously, Richard Strauss played less of a part in her repertoire. She was eventually recruited by István Kertész during his all-too-short time as Generalmusikdirektor in Cologne, after which I regretfully saw a good deal less of her.

12   *Norma Burrowes*

Another in the line of soprano goddesses came my way in the early 1970s. While still very new, Norma Burrowes was launched by a top agent as an up-coming Queen of Coloratura. She certainly went high and was very agile up there, yet hearing her I wondered if that was really her thing and how long she should go on doing it. As did she. I went to see and hear her at Covent Garden as the coachmen's mascot Fiakermilli in *Arabella*, and after the show she confessed to me that she couldn't wait to stop doing "all that dancing on tables". She was meanwhile revealing the loveliest lyrical talent (how else should I have met her?), and her singing was for a few years a lesson to me in purity and musical purpose. She remodelled my whole idea of 'intonation', which with her meant nothing so negative as 'not singing out of tune' – it meant singing positively *in* tune, with herself and with possibilities in the listener, the common factor being the natural harmonic series that underlies all music of definite pitch. During my time with the publisher in Vienna, I'd been deeply moved by Bach motets sung in 'just intonation' by the Akademie Kammerchor without keyboard or any other continuo instrument. I was made to realize (thank you, Basil Lam) that *a capella* is wrong for those works, not least because at times the tenor part goes below the bass part, producing false harmonic progressions unless the bass is doubled at the lower octave, but I still hankered after the sheer wonder and purity of such singing. In Norma I found it again. One most memorable occasion was when I had sat through a whole act of *Die Entführung* at the Met., putting up with the stars Edda Moser and Nicolai Gedda; each sang in some purely private scale of their own, the only palliative being the ever-reliable Kurt Moll, solidly in tune as Osmin. Then Act 2 opened with Norma's magically pure intonation. It was like coming home.

A different second-act revelation came when I went to *Der Rosenkavalier* at the English National Opera. That time, the predominant impression through Act 1 was that I didn't recognize the work (which in my Oxford time I'd briefly held to be the greatest music ever written, having chosen a score of it as part of my college prize when I got my First). Not until Norma entered as Sophie in Act 2 did I hear Strauss. The problem hadn't, after all, been the English translation: it was just that a Strauss phrase is a Strauss phrase and must be turned like one. If singing it in English makes that harder, tough. Norma was yet another perfect Strauss singer, who learned for me various almost-unknown songs such as *Das Bächlein*, neglected perhaps because of its dedication to Reichsminister Dr. Josef Goebbels and its closing '*Der, denk ich, wird mein Führer sein*' (He, I think, shall be my Leader – the poet, probably not Goethe, wrote a century before 1933 and so was innocent of the implications). Her coloratura was perfectly in place, but also perfectly incorporated in a finely-spun line. The *Ophelia Songs*, too, were memorable, with a unique pathos and yet a dignity; there was an echo of the Marschallin in the way she delivered the final '*Gott sei mit Euch*' (God be wi' ye).

Norma's wasn't a big voice, and it had a very slightly white or girlish colour, but it could say things with a clarity that stopped the heart. I came to look on it as a 'speaking' as well as a 'singing' voice, which was my highest accolade; hadn't Chaliapin once complained to Piatigorsky that too many instrumentalists concentrated on making their instrument 'sing', when it could even be made to 'speak'? One momentous evening was spent in the Albert Hall at a Promenade Concert performance of *The Magic Flute*. In that great cavern her voice suddenly opened up as I'd not heard it, seeming to fill the hall right to the remotest gallery. Even so, I suppose, did Madame Albani make herself heard at the back of the nineteenth-century Crystal Palace, not by decibels but by quality and projection.

Among other composers, Norma took on Holst and his set of twelve songs to poems by Humbert Wolfe, in particular giving the extraordinary one about the giant star Betelgeuse a cold mystery that chilled the spine. These unusual songs showed the full range of her expressiveness, from the intimacy of *Things Lovelier* and *The Dream-City* to the stark finality of *Journey's End*. And a minor composer, William Bardwell, was bowled over when he heard what she had found in his short Machado cycle, *La lechuza* (The Barn Owl). Remaining with the same poet, she was a worthy successor to Dorothy Dorow, Elizabeth Harwood and Mary Thomas in Dallapiccola's *Quattro liriche di Antonio Machado*, a favourite piece of mine, but I valued most of all her performance of Fauré's *La Bonne chanson*. It was the only one I ever heard that came close to the serene beauty of Suzanne Danco's recording from the 1950s.

In most of that she was aided and abetted by her conductor-accompanist husband Steuart Bedford, on whom I looked as the prince among the accompanists of the day. Alas, when the marriage broke up, Norma, too, went into a long period of uncertainty and vocal problems. In a very frank interview for the *Guardian*, she said straight out that she could only sing well when happy (the shadow version of what Maureen Lehane had said to me years before – "so long as I can sing, I'm happy"). Norma had for a long time not been happy. Her last BBC programmes were made with David Harper, and still contained lovely things, but she was on a downward curve and finally suspended her career to discover family life with the Canadian tenor Emile Belcourt. She emigrated with him to Toronto, at which point her singing career appeared to be over. I treasure the memory of my small part in it.

Part Five

Celebrating the start of the Vienna Festival broadcasts on WNIB at Chez Paul,
1992: Gernot Huebl, Vice President, Lufthansa (the sponsors), Dean Grier,
Helga Kopp (series producer) and Clemens Coreth (Austrian Consul General)

... and After

1   Sixteen Years to a Page

The Chief Producer years involved some very routine activity such as trying to keep down the store of used and now unwanted recordings.[1] Some of them showed a most remarkable capacity for survival – one instruction after another to 'wash' them would at the next inventory prove not to have been carried out. It prompted me to formulate Black's Law, which in its final, most succinct version runs: 'things are present in inverse proportion to your need for them'. In plain English, what you yesterday stumbled over, cursing, you today seek in vain, likewise cursing. An equally vast amount of much more congenial work was involved in coordinating an ever-expanding intake of radio recordings from abroad. That in its turn brought an experience of the American 'market', which proved so engrossing that I now devote an entire section to it.

With a merger of the Music Programmes and Gramophone Programmes Departments in 1982 there was, as in Peter Gould's smaller department, a Parkinsonian need for two 'assistant heads', and along with my opposite number Arthur Johnson from Gramophone Programmes I became one such 'Executive Producer'. Ever since that first promotion in 1971, I had managed to hang on to a sizeable amount of programme production; it was what I was best at, but also, I suspect, a main reason why a 1980s-style Management Audit soon decided there was one Executive Producer too many. This man should have been organizing people and crunching numbers, not enjoying himself doing the work of a mere producer. My career as a BBC official ended in 1988; I left four years early (at 56) and was free that much sooner to go on and develop new skills. One was still in programme-making, but this time the 'right' side of the glass; at long last I was required rather than forbidden to speak at length into the microphone as author. That very enjoyable if intermittent activity ended in 2003 after the publication of my book on Schubert (another case of post hoc non propter hoc). My later book on Rubbra failed to work the same oracle. For a very long time I had also been jotting down thoughts on a variety of musical subjects and figures, some of which have finally emerged from under their bushel to find their way into this book.

End of story. Almost …

NOTES

1   However, as one decade merged into the next, fresh names constantly gave
cause for renewed rejoicing. I still remember a Christmas Day recital by the
baritone Brian Rayner Cook and his pianist Antony Saunders, and an all-
Schubert programme, three years later to the day, by the majestic yet humorous
true-contralto Ann Collins; those were prestigious 'placements' for such still-
young singers.

André Tchaikovsky (Milein Cosman)

2   An American Dimension

By the middle 1970s the foreign recordings work was bringing me into contact with some great American orchestras. The first influential man from the other side was the agreeable Dick Kaye from WCRB, Boston[1] – an 'Eastern seaboard' American, then, but (for all his thorough musical education under figures going way back into the great names of Germanic scholarship) distinctly foreign in his pawky forthrightness. He had the Boston Symphony Orchestra to offer, and despite technical and contractual hurdles the transcriptions of their concerts began to be heard on Radio 3. They set an exemplary standard and offered a chance to hear not only the orchestra of the day under Seiji Ozawa but also performances under previous Music Directors from Koussevitzky onward. I greatly enjoyed concerts from seasons with the underrated Charles Munch (no mere French specialist nor just a conductor, since in his time he had led the Gewandhaus Orchestra) and one or two under Pierre Monteux, and vividly remember the oldest Boston tape we used, a stunning if eccentric performance of the Beethoven Choral Symphony under Koussevitzky: in the slow movement, the running violin lines at the main theme's third appearance can never have been played so elegantly.

Dick later widened his scope and came up with chamber concerts from Tanglewood. They often featured a truly outstanding violinist, Joseph Silverstein, who had led the orchestra for many years. He was already known this side of the Atlantic from the various concerto performances we broadcast in the course of Dick's 'seasons', starting with one of the Elgar concerto, which the discerning John Douglas Todd had spotted as outstanding. Eventually I worked with Joe in our studios, and his playing is one of the pleasantest memories from my entire BBC time. It was at a level to which Wilf Lehmann had sensitized me in my fledgling days.

Our one live relay from Boston featured the premiere (in fact the second performance, because the time-difference between Europe and the States meant we always relayed the middle, afternoon one of three concerts) of Leonard Bernstein's engaging *Divertimento*. Dick Kaye was a hands-on manager in matters technical, and the explosive energy he deployed in making the relay a success revealed a new side of him. Ozawa threw me a curve when he decided after Thursday's concert that the Bernstein hadn't attracted enough applause: he firmly intended to change the programme order on Friday, when it would be relayed to most of Europe. Told of this, I had urgently to apprise the orchestra's manager, Tom Perry, of all the behind-the-scenes arrangements made by radio stations sharing the broadcast, with a script circulated ages beforehand, timed to the second and stuck to down to the last comma. A change of order at that stage would carry the risk of chaos for those carrying (and paying for) the relay. Somehow I got this across forcefully enough for him to persuade the Maestro to reverse his decision. Phew! I also remember a typically dignified and musical Beethoven C minor Piano Concerto from Rudolf Serkin – one of his last – and, un-broadcast on the Thursday evening, a Mendelssohn Violin Concerto from Isaac Stern that left me infinitely grateful that it hadn't been his concert we relayed.

Soon we also had some outstanding archival programmes based on Georg Szell's years with the Cleveland Orchestra, including a classic account of Beethoven's *Missa Solemnis*. An extreme rarity was the Elgar 'Cello Concerto played (first with Lorin Maazel and later with Andrew Davis) by the supreme 'cellist Leonard Rose. He had been the major star among the countless gifted pupils of the work's first performer, the British virtuoso Felix Salmond. But when Salmond settled in the USA to teach at New York's Juilliard School and Philadelphia's Curtis Institute he never discussed the Elgar with his pupils. He had been so upset by the failure of the premiere (which came about because Elgar's fellow conductor at the concert, Albert Coates, hogged virtually all the available rehearsal time for a Skryabin premiere) that he thenceforth suppressed all thoughts of the music, which should have been one of his greatest triumphs. Rose had learned it off his own bat.[2]

A visit from Dick's opposite number representing the Chicago Symphony made a different impression. Dean Grier acted as both the orchestra's Media Director and the overseas liaison man for radio WFMT, one of the most prestigious USA music-broadcasters. There was something of the artist manqué about Dean, an elegance and a trace of wistfulness that blended remarkably with his total grasp of business method. Not until I'd known him for some years did I discover that he was married to a composer, Lita (Dubman) Grier. Ominously, he was also a chain-smoker.

Dean's was a friendship I valued above most – in fact during the years we worked together I reckoned him my best friend, despite the thousands of miles between London and Chicago. It was not quite an attraction of opposites, but certainly some sort of Platonic working-together of complementaries, a little like that of Bond and his CIA opposite number. And of course he was Virgil to my Dante as after far too long I finally began to discover the States. I have so many pleasant memories of him – his generosity, his down-to-earth cheerfulness – the sign in his office "*Ici on mange bien*" (One eats well here), the "Hello?!..." that came down the line when he didn't get the response he expected, the way he handled everything, and the cry, which I heard often enough, "Oh, you Brits!" (His other favourite notice, "Be reasonable, do it my way!", looks less funny in the light of George W. Bush.) It was clear that however good a business man he was, Dean genuinely loved music. After his abortive visit to Hans Keller to explore broadcasting possibilities on behalf of WFMT's programme director Norman Pellegrini, Hans wrote to me "what a nice man – but why is he so obsessed with not being a musician?" (I think the reaction to Hans at the other end was "what a fascinating man, but why is he so obsessed with money?").

Dean, like some other cultured Americans, had virtually no knowledge of foreign languages (an ungrateful comment, given the generosity with which he time after time invited me to benefit by his intimate knowledge of that most idiosyncratic language, French Haute Cuisine). I don't know if Mon Ami Dragiša ever tried the "*de quelle pays êtes-vous?*" routine on him; if he did, it may for once have failed to work, since Dean wouldn't have known what he was being asked. The Chicago tapes also had hurdles to surmount. By then our technical people were more understanding about the discrepancies between British and American practice, but Solti, as Music Director, was worried that broadcasts of the orchestra's concerts might affect its record sales, so each list had to be run past the eagle eye of Ray Minshull at Decca in London (who raised scarcely one objection). There was also sponsorship, in those days a taboo subject for the BBC: it would have been quite impossible under the Charter to say (which would have been true but ambiguous – who paid whom?) "Sponsored by ...". After careful thought and reference to the upper echelons of Management I finally arrived at a formula that satisfied the proprieties – 'the overseas broadcast of the concert was made possible thanks to support to the orchestra from ...'. It was thus made clear that though money had changed hands, it had gone not to the BBC but to the orchestra. Later, in the case of Washington National Symphony Orchestra, tapes sponsored by a firm of financial consultants named Mars, I resorted to, and got away with, a devious arrangement whereby a British firm of the same name but in a different and yet-stickier line of business carried (to mix metaphors) the can. A mere year or two after my departure one would see the *Radio Times* blithely sporting the legend 'Sponsored by ...' for concerts by BBC orchestras.

Like Dick Kaye before him, Dean expanded the range of his offers: Milwaukee had a more-than-respectable orchestra, which we broadcast a good few times, including the best performance of Mozart's 'Haffner' Serenade I have heard, under Sir Charles Mackerras. There were series from the Philadelphia Orchestra's recent seasons, and one from St. Louis, as well as odds and ends from places even farther afield such as Dallas. We also began to take live relays of the Chicago Symphony's concerts, about one a year. The orchestra's diary showed the same pattern as in Boston – a concert on Thursday evening, one on Friday afternoon, and a third on Saturday evening. The Friday ones were mostly attended by older subscribers, many of them chocolate-unwrapping, programme-rustling, blue-rinse, immensely-moneyed ladies at whom Solti's programming assistant Peter Jonas launched, first time out, a pre-emptive strike beginning "This is an historic occasion!" (i.e. "Don't rustle or cough!"). The Fridays were in all other respects ideal candidates for broadcasting to Europe; the time-gap between the mainland and Chicago, seven hours, placed them at just the right point of the European evening, and the BBC could handle a GMT start an hour earlier.

We began in 1978 with a concert offering the perfect blend of attractions: brand-new work, great soloist, and major classical masterpiece that managed not to be one of those one heard too often anyway. Easley Blackwood's Fourth Symphony was very thick and very loud: I had problems with its average noise-level until a day or two after my arrival I stood on a platform of the Chicago 'subway' (in fact an overground service) and experienced the impact of trains arriving simultaneously from both directions. Then I understood. (What would it have been like underground?!) The concerto was Grützmacher's concoction of Boccherini in B flat, with no less a 'cellist than Janós Starker returning to the orchestra where before his mutation into a Distinguished Professor at Indiana University he had held the last of his posts as principal 'cellist. He was genial, if very much in passing: Dean was the liaison with the performers and was obviously in charge. He could even restrain Sir Georg when a BBC-length opening announcement prompted the great man to growl "Dean, ve got to get dis show on de road".

But the undying pleasure of that first visit was Mendelssohn's Scotch or Scottish Symphony, heard six times at three complete runs-through and three concerts: given such playing, I'd gladly have listened to six more. I also covered for Radio 3, eventually writing the broadcast script, the Lyric Opera world premiere of Penderecki's *Paradise Lost*. It was pretty and effective, but what I recall after all this time is that at its very opening an immensely distinguished American actor, Arnold Moss, declaimed Milton's opening lines: I couldn't believe my ears when at a late rehearsal I heard "Of man's first disobedience, and the fruit/Of that forbidden tree WHERE mortal taste ..." I told myself it was a slip of the tongue and wouldn't happen again – but it did, and I somehow lacked the courage to chip in. "Da guy from da BBC sez ya got it wrong, Arnie" – unthinkable. (Or indeed to approach Lyric's Director's P.A., an intimidatingly vital and attractive former colleague who had been Eleanor Warren's secretary, so that she might try to get something done about it.) The bloomer bloomed on, right down to the broadcast, after which I began to face another unthinkable – the reaction of Bob Simpson, a passionate Miltonian, on my return. I needn't have worried – Bob wasn't going to waste his time listening to the latest Penderecki.

Later relays were of Beethoven's Choral Symphony, down a broadcast line of dubious quality; and then Mahler's Eighth, when disaster struck: someone in the New York communications headquarters of the phone company AT&T decided that symphonies last an hour and pulled the plug thirty minutes early, favouring the European listening public instead with a commercial for baby milk. An all-Prokofiev concert in 1982 came right at the end of the season around the time when the clocks change. Somehow Dean and I between us managed to get that wrong, and long after the *Radio Times* and several major European broadcasters had advertised the relay we realized that the States were not, as I'd thought, in daylight-saving, whereas we were. Under conditions of total secrecy we recorded the Thursday evening concert and broadcast it on the Friday afternoon, announcing it to European listeners as a recording of a 'live event' – or rather to those who remained, the Germans having primly opted out of broadcasting a 'mere tape'. For the only time, I left Chicago in deep depression: it was the sole cloud on my relationship with Dean, for I had taken his word about the time situation, he being on the spot. Collaboration and friendship survived.

The Mahler broadcast stays in my mind for another reason. I'd noted the different ways in which BBC balancers and WFMT engineers reflected their respective orchestras' sound, and though a total amateur in matters of microphone balance I used the plane journey to Chicago to read carefully through the score trying to work out what I should do were I in some fantasy or birthday world placed in charge of mike-placement for this 'Symphony of a Thousand'. I'd come to feel that the Chicago preference for predominantly central mikes slightly short-changed the world-class violin and 'cello sections, which extended right to the edge of an unusually wide platform. By touchdown at O'Hare Airport I had a scheme worked out in my mind, but of course no thought of persuading WFMT's people to implement it rather than their own ideas: they 'balanced' the orchestra week-in, week-out in a hall that was not without its problems – basically, a rather dry sound and unusual width. The understanding at these relays was definitely that they were in charge, whereas over the microphone presentation the station's cultural manager Norman Pellegrini deferred, if reluctantly, to my wishes, which soon extended to our taking an announcer with me. (After Norman had presented the first relay in 1978 there had been comment within the BBC's four walls that 'it sounded American'. Dammit, it WAS American …)

So at ten in the morning of the first of many days' rehearsal I walked into Orchestra Hall reflecting on my grand plan. I looked about me – and there were the mikes, set out almost to the nearest foot as I'd imagined placing them! Mitch Heller and I have been fast friends ever since that moment. He is one of the world's great orchestral 'balancers' and since the States is constitutionally freer of age-ism than we are he still has the occasional chance to prove it. Long may the arrangement continue.

I date the beginning of the end of my BBC career from the day early in 1987 when Dean rang and said, "Leo, as from next Monday I'm no longer with the station". That proved the start of a steep decline in WFMT's standards and prestige. He set up his own company, Intercontinental Media Inc., and we both hoped after my own departure that we might find Anglo-U.S. projects on which to collaborate. But it never quite happened, and when he came to London he was usually too hectically busy for anything but a phone call. Then one day in October 1997 Mitch rang with the news that Dean had had a heart attack and died, aged only 58. Bearing in mind what he also contributed to British broadcasting, I offered an obituary of him first to the *Times* and then to the *Independent*. Neither saw fit to print it.

One very seldom encounters true generosity, and Dean deserves his place in this memoir.

NOTES

1   WCRB refers to Charles River Broadcasting, and (later) WNIB to Northern Illinois Broadcasting. On the other hand, according to its co-founder Rita Jacobs, (the also later) WFMT refers to nothing at all – "it was just a nice combination". Thanks to Don Tait for this information.

2   The information comes from Rose's long-time assistant, Channing Robbins.

3   Imrat and Other Pandits

Towards the end of the 1960s BBC Radio at last began to find Indian classical music something to broadcast rather than merely talk about. The leading light was an older composer-producer named Ivor Walsworth, who had been a high-up in the Transcription Service until a serious illness, after which he was found work in the tranquil air of Music Division to tide him over until retirement age. Once, he was unable to be at a recording and asked if I'd be interested and free to look after it. I had virtually nil knowledge of the subject, but agreed, trusting that I could manage things like settling a time for them to begin, an explanation of what the red light meant (there I'd had practice with the beautiful Soviet pianist Bella Davidovich, whom I'd persuaded not to begin delivering Chopin's 24 Preludes until 'krasnoye lampuchka'), and some signal to show that they might begin to think about wrapping it up. As luck would have it, the first maestro or Pandit (Douglas Smith was usually the announcer and knew about forms of address) was Imrat Khan. Less world-famous than Ravi Shankar, he proved a formidable performer but an utterly charming man. A young colleague named Jamila Patten (née Singh) reassured me about that, telling of a party where he'd played and saying the atmosphere had been one of "Hello Mrs. Banerjee, what about my paratha?" I took to Imrat straight away and found him a joy to work with, even if the very long opening slow Alap in his major rags always made me fidget a bit. Once the tabla player came in and things speeded up even a little, I couldn't get too much of it, which was just as well given great Indian music-makers' inborn tendency to lay on just that. We even took the risk of an 'open-ended' programme with no set finishing time; but Imrat was westernized enough to know the kind of length we liked, and began to wrap it up just as I was beginning to hope he would. It always took a fair while to get going, but time wasn't of the essence. At one session he indicated his imminent readiness to record by swallowing something unidentifiable and saying cheerily "Horlicks!" into the mike. I reassured myself that, whatever trouble Controller Newby had in his time had with the Vice Squad over Henry Miller's F-word, the Drug Squad was very unlikely to descend on Studio I, Maida Vale.

Imrat mostly played the sitar, but once favoured us with a long and amazing solo on the larger and deeper-sounding surbahar. The cumulative solemnity of that music was something I'm glad to have experienced, but, given my western time-scale, my favourite piece from his repertoire was a cheery number called *Bhopali*. It took him a mere ten minutes to negotiate and livened things up no end, having the catchiest of refrains and seeming to be based on a rag that amounted to a normal Western major scale.

I had a less jolly experience with another leading sitar player, Mahmud Mirza, whom Walsworth had booked with a tabla player even younger than most. The rehearsal went all right until the lad began to use his tabla to tell what was evidently a highly coloured story. I was fascinated by its sounds, the maestro or Pandit wasn't; clearly it was not what the young man was there for – whether because of the story or because it threatened to detract attention from his elder and better I had no way of knowing, since I knew not one word of any language from the sub-continent[1] and he spoke virtually no English. With great dignity he gathered his things together and walked out. I could only follow him down the corridor and try to reassure him that Pandit Walsworth would surely be glad to see him again some time.

The Ali Brothers (Nazakat and Salamat), supremely relaxed-sounding Pakistani vocalists, I only heard but never met; they sounded as if, Harpo-like, they'd recorded leaning casually against a wall pleasing themselves. Their style placed them alongside the revered Cockney comedians of my youth, Flanagan and Allen (whose most famous number was *Underneath the Arches*), and (had I but known it) the future jolly oldsters of the Buena Vista Social Club, whom of course I nicknamed Llanagan y Allende.

NOTES

1   Not quite true: at school the music-master Bill Neve had told me of his Indian batman during wartime service in Photographic Reconnaissance, and of finding a cup of tea the man had made so repulsive that he said to him "but this is peshad!" [pee]. To which batman replied in the most matter-of-fact and reassuring way, "Oh no, Sir, it is not".

4 *Michala Petri*

I have Paul Hamburger to thank for one small but enduring revelation after he took over the BBC's live Wednesday lunchtime *Concert Hall* series from Eleanor Warren. The title reflected the venue in Broadcasting House, and the programme began as a vehicle for the broadcasting debut of artists who had lately passed their audition. In the fullness of time it was realized that the combination of 'live'-with-audience plus recording off transmission was too severe to allow most debutants to do themselves justice, and the series was from then on only occasionally a showcase for presenting new talent. One day Paul approached me to ask if I'd stand in for him that week, as I occasionally did when he was double-booked or when the programme featured a singer who'd asked for him in his other capacity as accompanist. But in this case, he said, it was just that this week's programme was to be given by a recorder player, and it was an instrument he couldn't stand. Viennese musicians of his generation liked their sound rich and colourful, which often boils down to vibrato: Hans Keller would have reacted no differently (he for his part showed a marked distaste for even the slightly meatier transverse flute).

I already knew of Paul's recorder player, a seventeen-year-old Dane named Michala Petri, and what I'd read had made me send for and have broadcast a Norwegian radio tape of her. I was perfectly happy to stand in, and spent a magical couple of hours as this slim, modest girl performed her wonders of articulation, agility and timing on a range of recorders, which she tucked into her corsage to keep warm when not in use. Her programme included a hilarious recent piece by Berio that sounded like a budgie having a nervous breakdown and enjoying it, as well as Dutch Baroque music of hair-raising virtuosity and a Classical sonata. To my secretary's great amusement, I spent the rest of the day wandering about in a trance hardly matched since the time when as a teenager I'd heard a broadcast of *Die schöne Müllerin* by Pears and Britten. The great recorder-playing name of the time was Frans Brüggen, who went on to become an early-music conductor, but something about Michala Petri's sound world captivated me and still does. The word for it, which came to me much later, is 'crystalline'. Her mixture of innocence and stunning maturity at seventeen was something I would not come across again until nearly thirty years later I watched the young Russian Maria Sharapova winning her first Wimbledon title (but that was only on television! And Michala doesn't scream as she plays). There had been enough bad imitations in the meantime, and there will be more.

Michala was the star turn in a family trio consisting of herself, her harpsichordist mother Hanne and her 'cellist younger brother David, who eventually (when grown, as she wrote to me, to 'two meters') became neither a soloist nor a member of a quartet ("he is not very workfull") but a member of the Hallé Orchestra. Even compared to that hard-up orchestra's 'workful' schedule, the ones Mrs. Petri arranged for the trio's tours were inhuman, with up to two hundred concerts a year, mostly in tiny venues paying a pittance. In a letter, Michala wrote to me of being toted around the German Democratic Republic and feeling terribly sorry for the people there. They might well have felt sorry for her. I succeeded in persuading the Corporation's short-lived classical music label, BBC Artium, to take on the first LP she made in Denmark. But it turned out that the rights all lay with the original company, who didn't pass on any of the royalties on British sales, so that apart from the publicity she was no better off for the deal.

In the end the touring became too much, the trio disbanded and, once recuperated, she was free to concentrate on her solo career. She was taken up by the Academy of St. Martin-in-the-Fields, with whom she was about to make a first CD when I met her again, and since then has never looked back. I know she valued that crucial British broadcast debut with its sympathetic, appreciative atmosphere, and for my part I felt and still feel in Paul Hamburger's debt for an experience that turned into a friendship. It is alive to this day.

5   *Doris Soffel*

The last major artist illumination of my BBC years was the German mezzo-soprano Doris Soffel. I'd heard her several times on foreign tapes, though not yet on the commercial Bach recordings she'd made with Helmut Rilling in her early days, and had been struck by the timbre of the voice and the purposeful way she used it, slightly 'home-made' though it seemed to be. It recalled one or two powerful if unpolished communicators from the past, notably a mezzo-soprano named Helen McKinnon from the days of the 'GTS recitals'. With this voice, however, I came in time to sense subtleties and sensitivities that made me want to get to know its owner better by producing her in a programme. I eventually discovered that, like Hans Keller's enthusiasm Jennifer Smith, she had also learned the violin, so she knew about variation of vibrato.

She came onto Howard Hartog's books at Ingpen & Williams: after all this time he had a shrewd idea what I'd like, and when Doris was due here for rehearsals of *La clemenza di Tito* at Covent Garden in 1983 he offered me her for a studio recording. She sent in a distinctly short but musically substantial programme including Schubert's amazingly sinister song *Der Zwerg* and a good Brahms group. So I bit, and booked Roger Vignoles to play for her. We met on the day in Studio 1, Maida Vale, she a fairly buxom blonde with a forthright manner, whom my mind's eye could see in white knee-boots extolling the virtues of the newest German fitted kitchen. She was on her guard, having no idea what degree of musical sophistication or ear she'd be dealing with, and it took some time to get the sound right. She came into the control cubicle and listened, as I thought, a shade hypercritically, but in the end the studio manager contrived something she was prepared to countenance, and off we went – very well, as it turned out. She was clearly relieved. Having disposed of the agreed programme, she wanted to go on, producing a set of Schumann Hans Andersen settings (in translations by Chamisso) that I didn't know, and which turned out to be sensational. I suppose she must at least have looked at them beforehand with Roger, just in case. Preparing to record *Der Spielmann*, she said in a tone I've never forgotten "*Jetzt kommt ein Wahnsinn!*" (Now for something totally crazy!). It was too. Even with the extra music we got through in short order and she invited us both to eat with her at her hotel in Kensington. At one point she asked me "How do you keep so fresh after all these years of recording people?". To which I said that such as she made it very easy. This she obviously liked. As we parted I told her "You're a great artist".

The next year she returned for an all-Schumann recital with Aribert Reimann at the Wigmore Hall, which we recorded. It included the entire Justinus Kerner cycle Op. 35, sung as to the manic-depressive manner born

(Kerner and Soffel, Swabians both!) and Goethe settings, mostly obscure, including *Lied Lynceus des Türmers*, so far as I know the only Lied setting of a text from Part 2 of *Faust*, which she and Aribert between them made into something colossal. The Kerner cycle had long been among my favourite Schumann songs, thanks to the advocacy of Thomas Hemsley, who'd given their first British broadcast or even performance, early in my time as a producer. He and Paul Hamburger recorded them again, once we were working in stereo. I also got Barry McDaniel to record them during the early 1970s. Recording Doris's recital took my mind off the Chicago Prokofiev disaster even then unrolling. We went afterwards for coffee somewhere near the hall with one or two people from the Goethe Institute. They presumably were the promoters of the concert and so of German culture in this country, one of whom confessed that Justinus Kerner was a poet he and indeed nobody else in modern Germany had heard of. (Kerner was a doctor and a good friend of Mörike.) This time my parting shot was to tell Doris to take it easy now and then – one couldn't live life two hundred per cent the whole of the time. Why I suddenly divagated onto her personal life I don't know – there was certainly a strong sympathy there.

A great swathe of operatic roles kept her busy, the old opera-recital antinomy asserted itself yet again, and the Lied evidently dropped back from her repertoire. I grew sick and tired of seeing prizes for Lieder records go to singers without half her weight and content, or Wigmore Hall recitals given by those of still less distinction. But she'd chosen her path, her agents had, the world had.

In 1992, after a decade away from the London concert platform, she returned to give an evening recital at St. John's, Smith Square. It was obvious that she had lost none of her vocal quality or her ability to convey emotion – not only the over-wrought, desperate emotions so beloved of Lied composers, but that rarest thing, joy.

Postcript: How It Looks Now

How different everything has become! Better, worse – who am I to say? Different, certainly. The sheer range of music on Radio 3 is crucial and to my mind more influential even than varying trends in presentation or the substitution of fixed-length 'slots' for constructed programmes that were oftener than not allowed to be precisely the length they had worked out at. With all of 'world music' to choose from, the old 'core repertoire' gets that much less of a look-in, while stations like Classic FM seem determined rather to contract the range, which of course also squeezes out a vast amount that's worthwhile. Do people rush to appreciate other musical traditions when they no longer know how to listen to their own?

Sophisticated programme-making was the essence of my BBC work, even after promotion into the ranks of the supervisors and executives. Those tailor-made broadcasts found a resonance among listeners but are unlikely to be heard again, since programmes as such are seldom repeated, only occasional performances that went into them. As a result, fewer and fewer people now even know that any of this went on. What I managed to initiate during my twenty-eight years is on the one hand a source of lasting satisfaction, but, on the other, of some sadness, in that I thought I was breaking new ground and paving the way. As it's turned out, it wasn't a way anyone wanted to follow. Broadcasting, overall as well as in detail, is a field where you drop a pebble down a well, wait for the faint splash, and then proceed to Next Business.

This memoir's litany of famous and less-famous names would amount to little more than an exercise in name-dropping unless supplemented by a hint, at least, of what went on before the names ever came into the studio. Looking back, I realize that programme-making took me deep into something remarkable – deeper even than I knew at the time. I thought I could scarcely do better in explaining what I mean than by quoting the preface to my 2003 book, *Franz Schubert: Music and Belief*:

> Uniquely memorable moments came seated in a silent reference library experiencing with my inner ear unknown German songs as they might sound when sung by some particular one of the musical young singers who in those days still enjoyed the priceless advantage of time to develop and mature.

But then in the collected sermons of Father Cormac Rigby, long a Radio 3 colleague, and a man who knew a deep level of reality from at least three different directions – movement, philosophy, priesthood – I was struck by a passage which came nearer still to the place where I had been during those programme-making years:

> It's not a time for going deeply into oneself, but a time for leaving oneself behind … I find it because, for a short time or a longer period, I have gone to find it – a time and a place set apart.

What Cormac meant by 'it' was 'time to fully open one's heart to God and to listen to whatever He wishes to say': mentioning my programme-research of the 1960s and '70s in the same breath, I realize that I am placing myself on the level, not of Father Cormac, but of the medieval juggler who went to a church and, having nothing else to offer, performed his routine in front of the Virgin's image. So be it. Very few people are cut out for the priesthood, but vocation is vocation and mine was as a producer of radio music programmes.

It did indeed come down to time and place – the time still a Reithian time when content and standard mattered and audience figures didn't, when one permitted oneself the luxury of thinking, not that the listener was irrelevant, but that if one's programme minutely changed or illuminated a single listener's life it had justified itself; the place, one where unusually cultivated minds could take their time learning a special craft, the craft of broadcasting. The writing was well and truly on the wall when one of the first internal documents about economies, long before the end of the 1960s, used the phrase 'the final 5% of quality not audible through the loudspeaker'. Audible to whom? So I occupy a middle position between that of Hans Keller, who declared 'broadcaster' a 'phoney profession' (in the sense that the verb 'broadcast' is transitive not intransitive – one broadcasts *something*, rather than broadcasting in vacuo for one's own pride and self-satisfaction), and that of Stephen Hearst, who vehemently denounced any such idea, being himself an outstanding deviser of broadcasts right up to the level of television series by men of the stature of Alastair Cooke. Music broadcasting was not an art, but certainly a craft whose working material was an art, and the aim was to draw the imagined listener into a different world by the most careful choice of music, of performer, and of introductory words.

The late Ernest Warburton used to speak contemptuously of 'men with a pile of CDs'. That showed his age; but it also spoke for my still more considerable age. Once retired, I was then invited to make occasional programmes that relied principally on – yes, a pile of CDs, if also on revivified 'live' performances from the Archives. 'Do I contradict myself? Very well, I contradict myself.' No more than Roberto Gerhard am I 'a slave to consistency', and the *laudator temporis acti* is rarely the most useful member of society. One must always look forward.

Part Six

Leo Black (Milein Cosman)

The Making of a Music Producer
or *Leo Black and How He Got That Way*

1 *Family Matters*

As Leo Rosten's indomitable if eminently imitable Hyman Kaplan put it, 'First, I Was Born'[1] – on the twenty-eighth of July 1932 to my good Fabian Socialist parents in the Neasden Humanist Nursing Home, where they came round in the evening to ask "Have you had your options open today?". My mother with her teasing sense of humour would have been in and out of her element there. After having either my elder brother John or me she sprang a serious puerperal fever, what Mistress Quickly called a burning quotidian tertian, and the third or fourth time her temperature shot into the middle 100s the jolly doctor said "Well, well, what are we up to, Mrs. Black?" – to which the jolly Mrs. Black replied that she was trying to see how many times she could rise on the third day without ascending into heaven. For grace under pressure I rate that somewhere above my own best effort in Vienna's Wilhelminenspital, to be narrated in due course.

The home address on my birth certificate is 10 The Avenue, Brondesbury, a grey-brick house that, seen in passing, looks surprisingly like 112 Chetwynd Road, Kentish Town, jointly bought in 1984 by Felicity and myself. As to my names, a mere eight letters were thought adequate (John had fared as badly – a letter more, a syllable fewer). Confusion was inbuilt from the start. At elementary school, having read *The Boy Mozart*, I for a while took my first name to be short for Leopold, much to classmates' amusement, while later, well into my very-young-looking thirties, the combination of Christian name and surname more than once prompted elderly and presumably purblind Anglo-Austrian ladies to ask "Are you the Mr. Leo Blech who conducted that wonderful record of Beethoven's Violin Concerto with Fritz Kreisler?" – it had been made a bit before I was born. To worse-confound the confusion, ever since student days in Oxford I have from time to time been mixed up in people's minds with the outstanding oboist Neil Black, a fellow student for whom I wrote cadenzas when during my final year he played the Mozart C major Concerto with Jack Westrup's University Orchestra.

My father was born in 1889 into the large family of a Jewish cobbler, Jakob Schwartz, in what was then Russia but is now again, and I for one hope permanently this time, Poland. He was originally Ischaiah, but immediately on arrival at the London docks in 1895 that was anglicized to Charlie by relatives already settled here. A bright youth, he grew up in legendary parts of the East End like Cable Street, with friends like Lewis Silkin, later Minister of Town and Country Planning in the post-1945 Labour government and eventually a Baron. Once, near the end of Dad's life, we walked round the area in search of traces, but he no longer recognized anything. What he did still acknowledge was the singing of Bud Flanagan, to whom he accorded his ultimate accolade, A LOVELY BOY.

He should have become the Rabbi – it was cooking nicely but one day, aged about 13, he came home from school to announce that religion was superstition and what counted was science. Great cries of "oy-veh!" but he was not to be moved. He got himself into Queens' College, Cambridge, crowning his time there with the college's best maths degree of the year. His British naturalization papers were issued on 8 September 1911, but he sat out the first nine months of the war with his provocative German-sounding surname.

The difficult question of military service soon arose, for as a pacifist he was totally against the war. That got him consigned for a while to Wormwood Scrubs, where I believe he was forcibly fed. As boys, we weren't regaled with heroic stories but it was there in the background: I think Ma wondered how much of his later depression and difficult temperament went back to his time in the Scrubs.

He had a strong vibrant voice, which would have made him a viable synagogue Chozzen had he gone on with Judaism. It struck one or two qualified people as worth training, and in the 1920s he and my mother spent several months in northern Italy so that he could take lessons from a Maestro Caronna, who had in his time coached Caruso. He acquired the elements of bel canto, which for the rest of his life made him extraordinarily intolerant of any other type of voice-production. His ideal among singers was Gigli (another Lovely Boy, invariably known in the family as Beniamino); Peter Pears in particular could drive him into a frenzy, and very few singers indeed passed muster. His great tribute to Janet Baker when she came along was "She's the only one who produces her voice right". In 1944 he contributed a very slim volume, *The Educational Reconstruction of Education*, to the left-wing Gollancz catalogue; it contained many humane and sensible ideas that were later put into practice, though R. A. Butler's White Paper of 1943 had anticipated them.

By now my account of him has quietly introduced a wife – and what a wife! – born Phyllis Beckett in 1895. Her father Tom came from Yorkshire and worked in a grocery, and by 1901 they were at 7 Jamieson Road in the Wavertree district of Liverpool, a very poor and disorderly area, or so we were told. He drank a lot, to the point of 'the D.T.-s', passing on the habit though not the consequences to some of the next generation, and to my mother an understandably strong dislike of drunkenness, which didn't however prevent her enjoying a drop of 'mother's ruin' in her declining years. Ma got herself by native wit, diligence and, I imagine, good teaching somewhere, into Liverpool University, whose student songs she still sang around the house late in life. She qualified as a history teacher, standing in at places as classy as Shrewsbury School, where Neville Cardus would have been the assistant cricket professional at about the same time.

She and my father met at a Fabian summer school, and were married some time after she began to teach history in Newport, Mon. The Newport connection is a nice case of 'it's a small world', for both my wife's parents were born there. Much work for the Labour Party was done from the back of a lorry – they saw horrendous poverty in Newport during the mid-1920s, which would have reinforced their childhood experiences, and he'd have been at his most presentable getting righteously indignant as he tried to do something about it. In those days women teachers were strictly forbidden to marry; my mother kept her marriage a secret for a while, but finally had to give up teaching. They were also paid a lower rate for the job; one reason for resuming her career later in life was that she'd always fought for Equal Pay and wanted to be there when it came – as indeed she was.

With Dad's singing career aborted, his brief business career followed, using that excellent Maths degree (so far as I know, he had no accountancy qualifications). Their circle of acquaintances at the time included the theatre producer Henry Cass and the composer-cum-music-publisher Maurice Jacobson. When I was at a loss to find a job after leaving Oxford with two seemingly useless degrees, both men were enlisted to advise us. Jacobson I found patronising, where Harry Cass was all too practical, telling me to write to Sidney Bernstein at Granada Television and say how good I was, with ideas for programmes: "If it means saying you'll get Mozart to appear, then say it!" I didn't.

NOTES

1   The American humourist Leo Rosten (1908-97) first published pieces on the 'night-school' English lessons of the Ukrainian immigrant H*Y*M*A*N K*A*P*L*A*N in the *New Yorker* in the 1930s under the name Leonard Q. Ross. In book form they were my favourite adolescent reading. Rosten followed this up with *The Return of H*Y*M*A*N K*A*P*L*A*N*. I have also much enjoyed another book of his, *The Joys of Yiddish* (1968).

2   *Amersham*

We moved to South Kenton and in 1938, by a second wisely pre-emptive move, further north-west to Amersham in the southern Chilterns. After much scanning of the 'Vacancies' pages in the *Times Educational Supplement* Dad had rejoined the teaching profession as senior maths master at Wycombe Grammar, a half-hour bus ride away. Schooling was at the 'elementary', which may have been called Amersham Common but they did teach one English – parsing, précis and all. Turned ten, I went on to Dr. Challoner's Grammar School, which was then co-educational. By 1938 it was legal to be a married teacher, and Ma, too, had begun working again, at Hendon School. When the Blitz began Dad insisted that she stop. Around the end of the war she was actually teaching history at Challoner's. That she was a brilliantly entertaining teacher I know, not only from my own recollections but from a former schoolmate who's emphatic about her ability to interest him in her subject.

We were vegetarians, until wartime and rationing; that wasn't just to do with pacifism, and in my father's case it outlived it, for what he picked up about Hitler changed his lifelong views about meeting force with force. A careful protein count on the outbreak of war led to the conclusion that we'd better use the meat ration rather than exchange the coupons for extra cheese or whatever it was one could have.

My early fascination with music came from overhearing our friend Francesco Ticciati, a brilliant pianist who had studied with Busoni but later emigrated from Mussolini's Italy, and from listening to the radio and records. Beethoven's Seventh Symphony I recall vividly, especially its hypnotically repetitive slow movement. By the age of six I was showing enough interest in the piano for my parents to decide it was time I learned to play. The chosen teacher, Constance Dupré, was a Ticciati pupil. And here there was a fateful surprise. For some reason, I imagined a piano teacher as a grey, severe elderly lady; why that should have been I don't know, since at six I hadn't even started to go to Amersham Common, whose staff indeed included several such ladies (very nice people, as I later discovered!). Be that as it may, on the Sunday morning in question I was told that Miss Dupré had arrived, and made a tremulous entry into the sitting-room. There at the piano sat a definitely young person, whom even my six-year-old eye could diagnose as distinctly pretty. The light of a fine summer morning added to the effect, nor did her manner put me off. Who knows what lifelong precedents and norms established themselves in that brief moment of epiphany during the summer of 1938?! (As Luther put it, *Frau Musica*.) I've no idea how good a teacher she was. My 'lovely tone' was regularly praised, but that could have had to do with the Bechstein grand pianos, formerly Artur Schnabel's property, which Francesco had the use of and stored with us. From such instruments even a little squit, Herbert or Bluebottle like me could conjure up something presentable. Busoni's school was, moreover, renowned for its cantabile and disdain of sheer muscular power; about the latter I learned later, from a tough and admirable Leschetizky lady named Dorothy Hall. Francesco's playing showed the Busoni penchant for extremely fleet tempos, but I don't blame him for a chronic tendency to hurry in my own! To give my musical education a good technical founding he himself taught me 'rudiments' (staff notation, basic chords and so forth), which he made seem very easy and obvious. He died soon after the end of the war though the name lives on – his 'cellist son, Niso, was active in propagating the Alexander Technique that has spread among British musicians such a plethora of half-truths about body-use or non-use. And even as I write, another bearer of the name, presumably a great-grandson, with the first name Robin, is rapidly acquiring a reputation as the latest brilliant young conductor.

The same fascination with music also led from around 1940, when I would have been a precocious and musically ambitious seven, to attempts at composition, which continued until just after the end of my studies at Oxford. My musical penchant, combined with a distinct weediness, academic prowess and a tendency to twitch, might have been expected to provoke ridicule and bullying from the rustics discharged for their pensum of daily education by the little green Leyland bus that laboured noisily up the steep hill out of Chesham, its minor sixth rising in pitch with the gradient. But in fact I had no problem from that quarter: local youths belting past on their bikes as I played tended to clap and call out encouraging things. During a spell of jogging in the Westbourne Park area of London during my late thirties I noted a similar tendency on the part of black men I ran past – they'd call out "Hey, great, man, keep goin'!", while white yobs were more likely to jeer. There was an occasional tendency to pick on us as Jews. It might seem strange that in a place brimming with names like Deitchman, Wolchover, Indermühle and Minkovich two boys called Black should have been singled out. But as a convinced atheist Dad did keep us away from 'religious instruction' lessons, so I can only think that whereas 'atheist' meant nothing to the others, 'Jew' was known as a different race and religion, the more pejorative aspects following by association. In any case, John's elder-statesmanly advice, "When they do that, call them Christian Gentlemen", usually stopped it in its tracks.

3 Don't Mention the War

Once the 'phoney war' was over, the Blitz was audible enough from twenty-five miles away to make us thankful that Dad had had the foresight to get out of London while the going was good. A curious episode was that of the 'evacuees'. The closing years of the twentieth century saw various published accounts of the trials and tribulations of displaced children from places like the East End of London. These were meant to wring the withers of the tender-hearted half a century later, by which time their out-of-London hosts would be safely dead or have forgotten about them. To me the wither was over the other foot, for the invaders were incredibly tough and streetwise and at times made our lives a misery. Snowballs with stones in them were virtually weapons of mass destruction, particularly when rammed into one's eye from behind …

One fine morning in June 1941 we went for a walk, and as Dad and I reached the top of a hill he told me Hitler had invaded Russia. That, he said, will change the course of the war and will probably mean we don't, after all, lose. Given our part-Jewish background, there had been serious thought of sending John and myself to Canada for the duration, but it came to nothing: many parents must have had a change of mind after the sinking of the *Arandora Star* with a boatload of internees on its way across the Atlantic. From mid-1941 onward, 'Aid to Russia' became a major money-collecting preoccupation, successor to the campaign that had helped finance the building of Spitfires and Hurricanes for the Battle of Britain. 'Open a Second Front Now' was a slogan often seen daubed on walls. Finally, in 1944, D-Day came, as endless convoys of planes flew over the school during a woodwork lesson with Taffy Owen. Amersham was just within range of the V1 'flying bombs' the Luftwaffe unleashed on England a few months later. The only time one came really close, as I played in the field at the back of the house, I flung myself to the ground not before but after the bang, a pointless manoeuvre that would have greatly alarmed my parents had they seen it. The far more deadly V2s didn't come so far West but could be heard exploding in London all that distance away. The morning after the first one, Dad, who had a good ear, summarily vetoed my intended visit to the city to watch a late-season cricket match at Lords.

When the war in Europe ended in 1945 I was three months short of thirteen. VE Day was quite a celebration, but for us, who'd lived so long with the serried red ranks of Victor Gollancz's Left Book Club on our shelves, parading titles like *Guilty Men* (by 'Cato', in part Michael Foot, later leader of the Labour Party), the victory of Clement Attlee at the ensuing General Election occasioned a still better one. I recall a Conservative MP, Sir Thomas Inskip, as for some reason particularly 'guilty', though the book's main quarry was far bigger – no less than Prime Ministers Ramsay MacDonald and Neville Chamberlain. We heard of the Japanese surrender while on holiday in North Wales, having a few days earlier read in the newspaper (the liberal *News Chronicle*) about the first atom bombs. My father had suffered during the First War, seen the Second follow a mere twenty-one years later, and now the prospect of a third, nuclear, world war became the supreme imagined horror, outweighing even the relief of knowing the second to be safely over. As a hyper-critical adolescent I formulated the thought, "You only worry about the Bomb if you've nothing else to worry about". In fact, he was living disproof of that, having room and to spare for both.

Visits to London an hour away on the Metropolitan line were now more possible, though during lulls in the bombing we'd already dared to go 'up to town'. Leaving good and early, the 'workmen's return' cost something like one and threepence, or 6.25p in present-day currency (not allowing for inflation) – though first catch your one and threepence. Alighting at Baker Street, our first move would be for breakfast to the nearby Express Dairy, whose blue tiles and window lettering are still a memory, as are the great gaps in the buildings the other side of the street. I went to one or two memorable concerts. Not that Amersham was without music, even apart from its distinguished temporary residents: I recall the Blech String Quartet, led by the future founder of the London Mozart Players, giving a concert in the church hall in their blue RAF uniforms, and a pianist of the calibre of Frederic Lamond playing in the British Restaurant in Chesham.[1] But what I heard in London just after the war was world-class, namely two Albert Hall concerts, one of them a piano recital by Artur Schnabel. Having lived for years with his pianos, I at last experienced the great man himself, and can still feel the rolling arpeggios near the start of Beethoven's A flat major sonata Op. 110, heard from far up in the gallery. Then, on my own, I heard the Philadelphia Orchestra during its first post-war visit. It was my first great orchestra, indeed one of the first orchestras of any kind I heard live – though there had been the one playing the Brahms Requiem on a famous occasion when we arrived late at the church in Old Amersham and trooped down the aisle under the gimlet glare of the soprano Margaret Field-Hyde. The soprano in that work has enough to make her edgy, what with sitting silently through the early movements before having to deliver a horrendously difficult solo of what needs to be celestial beauty. Having trooped, we found ourselves sitting right over the timpani, at which point Ma remembered that she'd left some jam on the stove. Not daring to un-troop prematurely after such an entrance, she mentally wrote it off, only to find on getting home that it was perfect to the minute. "How long did you give it?" – "The length of the Brahms Requiem minus a few minutes for being late plus getting down to the church and back". It was an opportunity she never missed.

The Philadelphia Orchestra, however, was something else. My abiding impression is of the spread G-major string chord at the opening of the *Mathis der Maler* symphony, my first piece of 'modern' music and one that lit a spark of sympathy for what during my Oxford time Thomas Armstrong was to call "the grey hand of Hindemith".

NOTES

1   'British Restaurants' were a chain of cheap, state-run eating places where one could find a desperately mediocre meal despite the rationing system. As late as the start of the 1950s I still frequented the one in Oxford when really hard up.

4 *Cheltenham*

Our family moved to Cheltenham in the late summer of 1946, Dad having applied for and been appointed to a job at one of the Emergency Training Colleges set up to recycle returned soldiers into urgently-needed teachers. Volunteers for that selfless public service were of course assured that with the programme once concluded they could safely reckon on returning to jobs as good as those they'd given up. And of course with a maths teacher aged sixty there was no way that was going to happen in a Fabian Socialist as distinct from Communist country. Sure enough, when it came to it Dad eked out his final working years filling in wherever he could, for example in Nottingham, which was a long way from home and meant we only saw him at weekends.

As our introduction to the West Country, the train drew out of the tunnel before Chalford and clouds of smoke dissipated to reveal The Golden Valley. A good twenty years before the infamous Beeching there were more stations than there are now, Brimscombe having its own stop, and the train's sedate progress towards Cheltenham offered every opportunity to take in an enchanting new very green landscape. I've returned to the area many times for one reason and another, mostly to do with friendships, and it never ceases to delight me.

Next morning we enrolled at Pate's (= Cheltenham) Grammar School, centrally situated next door to the Cheltenham Original Brewery, whose typical tannin-y, hoppy smell is still indelibly linked in my mind to CGS. Pate's, unlike Challoner's, was at that stage single-sex, and without all the very bright girls the academic standard was even less challenging. I maintained my accustomed top-of-the-class with no trouble, for the moment taking no part in school music. Dad had arranged for me to have piano lessons with the music master at Cheltenham College, George Loughlin, since there was an organ in its chapel: with the likelihood of my becoming a professional pianist receding, it would be good for my education if I learned that instrument too. I did so for a while, never really achieving the hands-feet coordination necessary to use the pedals to much effect. Loughlin added to my mish-mash of piano styles an element of 'Matthay' and took me through the history needed to pass School Certificate (the predecessor of O-level) in music. What with one thing and another, it only emerged a few weeks before the exam that I'd been studying set works from the wrong syllabus (Oxford and Cambridge instead of Oxford) – which made not a blind bit of difference, since I got my mind round the new ones in a week or two and emerged, as in all eight other subjects, with the top grade. Revolting little swot.

Eventually the CGS music master discovered me, and with the mildest of reproofs for having hidden my light under a bushel we became fast friends, for

William Neve was the kindest and most amiable man I've ever met, full of the enthusiasm without which teaching is purgatory, and being taught little better. He even converted me to Gilbert and Sullivan, at which I'd always followed my parents in turning up my nose. I was roped in to play the orchestral piano in *Trial by Jury* and thoroughly enjoyed it, discovering that in music I become enthusiastic about almost anything I do regularly enough.

Cheltenham had the edge over Amersham when it came to landscape, the Cotswolds being more clearly and closely on show than the Chilterns had been. Nothing else was as idyllic as that first swathe from Chalford to Stroud, but the low sweep of Cleeve Hill rising to a thousand feet or so from straight behind the college's wartime-surplus buildings on the outskirts of the town has become a template for my perceptions of the country. And the uniquely evocative Elgarian sweep of the Malverns could be seen from up on Cleeve. A handsome town, Cheltenham had already thrown off its choleric-retired-colonel image. The City of Birmingham Orchestra, conducted by George Weldon and later by Rudolf Schwarz, gave regular concerts in the Town Hall: I have a recurring memory of its leader, Norris Stanley, sweating as he laboured at the across-the-string arpeggios that lead from the cadenza into the recapitulation of the first movement of Mendelssohn's Violin Concerto. On the next level up, Alfredo Campoli played the Elgar Violin Concerto at the yearly Music Festival, where a concert by the chamber ensemble of the English Opera Group offered a first hearing of the Schubert Octet. The Hallé Orchestra came to play Elgar's First Symphony and I was allowed to be at a rehearsal. I can still feel the atmosphere as something one could cut with a knife, such was the concentration, but when at the pianissimo end of the slow movement a percussionist dropped a cymbal, Barbirolli merely said "Be very careful tonight, will you?". They also gave one of the earliest performances of Vaughan Williams's Sixth Symphony at the Festival, and I aroused amazement at school the next morning by reproducing at the piano its opening F minor scale contradicted by an E minor chord.

The town also had a competitive music festival, where I acquired a rather strange record: I won the sight-reading class, entered again the next year and found awaiting me on the stand a Kabalevsky Sonatina I knew already. Over-confidence made me play it so fast and so wildly that I was way down the list when adjudication time came. I must already have sensed something unusual about Schubert, because my *molto sostenuto* rendering of the first movement of his A major sonata D. 664 was come down on by the adjudicator as atmospheric but really not viable. At least a setting of A. E. Housman got a creditable mark in the composition class from a major musician, E. J. Moeran. A brief and sobering contact with my musico-cricketing idol Neville Cardus came at a symposium in the Town Hall during the Literary Festival. His autobiography being my bible at the time, I stood up and asked for advice to a young man hoping to follow in his footsteps as a critic. It came: "Marry a rich wife!".

Some time around then I sat my last Associated Board exam in piano: distinction of course – indeed, it earned me something called the Samuel Aitken Memorial Prize for the highest-marked Grade 8 in Gloucestershire. A still less likely achievement was an essay prize, for which I'd chosen, God knows why given my anti-Imperialist upbringing, Cecil Rhodes. I must have spent at least a week boning up on that.

Having continued to satisfy examiners, this time in Higher School Certificate (the equivalent of A-level, main subjects Music and English, secondary subjects French and the Latin that was still required for Oxford or Cambridge entrance), I was awarded a 'state scholarship'. This was enough to support me at University and I was consigned to my second choice, Oxford. Dad plumped for Wadham College on the grounds that it accommodated both the Professor of Music, J. A. Westrup, and a Professor of English, namely its Warden, Maurice Bowra. The legendary Bowra proved of no use whatever to the likes of myself, nor I to him, since he preferred his young men pretty, interesting or rich.

5 *Oxford*

I arrived at Wadham in late September of 1950 and lived in college for my first year, tucked away in true state-school-commoner fashion in the deepest recesses of the back quad – the other side of the wall from the King's Arms, where I never in my five years set foot. For four further years I lived in 'digs', first in the purlieus separating the Cowley and Iffley Roads, later near the railway station, and finally in a very nice room in the centrally-located Walton Street. The mix of students took in public and state school, but, even more importantly, post- and pre-National Service. The most senior students had served in the War, I was pre-everything. Wadham was pleasantly free of rank snobbery and body fascism, and the honours music course, then in its second year, made for agreeable work. As I embarked on it, Schoenberg was still alive but you wouldn't have known. Tutors included Bernard Naylor, composer of some good choral pieces, and for history Frank Harrison, at that time producing – hot off the press – works he'd edited from the fifteenth-century Eton Choirbook. We sang them through at Jack Westrup's informal one-voice-to-a-part 'chamber choral' group in the lecture room of the Music Faculty next door to the Holywell Music Room, giving their pretty hilarious First Performances in Modern Times. Westrup was a very knowledgeable and friendly man, with a dry, almost clownish sense of humour that appealed to me: we got on well, though I remember virtually nothing he said.

For harmony and counterpoint I was next in the sympathetic hands of Edmund Rubbra, who had the keenest of ears and unfailingly spotted the passages in exercises where one had simply failed to hear things accurately in one's head. He was far less permissive than Bernard Naylor. His lectures on Bach's '48' were a byword for meticulous derivation of everything from the first few notes of the piece – something of a joke to us in view of the minimal amount of Bach he'd covered by the end of a term, but illuminating and a sign of his own scrupulously organic musical mind. During my last year I wrote for *Isis* a piece about his Sixth Symphony, which showed the young graduate trying very hard to be mature and sociological beyond his means, and managing merely to sit precariously on a number of fences. I'd heard the piece once, had no means of checking my impressions, and to all intents and purposes could have written the article without having heard the music at all. My former tutor was philosophical about what I'd said; half a century later I found it surprisingly perceptive, for all its subaltern presuppositions and begged questions, and appended it to the book in which I far too late tried to make amends for twenty-eight BBC years with my mind anywhere else than Rubbra.

Bernard Rose set off rather faster through the pre-history of chamber music, pausing only to savour the asperities of Purcell's Fantasias; but once he hit

Haydn's string quartets he, in turn, became so enthusiastic that by the end of the academic year we were still on Haydn. Egon Wellesz's cherubic presence offered a whiff of the cosmopolitan, and the Professor took a valuable score-reading class.

The Oxford University Musical Club and Union was active, with weekly concerts by its members in Europe's oldest purpose-built concert hall, the Holywell Music Room contiguous with Wadham. I took part in a small way, both as pianist and in a still smaller way as composer. Oxford was, all in all, a comfortable continuation of schooldays, with nothing more disturbing than Hindemith or Bartók to remind us that music had meanwhile moved on through the holocaust and into the second half of the twentieth century. One exception was when a priest named Dr. Peacock appeared out of nowhere with a class on recent French music. He showed us a Boulez piano sonata which none of us could make the first thing of, maintaining that it exemplified the traditional French virtues of clarity, economy, elegance and something else equally unlikely. We were all too polite to say "Pull the other one, it's got antique cymbals on it". Contemporary avant-garde developments in places like Paris and Cologne were unknown to us, with Boulez an enigmatic newcomer and Stockhausen yet to heave over the horizon. Even the name Olivier Messiaen meant nothing, whereas for Londoners like Richard Rodney Bennett and Susan Bradshaw and for Richard Hall pupils in Manchester like Sandy Goehr, Harrison Birtwistle, Peter Maxwell Davies, Elgar Howarth and John Ogdon, he was the obvious port of call, the rudiments once mastered.

And so three years passed as in a slightly lonely dream, with First Class Honours materializing at the end of them in 1953, for me as for five others out of a class numbering little more than a dozen. 'What then, sang Plato's ghost, what then?' On leaving, I resolved that in the unlikely event of my ever qualifying for any version of *Who's Who* I'd describe myself as 'self-educated after Oxford', but now view that as ungrateful. I'd absorbed from somewhere a certain humanistic approach to great music, a belief in its connection with personality and human depths that helped save me from becoming a 'musicologist' and stood me in good stead when at long last I came to write a book.

'Research' was the logical next step. I'd been enthralled by a Third Programme series, the brainchild of Robert Simpson, on Mozart's Vespers and Litanies, and now got it into my head, as a fatal non sequitur, that his predecessors as Austrian church composers offered a viable field of research for a further degree. My alternative idea was the relationship between instrumental and vocal music in Schubert, which Jack Westrup said he'd personally choose of the two, but there's no warning some people. Given the eventual course of my life, it's ironic that I saw that door open so early and chose not to go through it – but probably it would have been too soon.

A year later I returned from a deeply depressing visit to Vienna and Salzburg that had involved examining what looked like forty totally identical masses by note-manufacturing machines such as Giuseppe Bonno. I determined to chuck the whole thing in and see if I could spend my yet-another year, already agreed, on the Bachelor of Music, a so-called composition degree. Wellesz continued as my supervisor, showing me a few ways in which my attempts could be improved, and coming out with the odd memorable saying. When I'd been listening to Berg's early music and commented on its overwrought emotional level, asking "does it always have to sound as if he was going mad?", Wellesz said "But zey vere all mad. Zat vas vy I left zem." It took me a long time to discover that, so far from having occasion to 'leave' the Second Viennese School, he'd come no closer to joining it, some early lessons with Schoenberg apart, than when he produced the first provisional biography of Schoenberg up to the middle 1920s. The Master had been tolerant of that, but distinctly sniffy about him elsewhere. (My editor, who also studied with him at Oxford, remembers being told how Bruno Walter had perceptively warned Wellesz that, thanks to Schoenberg, "things were getting into Berg and Webern's music" that shouldn't be allowed into his.) One Wellesz saying I still relish is actually by Richard Strauss, that fullness of scoring in operatic composition must depend on how many people occupy the stage at any given time.

Another that struck home came when the No. 2 in the Faculty, Thomas Armstrong, a Churchillian figure whom despite occasional pomposities and archaisms I liked and respected, had been persuaded to review an OUMCU concert with student compositions, mine included, and weighed in with his 'grey-hand-of-Hindemith' routine. At the time I was writing a weekly column for *Isis* and indulged myself with a distinctly sentimental, self-pitying piece on behalf of young composers, asking in effect "Why do we do it?". At my next tutorial Wellesz surprised me by saying he'd read me, and quoted as a real answer to my rhetorical question a saying of Hofmannsthal's: '*Ein Zeugnis, dass ich hier war*' (A witness that I was here). At the time I thought "Why should it matter whether I was here or not?", but now see they were right. If one has anything in the least unusual one ought to try to pass it on in some shape or form. Composition was running out, but programme-making and finally writing would to some degree replace it.

Wellesz's most memorable remark to me came, however, after he'd had the goodness to turn out on a bitterly cold night and watch me play the Old Shepherd in, appropriately enough, *The Winter's Tale*. When next we met he summed up my acting ability with "you vere very good – you looked so much younger zan you usually do". When he heard I was off to Vienna to train with Universal Edition, his succinct advice was: "Keep your eyes open. And your ears." I tried.

6   Before and After Vienna

In true Jim Dixon style I took my hilarious leave of Oxford during the summer of 1955 at the British Musicological Congress, where with students and fellow-graduates I did a variety of menial work. There were incidents, as when I managed to put down a chair-leg on a priceless eighteenth-century violin incautiously parked by a professor, David Boyden: what would have happened had it come to any harm I hate to imagine, but by some miracle it hadn't. The climax came when the congress's sole slide-projector was needed for two lectures that were scheduled simultaneously. I was on duty at the one presided over by Jack Westrup, and when I said "It's being used already" he was unwise enough to reply "It can't be, we need it here!". The Leader Had Spoken, the dutiful squaddie marched off into the next room, unplugged the projector and carried it out even as a great medievalist was in full flow. We gathered that he had been Not Best Pleased. He struck me, on twenty seconds' sight of him, as a dead ringer for Groucho Marx, so the fantasy in the ensuing letter to Hugh Wood can be imagined. My overall conclusion from the event was that musicologists show very little interest in or talent for music; the Germans' overall conclusion as they departed was "Next year ve vill show ze English how to run a congress".

Down from Oxford with my convertible BA and non-legal-tender B. Mus., I spent much time agonising over the prosaic question, "Who'll give me a chance to earn my living?". The BBC was initiating a system of 'general traineeships'; it threw up people of the calibre of future directors of networks, so not surprisingly my application got me nowhere. Or just a little way, for they wrote back that 'in view of my special qualifications' someone would talk to me. I duly visited London in May 1955, a few weeks before going down, and have never forgotten walking for the first of thousands of times along Portland Place towards the Holy of Holies, Broadcasting House. I was seen by Frank Wade, who was fairly high up in the Music Division hierarchy; he spotted that I was too young and green to be thrown straight into even the sedate world of radio broadcasting. "How would you cope with temperamental artists?" he asked me, and I had no idea. I took myself off to the zoo, hoping to see the geckos, but that didn't work out either.

I tired of applying for university posts after two interviews. One of them, for Aberdeen, turned out prosaic in the extreme, the other, for my Alma Mater, memorable if traumatic. In order to apply, I'd postponed the idea of going to Vienna to train in publishing with the modern-music publisher Universal Edition, sole catch from what had seemed an endless trawl of job applications. Two glittering degrees, no 'glittering prizes' (which is the sort of cliché that establishes itself among the worldly-wise: I'd done the wrong subject). Vienna was agreed after a mildly thorny interview with Universal's senior director, Dr. Alfred A. Kalmus, at the office in Great Pulteney Street, London w1; I distinguished myself by answering the question "Do you speak German?" with "*oui*". I'd read people like Abert and Jahn on Mozart, not to mention all those poems Schubert set, but speaking was another matter.

The Oxford interview was friendly enough, despite a battery of faculty members known and unknown scrutinising me, and unlike Kingsley Amis's John Lewis I didn't 'hear someone saying "no" loudly as I went out'. I went off and had tea with another applicant, Denis Arnold, who much later became not merely a lecturer but even the Heather Professor. Our chances were scuppered by the very-last-minute arrival of an application from an American full professor, Fred Sternfeld. Wellesz it was who'd laid it on the line, with registered letters arriving at our Birmingham house late into the night, that I must at all costs risk offending Kalmus by postponing my departure for Vienna, though he'd also warned me that Oxford elections were always unpredictable. As Faculty Board chairman and retiring lecturer, he said, he 'didn't vote and had to be impartial', but Bernard Rose reported his saying of Sternfeld "he comes from a very good family". The turn-down left Bernard, my more faithful fan, very angry – he wrote to me that he'd walked out of the appointment board, and bitterly regretted the loss of 'a chum to hold my hand when I grow old'. He did, however, say when asked some years later that he no longer felt that way and that Sternfeld had done a good job. I cherish all-the-more ambivalent feelings about Wellesz, who was gentle and utterly charming but perhaps a shade weak and certainly a shade vain ("I go next week to Rome, to RECEIVE A DECORATION"). My private jury is still out on how good a composer he was; I liked his Octet enough to instigate more than one BBC broadcast.

I sat out the time till Vienna by working in Kennington as clerk for the DMC Thread Company, British agent for the major Alsace manufacturer, Dollfus-Mieg. It was an agreeably undemanding spell at a time when I should have been stretched to my limits. During that time in limbo Hugh Wood gave me a copy of Bach's *Goldberg Variations*. Without access to a piano, I spent all my spare time studying it, often on the tops of buses. I'd always been an outstanding score- and sight-reader, the sort of not-uncommon academic who can sight-read anything and perform nothing, and when I finally went home to Birmingham I sat down at the piano to find out how far I knew the variations in terms of actually playing them. I lost the thread halfway through No. 28 (out of thirty), and still look on that as one of the major, if purely private, musical achievements of my life. It helps explain how I could later form such an accurate inward impression of any given singer performing new songs for the BBC. I also spent much time around then playing *The Art of Fugue* from an edition in the old clefs, and trying to play and simultaneously sing the original, mostly bitonal version of Hindemith's *Das Marienleben*. I should have been with Messiaen.

Oxford being off the agenda, Vienna was back on. In those days ordinary mortals went there by train, so I repeated a journey made during my research year, the length of the country starting with the long-drawn-out mountain fastnesses of the Arlberg, where the train stops at places with odd names like Dalaas. Like the entry to Cheltenham a decade before, the entry into Vienna through the woods along the Westbahn was and is magical, but I got a series of strange impressions during my nine months there. At least, the occupying powers had gone in the two years since my first visit. The UE offices in the Musikverein building were on the first floor, so a variety of practising noises at all hours accompanied my induction into the publishing business, which consisted mostly of sitting with people in their offices (though also down in the cellars with the packers and hire-library shifters), trying to follow what they were up to, such as the registration of orchestral hire-contracts in an enormous, age-old *Reversbuch*.[1] Production was sampled in the large multi-purpose room known as the Herstellungsabteilung; I watched the photographic production of printing plates and became all too familiar with the ammoniac smell of the duplicating machine. It was strange to hear Dr. Philipp, who ran that 'production department', speak in the most matter-of-fact tones of a nearby building '*wo die Gestapo waren*' (where the Gestapo were). The reprint on which I cut my teeth when left in charge of the linotype machine for a few minutes (it went wrong, of course) was Schoenberg's *Harmonielehre*. That was to figure prominently in my life a decade later. A first attempt to see into the world part of a new series for the recorder, *Il flauto dolce*, visiting printers and talking paper sizes and weights, felt unnatural and unsuccessful. The bosses thought so too. I at least had an agreeable set of colleagues keeping an eye on me, though to no avail, since I ate so badly and became so cast down about life in general that I eventually fell ill.

Social life was limited in the extreme, but a precious home-from-home just round the corner from my over-priced single room near the Ringstrasse was the roof-level flat of Ernst Kölz, virtuoso recorder-player and eight-till-five wage-slave in the Herstellungsabteilung. He couldn't afford a harpsichord and loathed the sound of the piano, so his upright had drawing-pins stuck into the hammers. The hospitality I received from him and his blonde wife Else was a life-saver, and I met some powerful personalities, above all H. C. Artmann, who was about to publish his Viennese dialect poems, the *G'dichta'r aus Bradnsee*. He would recite them to great effect until it was time to get bored and turn on the company with a snarl. Once back in England, I received a signed copy from him. Breitensee ('*Bradnsee*') lay within the larger 'Bezirk' of Ottakring (Wien XVI), somewhere I was soon to experience in the strangest way. Ernst and I even joined forces with a violinist, gamba player and singer to give a concert at an adult-education place, the Wiener Urania. A 'spinettino' was hired and as continuo player I was the one who never rested the whole evening through, playing nine works in all. Each performer's share of the takings worked out at around seventeen-and-sixpence in sterling, but the music (Handel, Telemann, a cantata called *Corydon* by Pepusch) was good. Around then we were also caught up in a concert to raise money for refugees from the Hungarian Revolution. I accompanied an American mezzo-soprano in 'Et exsultavit' from the Bach Magnificat (a good clomping piano part to shock the Kölzes!), but never saw her again. My donation of a white cricket sweater to a collection for the refugees reduced the UE receptionist to tears: those were 'their people' but she hadn't expected an English stranger also to feel in sympathy.

The other opportunity to make music in Vienna came from an introduction to a schoolteacher and amateur 'cellist named Professor Oberdorfer, who lived up in Gersthof, a wooded suburb at the end of the No. 41 tram line. Before and after the evening meal we'd play through the masterpieces for his instrument and piano, including a remarkably fine Reger Sonata in A minor. My one act of hubris was to try and sight-read the fugal finale of Beethoven's D major Sonata; as an attempt it was almost uniquely unsuccessful in my life as a born sight-reader, matched only when during my early BBC years I attempted to rehearse with the soprano Jeannette Sinclair Fauré's *La Bonne chanson*, whose piano part I'd never looked at. That brought home to me Fauré's amazing unpredictability in what comes over as eminently logical harmony; with the Beethoven it was rather my contrapuntal sense that was stretched beyond its limits.

Music to hear wasn't hard to come by; even the odd opera seat came my way. I was profoundly impressed by the Staatsoper production of Pfitzner's *Palestrina*, for in the mid-1950s Julius Patzak was still in enough voice to sing the title role. I can still hear his "*Ich glaube – nein!*" to Borromeo's "*So spricht denn Gott nicht mehr in Eurer Seele!*" (So God's voice, then, speaks no more within your soul? – I believe not!). It matched all too well a growing sense of hopelessness that was overtaking me in my middle twenties: as he stood there he was the quintessence of human loneliness. I must also have seen *Ariadne auf Naxos*, for I remember Hilde Gueden as a supremely balletic and charming Zerbinetta. At the time of the Hungarian uprising, the long-established Hungarian String Quartet led by Bartók's old colleague Zoltán Székely came for a concert, which because of the indignation against Kadar and his cronies had to be billed as 'Ungarisches Quartett (New York)'. In contemporary repertoire the *Die Reihe* ensemble had yet to get going, but its founder Friedrich Cerha was already active, conducting, for example, *Pierrot lunaire* with a soprano, Marie-Thérèse Escribano, whom I didn't greatly take to: Anny Felbermayer, seen and heard as Ighino in *Palestrina* and as Pamina, was more my classical cup of tea. Re-hearing Felbermayer's voice decades later I realized how little my sympathies had changed: she was a worthy predecessor of sopranos whose singing was to mean so much to me, particularly Elizabeth Gale.

For some reason, money probably, I didn't return home for Christmas 1956. Rather, my landlady packed me off in short order to a village in the Semmering where I spent a solitary few days. A few minutes into my stay in an icy room the chambermaid entered to say '*Muang wiad g'aazt*' (we'll light the fire tomorrow). In about February I began to feel peculiar, the very first sign being a sudden extreme tiredness on the tram down from an evening with the Oberdorfers. Eventually 'flu was diagnosed – the consensus nowadays is that it comes on suddenly, but that was then, not to mention there. My landlady again had other things on her mind, and after a farcical interlude when she disappeared as the doctor came to see me, I was carted off in an ambulance to the Wilhelminenspital, slightly up a hill some way out from the centre of the city on the 'outer girdle', a stone's throw away from Artmann's Breitensee. There I lay for twelve weeks getting weaker and weaker with an obstinate low fever that wouldn't go away, until finally they hit on the newish steroid cortisone, which turned me round within hours. After that, it was a matter of getting my strength back. There never was an authoritative diagnosis of just what had been wrong.

All that was an inauspicious opening to a career in publishing or anywhere else, but the atmosphere in the hospital ward was memorable, so too some of the views over towards Hungary and the birdsong in the early hours (I recall a pigeon or dove that yodelled); and exposure to the music on the tannoy brought me (over and over again) my second and decisive taste of Franz Schmidt, already recounted.

One Sunday afternoon just before the presidential election two men in dark suits burst into the ward carrying masses of red roses, to assail the assembled patients and visitors with *"Kandidat Schärf grüsst bestens"* – i.e. vote for Adolf Schärf, the socialist candidate to become Head of State. His right-wing opponent was a distinguished senior doctor, and after a moment's thought I asked the man in the next bed *"Na wos krieg' mer vom Denk? – a Spritzn?"* (what'll we get from Denk – an injection?, of which I by then had a wide experience to go with a certain command of the Viennese allotrope of the German language, nurtured during my stay in the ward). As a joke it didn't quite match my mother's best, but I was proud of it.

So long an inactive spell meant a correspondingly protracted convalescence at home in Birmingham. I read a lot, heard the first of Hans Keller's 'Functional Analyses', of Mozart's D minor String Quartet, K. 421, and was immensely impressed by a performance, several years pre-Jacqueline du Pré, of the Elgar 'Cello Concerto with János Starker and Barbirolli, a veteran of the work's premiere. They timed the finale's sudden transition from high spirits to deepest regret so that it was more moving than in any performance I've heard since. I was, of course, in a state to be moved.

NOTES

1   Given the presence of 'Mezzanin' and 'Halbstock', one had to ascend an amazing number of stairs before reaching that 'first' floor.

7 *London, 1958*

At the very start of 1958 I set out, full of hope and good intentions, to work at Alfred A. Kalmus Ltd., 24 Great Pulteney Street, London W1. Colleagues there were Stephan Harpner, soon to become Dr. Kalmus's son-in-law, a vigorous youngish man who did everything with what the Viennese call '*lauter Tschinbum*' (cymbals and big bass-drum); the sales manager Bill Colleran and his secretary Helen Levinson (half a century later still a friend under her married name), Dr. K.'s irreplaceable secretary Mia Herrmann, who kept us all in order and was nice to me in her slightly ward-sister way, and soon a vastly agreeable and entertaining Londoner named June Parks, who helped with the accounts and became my firm supporter and friend down the years. In more recent decades she has become an equally faithful fan of my 'cellist wife Felicity, who finds in her one of her ideal members of an audience, those who are taken somewhere else by great music finely played.

The UE's comprehensive 'new music' catalogue ranged from pre-1914 Schoenberg and Webern to Stockhausen's latest arcana and ephemera such as the works of Roman Haubenstock-Ramati, the firm's adviser on 'new music'; and it was largely up to me to get it (or anything else, such as the more user-friendly Kodály) performed in the British Isles by contacting conductors and others such as BBC staff. The principle was clear, the execution spotty, since while able to write a good letter if anyone could be found to type it in those years of carbon copies and messy erasure of mistakes, I was awkward and unforthcoming in making contact with people. Dr. Kalmus's eternal question when a performer's name came up, "Do you know him?", slowly drove me mad; for all his patriarchal dignity he was gregarious and very well versed in the ways of the world, whereas I'd had only five solitary Oxford years and a most peculiar few months in Vienna to fit me for the job.

There were compensations of course. Hugh was close at hand and, as mentioned, I was able to help in getting him his first offer of publication. Hearing of his engagement to a gifted young pianist, Susan McGaw, was a shot in the arm – or maybe across the bows, for I began to do extra paid work for Kalmus translating the avant-garde publication *Die Reihe*. Alexander Goehr had done the first volume, on electronic music, but walked out of the second, on Webern, infuriated by Karlheinz Stockhausen's arrogance over some detail of translation. A good deal of Volume III and its successors was of a pretentiousness that left me struggling to put it into some sort of English that would make any sense at all. I got the hang of it and eventually realized that translating rubbish is easier by far than translating stuff with something to say. The two sets of Webern lectures published as *The Path to the New Music* were, of course, a different matter, and at least it all led to an invitation from

Barrie and Rockliff to do Paul and Eva Badura-Skoda's *Interpreting Mozart on the Keyboard*. That I took to like a duck to water.

Relations with Sandy were resumed. He was by now married to Audrey and bringing up a pair of daughters in a house in Tooting. There I met some of his mates and fellow Richard Hall pupils from the Manchester School of Music, such as Elgar Howarth and Harrison Birtwistle; I also heard of others, including the legendary John Ogdon, for whom I soon spent an eventful evening turning the pages of an all-new-music recital, most of it in manuscript and some of it in pencil, with a fair amount of turning back and general jumping about. A little later, around the time we were both recruited by the BBC, Sandy roped me in to write replacement lyrics for a Mermaid Theatre production of Brecht's *Schweyk in the Second World War*, for which I imagine Hanns Eisler, composer of the incidental music, had recommended him to look after the musical side. I was delighted to be associated with a production that, for one, featured the most endearingly funny character from all my boyhood reading, and, for two, starred Bernard Miles, whose Buckinghamshire humour took me back to boyhood days in Amersham (I can still recite word-perfect one of his monologues about 'Ivinghoe'). I did however feel that the anti-Hitler satire boiled down to a crude and obsolete evening of 'Antifa Agitprop' from a safe distance. The Lord Chamberlain had yet to withdraw from the censorship of stage productions, so words like 'crap' and lines like 'Work it up yer arse' (even when addressed to Hitler) had to be removed and blander synonyms found.[1]

At that point Fate, in the shape of William Glock, intervened.

Such was the making of a producer: a relatively sheltered life, shadowed by nothing more tangible than the very distant possibility of perishing in one of Hitler's camps. Its exposure to music and at times to distinguished music-making could hardly have been better calculated to produce the kind of dedicated, slightly unworldly figure that prospered within the BBC during the years when, had we but known it, the Corporation was preparing to shed its skin. Exit Auntie, enter The Beeb. I think I know which I prefer, but then I Was There.

NOTES

1   At the BBC I heard the legend of a programme that during the war used a brief recorded excerpt from one of the Führer's Nuremberg rally speeches, upon which the honest and punctilious Accounts Department spent some time trying to put through the appropriate copyright payment to Mr. Adolf Hitler. As an example of unshakeable BBC routine, that would rank alongside the story of King Haakon of Norway arriving at Bush House to make his Sunday night broadcast to his occupied land. The usual commissionaire not being on

duty, his locum stopped the stranger to ask him his business. Being told he was Haakon, King of Norway, who came every Sunday, regular as clockwork, to speak to his people, the commissionaire politely enquired "from which studio, Sir?" and then rang the studio to say "A gentleman here says he's – er, what country did you say you was King of, sir?".

Appendices,
Bibliographical Note
and Index

Robert Simpson (II) (Milein Cosman)

Appendices

1 *Nikos Skalkottas*

A great imaginative novel could be writtten about the Greek composer Nikos Skalkottas, who lived from 1904 to 1949. As a young man – 'lively, ironic and combative' – he studied the violin at the Athens Conservatoire. After winning a gold medal for his performance of the Beethoven Violin Concerto, which according to contemporary accounts was distinguished by its exceptionally economical and discerning use of vibrato, he proceeded to Berlin, with every prospect of becoming a world-famous virtuoso. By the mid-1920s, however, he had decided to make his career as a composer. After a short period of study with Philipp Jarnach and Kurt Weill he went on to Schoenberg, who thought so highly of his talent that a quarter of a century later, knowing none of the music Skalkottas had meanwhile written, he named him among the few real composers he had taught in Berlin.

In 1933, shocked by the advent of the Nazi regime, Skalkottas left Berlin; after a time in Sweden, of which little is known, he returned to Athens, as Mozart had returned to equally provincial Salzburg after the double failure of his grand tour and his great love in Mannheim and Paris. For Skalkottas, ten years older than Mozart had been when his crisis came, there was a black period of three years when he wrote nothing. Then he broke into flower again, composing ceaselessly and, to judge by the size of his output, effortlessly. Genius is, among other things, an infinite capacity for taking pain and transmuting it to other people's pleasure. But the combative personality was, to all appearances, gone; there had been a withdrawal from the world, the onset of a divine indifference that, rather than inhibiting action, allowed something to speak through the hole where the ego had been; Mozart had reacted rather similarly after Aloysia Weber turned him down. And as Hans Keller once pointed out, Skalkottas was not concerned with himself even to the extent of critically destroying any of his music, as the comparably fluent and fractured Brahms had been. He composed; he played his violin again, for money, in whatever orchestra was to hand; he lived, if you call it living, and in 1946, at the age of forty-two, he married. Three years later he died. He had for some time been suffering from a hernia which he had not bothered, or not been able to afford, to have treated. A fatal omission: it strangulated, and not wishing to disturb his wife as their second child was about to be born, he paid the price.

His sets of Greek Dance arrangements (which first won him my sympathy when I heard them conducted by – whom else? – Walter Goehr) are as typical of him as are the modern dances in his vast set of piano pieces or the classical forms found in his chamber music. Generally speaking, there can rarely have been a greater disparity between how a composer's music looks likely to sound, and how it in fact sounds – which is to say that Skalkottas had an incredible 'inner ear'. Edmund Rubbra used to ask his pupils, "Did you really hear that in your head?"; Skalkottas's answer would always have been "Yes". His inner sound-world was busy and clouded like that of Charles Ives, totally chromatic like that of Schoenberg, yet rarely out of touch with the intonations of Greek folk music. To draw examples from his chamber music, there is a set of eight variations for piano trio, on a Greek folk tune, which obviously lies at the folk-like end of the range, an Octet standing somewhere in the middle, and a work such as the Third String Quartet which is nearest what one could call the Schoenberg end. Each shows a slightly different facet of the same many-sided crystal, the inexhaustible musical personality. Nor was it a matter of his style's 'changing and maturing'; among the violin music, a solo sonata from the early 1920s, one of the great works for violin alone, is almost like Hindemith but better-sounding (it anticipates the fugue in Bartók's solo sonata by a quarter of a century), while his last such work, the Second Suite with piano, is a kind of Greek atonal Wieniawski-brought-up-to-date. In giving the Solo Sonata a hearing, the advocacy of the Turkish Armenian-born British violinist Manoug Parikian was invaluable, for he was a true virtuoso with a lovely sound and a technique equal to anything. (When he recorded Bartók's Solo Violin Sonata for me, he had some slight trouble with a passage near the end of a movement, and self-mockingly put it down to "not having played enough Paganini Studies when I was five".) Since Skalkottas too had been a remarkable violinist, Manoug's total command of his instrument let the music speak as it truly should – showing Schoenbergian rigour and Mediterranean luxuriance, free-and-easy, exuberant, expert, unclassifiable.

My BBC work for Skalkottas took a variety of forms. I had first become aware of him from those Greek Dances, and during my UE time I tried to secure a performance of an ambitious hybrid work, *Fairy Drama*; the London Philharmonic eventually performed it, leaving me little less puzzled than before. Once I was at the BBC, the Rome-based singer Alice Gabbai offered a selection from a set of sixteen Skalkottas songs to poems by a leading contemporary writer, Chrisos Evelpidis. I found them extraordinarily melodious and haunting, with their eloquent vocal lines and complex accompaniments, and returned to the charge when Alice visited for a second time. I even had a group copied out for our own Maureen Lehane to sing in phonetic Greek. The distinguished writer Henry Reed contacted me to say how impressed he'd been hearing the songs; they'd made him want to translate their texts for an English singing version. That pleased me very much, as an admirer both of his satirical radio pseudo-documentaries – *A Very Great Man Indeed, Through a Hedge – Backwards, The Private Life of Hilda Tablet* – and poems of 'national service' such as *Naming of Parts* and *Judging Distances*. The matter got as far as his being provided with a complete copy of the Greek text and tapes of such songs as the BBC had recorded, but Reed died before it could go any further.

Manoug recorded for me not only that solo violin sonata but also the 'Wieniawski-type' late suite. Perry Hart and Margaret Major of the Oromonte String Trio chipped in with a duo for violin and viola, which Manoug and Amaryllis Fleming later supplemented with a couple of movements from a longer duo for violin and 'cello, and the Dartington Quartet contributed one of the quartets, doubtless heavily coached by Hans. Finally, there were those amazing Valerie Tryon performances of piano pieces from a set numbering no fewer than thirty-two, many of them in very up-to-date dance forms. I should imagine that they contain between them more notes than any comparable collection, with perhaps the exception of *Das wohltemperierte Klavier*, which is after all three times as long …

After the heady days of Glock's Lot, major twelve-note figures like Gerhard and Skalkottas have again receded into the background, which is a shame. Could we know and understand Skalkottas better, we might well find him equal in stature to Berg or Bartók (though harder to analyse or pigeon-hole than either). The Quiet Genius (sorry, Bob) remains the twentieth century's most mysterious great composer.

2   *Roberto Gerhard's Concerto for Orchestra, 1965*

Roberto Gerhard calls his work a concerto because 'ensemble playing, [its] distinguishing feature … takes the place of the soloist in the traditional concerto. As a result, one of the composer's tasks is to provide sufficient varied and exacting examples of "concerted action" in order to allow the orchestra to display the precision, versatility and artistic quality of its performance as a team'. The impartial listener might also find the title acceptable as a comment on Gerhard's inventiveness of orchestral sound. (The sheer speed at which things happen may even be an obstacle – as Mozart's more comprehensible colleague Dittersdorf said of him, "I could almost wish he were not so lavish in using his ideas. He leaves his hearer out of breath; for hardly has he grasped one beautiful thought than another of greater fascination dispels the first, and this goes on throughout. So that in the end it is impossible to retain any one …".)

As well as richness of sound, there is conflict: not just contrast, conflict – of moods rather than themes, since Gerhard constantly invents new sounds, new incarnations of basic moods, and rarely repeats anything. The Concerto is filled with sounds characteristic of him: echoes of Spanish dance rhythms, as of castanets; great static rasping wind chords like a vastly magnified accordion, recalling the traditional instrumental sound of the *sardana*, the national dance of the composer's native Catalonia; the threatening low brass and timpani glissandi that came in his recent *Hymnody*, seeming to reflect that work's superscription 'Strong bulls of Bashan have beset me round'; the celestial saw-mill sounds of *Concert for 8*, here most sinister of aspect. All these are more than sound effects: for Gerhard they are personal symbols, as cowbells had been for Mahler, deep-lying elements that reappear in a master's work, lived through, perhaps long ago, and transformed by submersion. The musical context ensures that they communicate at least some of their evocative quality.

The work starts *in medias res*, like Beethoven's last violin sonata or Gerhard's own Violin Concerto – almost as if it had begun some time ago but one had only just turned the volume up. The mood is frenetic; almost immediately the brass hurl in a motive that perhaps even Dittersdorf could have retained; with its whole-tone scale it could well be from Berg:

Example

One may find it odd that so striking a motive returns only by oblique hints: one may even be meant to. *It will return.* The opening mood persists, in various incarnations, for some 4½ minutes; then it is quite suddenly replaced by a different quick tempo, perhaps less uneasy, certainly more dance-like. This too stays long enough to establish itself (2½ minutes), and also ends as suddenly as it began: the violins, having arrived at a high G, hang there, endlessly. It is an uncanny moment, with something contemplative, timeless about it; but 'the most fleeting worldly thought disturbs contemplation', and soon, beneath the high strings, the bulls make themselves heard, and the giant-accordion chords, and later the sinister saw-mills – as if all that had been most troublesome were to pass sombrely in review before the mind's eye. The slow-motion tempo, with its vast, oceanic pulse, tries to persist, but now there is a battle of tempi on, and it goes on for a long time, running now one way, now the other. About twenty minutes in, the long-drawn violin lines seem to be winning, as if the end were to be as in the Bruckner Ninth or *Moses und Aron*; but the quick tempi gather themselves together (particularly the frenetic opening one), an indissoluble clinch develops and the catastrophe approaches – for, like Mahler's Sixth, the Concerto ends in catastrophe. The unmistakable motive suddenly returns on the brass: so literal a quotation in so non-thematic a work can bode only ill, and what happens next is a kind of musical anaphylaxis – re-infection touches on greatly heightened sensitivity and provokes in no time at all an enormous, fatal reaction. The music swells terrifyingly, then dies into the silence of extinction.

Paul Hamburger (II) (Milein Cosman)

Bibliographical Note

This is not the first book to refer to the Glock era, and readers could well follow up the issues it raises in five key sources: **Asa Briggs with Joanne Spicer**, *The BBC: The First 50 Years*, London, Oxford University Press [hereafter OUP], 1985; **Asa Briggs**, *The History of Broadcasting in the United Kingdom, Vol. 5: Competition*, London, OUP, 1995; **Humphrey Carpenter**, *The Envy of the World: Fifty Years of the BBC Third Programme and Radio 3*, London, Weidenfeld and Nicolson, 1996; **A. M. [Alison] Garnham**, *Hans Keller and the BBC*, Aldershot, Ashgate, 2003; and **David Wright** on 'The Glock and Ponsonby Eras, 1959-85' in *The Proms: A New History*, ed. Jenny Doctor and David Wright, London, Thames and Hudson, 2007, pp. 168-209.

Some of the main figures described in these pages were also authors, and readers might well want to follow up their writings too: five of the books by **Deryck Cooke**, *The Language of Music*, London, OUP, 1959, *Gustav Mahler (1860 – 1911): A Companion to the BBC's Celebrations of the Centenary of his Birth*, London, BBC Publications, 1960, *I Saw the World End: A Study of Wagner's 'Ring'*, London, OUP, 1979, *Gustav Mahler, An Introduction to His Work*, London, Faber, 1980 and *Vindications: Essays on Romantic Music*, London, Faber, 1982; **William Glock**, *Notes in Advance*, London, OUP, 1991; four essays by **Paul Hamburger**: 'The Chamber Music' and 'The Pianist' in: *Benjamin Britten: A Commentary on His Works from a Group of Specialists*, ed. Donald Mitchell and Hans Keller, London, Rockliff, 1952, an edition with extended commentary of *Twenty-one Songs [for Voice and Piano] by W. A. Mozart*, London, OUP, 1992 and 'Mahler and *Des Knaben Wunderhorn*' in *The Mahler Companion*, London, OUP, 1999; **Stephen Hearst**, *Artistic Heritage and Its Treatment by Television*, London, BBC Publications, 1981; three of the many volumes by **Hans Keller**: *1975 (1984 minus 9)*, London, Dobson, 1977 (reissued as *Music, Closed Societies and Football*, London, Toccata, 1986), *Criticism*, London, Faber, 1987 and *Essays on Music*, ed. Christopher Wintle, Cambridge, Cambridge University Press, 1994; **Basil Lam**, *Beethoven String Quartets*, London, BBC Music Guides, two volumes, 1975 (reissued in one volume, 1979); four works by **Robert Simpson**: *Carl Nielsen: Symphonist*, London, Kahn & Averill, 1979, *The Essence of Bruckner*, London, Gollancz 1967 (rev. ed., 1977), *Beethoven Symphonies*, London, BBC Music Guide, 1970 and *The Proms and Natural Justice*, London, Toccata, 1981; **Robert Tear**, *Tear Here*, London, André Deutsch, 1990 and *Singer Beware*, London, Hodder & Stoughton, 1995; and **Hugh Wood**, *Staking Out the Territory and Other Writings on Music*, ed. Christopher Wintle, London, Plumbago, 2008.

Other players in the cast wrote on a whole range of topics, in some cases copiously. The following is just a sample: **David Drew**, *Über Kurt Weill*, Frankfurt-am-Main, Suhrkamp, 1975 and *Kurt Weill: A Handbook*, London, Faber, 1987;

Alexander Goehr, *Finding the Key: Selected Writings*, ed. Derrick Puffett, London, Faber, 1998; *Leonard Isaacs, Five Lives in One*, Winnipeg, Good Cheer, 1996; **Ronald Lewin** wrote extensively on military matters for Batsford, Cooper and Hutchinson; **Howard (P. H.) Newby** penned over 25 novels, principally for Jonathan Cape, Faber and Hutchinson, as well as a BBC lecture on *The Third Programme*, London, BBC Publications, 1965; **Ian McIntyre** has written a number of studies, on Hester Thrale (Johnson's 'dear mistress'), Robert Burns, Joshua Reynolds and David Garrick, as well as on Sir John Reith, *The Expense of Glory*, London, HarperCollins, 1993; **Robert Ponsonby**, *Musical Heroes*, London, Giles de la Mare, 2009; **Cormac Rigby** in his later incarnation as 'Father' wrote several volumes for Oxford Family Publications: *The Lord be With You* (2003), *Lift Up Your Hearts* (2004), *Let Us Give Thanks* (2005) and *The Lord My Light* (2006); and **Ernest Warburton** published on Mozart's opera librettos and their sources, New York, Garland, 1992, and edited the collected works of J. C. Bach in three volumes with a separate thematic catalogue, New York, Garland, 1999.

As for **Leo Black**, his two previous books are *Franz Schubert: Music and Belief*, Woodbridge, Boydell Press, 2003 and *Edmund Rubbra, Symphonist*, Woodbridge, Boydell Press, 2008. His many translations include: *Die Reihe: Vol. 2, Anton Webern, Biographical/Analytical*, 1958, *Vol. 3, Musical Craftsmanship*, 1959, *Vol. 4, Young Composers*, 1960, *Vol. 5, Reports, Analyses*, 1961 and *Anton Webern, The Path to the New Music*, 1963, all for Bryn Mawr Pennsylvania, Theodore Presser Company in association with London, Universal Edition, as well as: Paul and Eva Badura-Skoda, *Interpreting Mozart on the Keyboard*, London, Barrie & Rockliff, 1962, Willi Reich, *Schoenberg: A Critical Biography*, London, Longman, 1971 and the much-enlarged centenary edition of Arnold Schoenberg, *Style and Idea: Selected Writings*, ed. Leonard Stein, London, Faber, 1975. Beyond that, and apart from many short contributions to *The Musical Times*, *Radio Times*, *The Listener* and *The Strad*, he has contributed widely to symposia and journals, notably on: 'Hugh Wood' in *British Music Now: A Guide to the Work of Younger Composers*, ed. Lewis Foreman, London, Elek, 1975; 'Die Aufnahme der Musik Franz Schmidts in England' in *Studien zu Franz Schmidt VI* (*Franz Schmidt und seine Zeit*, Symposium 1985), Vienna, Doblinger, 1988; 'Franz Schmidt und das musikalische Hören' in *Klang und Komponist* (*Kongressbericht: Ein Symposion der Wiener Philharmoniker*), Tutzing, Schneider, 1992 and 'Heimito von Doderer: An English View' in *Viribus Unitis* (*Festschrift für Bernhard Stillfried aus Anlass seines 70. Geburtstags*), Frankfurt and New York, Peter Lang, 1996. For the bicentenary of Franz Schubert's birth in 1997 he contributed a number of pieces to *The Musical Times*, Vol. 138: 'Raising the Dead (Lazarus)' (January), 'Wort oder Ton?' (March), 'Oaks and Osmosis' (June), 'The *Arpeggione* Sonata' (November) and 'Schubert, The Complete Voice' (December). He contributed 'Schubert and *Fierrabras* – a Mind in Ferment' to *The Opera Quarterly*, Vol. 14, No. 4, Summer 1998 and (in German) 'VDB (Voice Doubling Bass)' to the *Internationales Franz Schubert Institut Mitteilungen 26 sowie Bibliographie Teil II, Schubert durch die Brille*, January 2001.

Index